ETHNIC VOTERS AND THE
ELECTION OF LINCOLN

ETHNIC VOTERS
AND THE
ELECTION OF LINCOLN

Edited with an introduction

by

FREDERICK C. LUEBKE

UNIVERSITY OF NEBRASKA PRESS • LINCOLN

Acknowledgments for permission to reprint copyrighted material appear on pp. ix–x.

Publishers on the Plains

UNP

For

Christina

John

David

Thomas

Contents

Acknowledgments

The wisest of men, King Solomon, observed that of making many books there is no end. He might have added that as a book is made, the web of personal obligations is greatly extended. I therefore acknowledge my indebtedness to my wife and children for their patience and forbearance, to the University of Nebraska Research Council for a Senior Faculty Summer Research Fellowship, to Mrs. Mary Beck and Mrs. Georgetta Harris for their splendid secretarial services, and to my excellent colleagues, Professors James A. Rawley and Benjamin G. Rader, for their encouragement and counsel. Professors Ronald P. Formisano and James M. Bergquist graciously interrupted other plans and projects to contribute their essays to this anthology. My sincere thanks go to them and to the authors, editors, and publishers for their permission to reprint the articles as listed below.

FREDERICK C. LUEBKE
University of Nebraska

"The Influence of the Foreign-Born of the Northwest in the Election of 1860," by Donnal V. Smith. Reprinted by permission of the author and the Organization of American Historians from the *Mississippi Valley Historical Review* 19 (September 1932): 192–204.

"The Iowa Germans and the Election of 1860," by Charles Wilson Emery. Reprinted by permission of the editor from *Annals of Iowa,* 3d ser. 22 (October 1940): 421–53.

"Who Elected Lincoln?" by Joseph Schafer. Reprinted by permission of the American Historical Association from the *American Historical Review* 47 (October 1941): 51–63.

"Did Abraham Lincoln Receive the Illinois German Vote?" by Jay Monaghan. Reprinted by permission of the author and the Illinois State Historical Library from the *Journal of the Illinois State Historical Society* 35 (June 1942): 133–39.

"The German Element and the Issues of the Civil War," by Andreas Dorpalen. Reprinted by permission of the author and the Organization of American Historians from the *Mississippi Valley Historical Review* 29 (June 1942): 55–76.

"The Election of 1860 and the Germans in Minnesota," by Hildegard Binder Johnson. Reprinted by permission of the author and Minnesota Historical Society from *Minnesota History* 28 (March 1947): 20–36. Copyright 1947 by *Minnesota History*.

"Immigrant Vote in the 1860 Election: The Case of Iowa," by George H. Daniels. Reprinted by permission of the author and the editor from *Mid-America: An Historical Review* 44 (July 1962): 146–62.

"The Ethnic Voter and the First Lincoln Election," by Robert P. Swierenga. Reprinted by permission of the author and the editor from *Civil War History* 11 (March 1965): 27–43.

"Lincoln and the Immigrant Vote: A Case of Religious Polarization," by Paul J. Kleppner. Reprinted by permission of the author and editor from *Mid-America: An Historical Review* 48 (July 1966): 176–95.

Introduction

A twofold purpose informs this anthology of essays on ethnic voters in the presidential election of 1860. First, it gathers together a great quantity of factual information about immigrants and politics on the eve of the Civil War. Naturally, the Germans receive the greatest amount of attention. Not only did they rival the Irish in numbers in 1860, but they were also the most diverse ethnic group in America. The essays of this volume also offer much data about politicians and their perceptions of the democratic process, about political parties and the social bases of their support, and about political campaigning in the nineteenth century. Largely based on local sources, they offer impressive evidence that a large bloc within the American electorate was basically unmoved by the great national debates over slavery and sectional interest that plunged this nation into four years of bloody strife.

Second, and perhaps more important, the essays document the evolution of the historical concepts and methods that have undergirded the writing of ethnic political history during the past half century. Present-day studies in the history of immigrant political behavior differ radically from their predecessors in their assumptions about ethnicity, its components and their relative importance; the unity of ethnic groups and their place in American society; political issues and their impact upon the electorate; the sources of ethnic political history; and the methods used to discover and interpret data, both old and new.

Through the years the questions asked by historians have also changed. The earliest writers were fundamentally concerned with the question of whether the Germans elected Lincoln, that is, if their votes were decisive. Subsequent historians shifted the question to a simpler one of partisan preference—did the Germans vote overwhelmingly Republican in 1860? Much more subtle and more significant are the later efforts to determine how major subdivisions within the German ethnic group voted by comparison to the total voting population or to other identifiable collectivities. Still other historians have insisted that voting is but a part of political behavior; hence, we must continue to ask, as the earlier historians had, if Germans or other foreign-born persons were important in the shaping of Republican or other party platforms, strategies, nominations, and campaigns.

All the articles included here are intended to illustrate this development of historical thought and method. With the exception of the last two essays, all have appeared in historical journals during the past four decades. They are arranged in chronological order. Inevitably they are of uneven quality, but by no means does it follow that the best essays always appeared in the most prestigious publications.

Although historians had from time to time commented on the relationship of ethnic voters to the election of Lincoln in 1860, it was not until 1911, when William E. Dodd wrote an article entitled "The Fight for the Northwest, 1860," that the problem captured the attention of American historians.[1] Dodd pointed out that during the 1850s there had been a great influx of German, British, and native-born settlers into the Northwest and that the majority of them "were either hostile to slavery or jealous of the overweening power of the South." In order to weaken the natural alliance between the South and the Northwest, the basis of Democratic candidate Stephen A. Douglas's support, Abraham Lincoln and the Republicans had to forge a program attractive to the Germans and the other new settlers in the region. Since Protestant churches, characterized by Dodd as having been on the side of wealth and power, were unable to provide the impetus for a radical antislavery program, the Republicans were forced to turn to "worldly-wise" appeals for high tariffs and free homesteads. Republican idealism was thus sacrificed in order to win the Northwest and to defeat the Southern strategy of carrying the election into the House of Representatives.

1. *American Historical Review* 16 (July 1911): 774–88.

Dodd attributed a vital influence to the Germans in the election of Lincoln. Three states, he averred, "would have given their electoral votes to Douglas but for the loyal support of the Germans and other foreign citizens led by Carl Schurz, Gustav Koerner," and others. Moreover, he wrote, the property interests of the foreign-born voters "had not overcome their idealism"; they "saw in Lincoln, despite his silence or quiet disclaimers, the champion of the essential American ideals of human equality and freedom." According to Dodd, one vote in twenty switched from Lincoln to Douglas would have lost the Northwest to the Democrats. The votes of the "foreigners" made the difference. "The election of Lincoln and, as it turned out, the fate of the Union," concluded Dodd, "were thus determined not by native Americans but by voters who knew least of American history and institutions."

Despite the widespread acceptance it gained, Dodd's analysis was based on scanty evidence by today's standards. His assertion that the foreign-born vote was decisive requires evidence, first, that the "foreigners" did indeed vote Republican in 1860, and second, that their electoral preference was notably more Republican than that of the total voting population. To illustrate, if it is established that both native and foreign-born citizens in a given state voted 75 percent Republican, it can hardly be said that the vote of the foreign-born was distinctive. Moreover, in order to establish its decisive character, Dodd would have had to demonstrate that their votes in 1860 were significantly more Republican than they had been in the previous elections of 1858 or 1856. If, for example, 90 percent of the German voters in the Northwest voted Republican in the earlier contests as well as in 1860, again their votes can hardly be termed decisive. They would have been no more or no less significant than the votes of any other durable component of the Republican coalition, such as native-born farmers, Methodist abolitionists, and the like. Finally, Dodd assumed without evidence that the Germans responded to the leadership of Carl Schurz and other ethnic leaders and that they were moved to vote for Lincoln by their idealistic opposition to the evil that was slavery.

During the decade following the publication of Dodd's essay, his views found places in other interpretations of Lincoln and his times. A widely read book on the history of American immigration written by George M. Stephenson accepted most of Dodd's thesis but added an important emphasis on issues other than slavery. As an immigration historian, Stephenson was keenly aware of the importance of the nativistic Know-Nothingism that infected the 1850s. He also admitted that proposals for homestead legislation were potent among foreign-born voters. Yet he agreed that these matters were "eclipsed by the anti-slavery agitation."[2]

The traditional interpretation of the ethnic voter in Lincoln's election is summed up in the first article in this volume. Published in 1932, it was written by Donnal V. Smith, at that time a recent Ph.D. graduate of the University of Chicago. Concerned primarily with national politics, he offers a useful summary of factual information at that level. Smith's account is the familiar one: because of their aversion to slavery, the foreign-born voters of the Northwest moved en masse into Republican columns in 1860, dependent, as they were, on a few capable leaders like Carl Schurz, Gustave Koerner, August Willich, Nicholas Rusch, and Henry Scholte "to translate and explain political questions to them."

Smith's article epitomizes the assumptions, concepts, and methods of that generation of historians as they analyzed ethnic political behavior. Smith relied extensively on secondary sources, on newspapers oriented toward national issues, and on elitist evidence, such as the letters, memoirs, and papers of major figures, notably Schurz and Koerner. Repeatedly stressing that the Germans voted as a bloc at the direction of their leaders, he assumes that their campaign efforts were powerful creators of Republican votes. Such evidence as Schurz's extravagant self-praise is taken at face value. Moreover, few distinctions are made among the foreign-born generally, and sectional differences within ethnic groups are overlooked. National issues, such as slavery, home-

---

2. George M. Stephenson, *A History of American Immigration, 1820–1924* (Boston: Ginn & Co., 1926), pp. 118–33. This work was reissued by Russell & Russell, Inc., in 1964.

stead legislation, and federal support for railroad construction, are assumed to have had vitality for foreign-born voters, while ethnocultural issues like nativism and prohibition are considered to have been of little consequence because Lincoln and his supporters had cleansed the Republican record on this score in their national platform and in their speeches and correspondence.

Ending his article with an analysis of population figures and votes in the northwestern states, Smith rests his conclusion on his calculations that the number of adult males of foreign birth in each of the states in question exceeded the margin of Lincoln's victory. Like William E. Dodd, he argues that without the vote of the "solidly united" foreign-born, "Lincoln could not have carried the Northwest, and without the Northwest, . . . he would have been defeated." However, the fact that the number of foreign-born voters exceeded Lincoln's margin of victory in the Northwest has no special significance; the same could be said of many other ethnic, occupational, nativity, income, education, or age groups. Thus Smith's article, entirely typical of ethnic political analyses of a half century ago, introduces no time dimension to illustrate trends and permits no comparisons of ethnic preferences with other groups or with the voting population in general.

The earliest detailed examinations of German political behavior at the state level came in Iowa. Frank I. Herriott published several extended essays on the subject in the *Annals of Iowa,* the *Jahrbücher der Deutsch-Amerikanischen Gesellschaft von Illinois,* and elsewhere just before World War I. His studies provided the groundwork for a master's thesis completed in 1940 by Charles Wilson Emery at the University of Iowa. Originally published in the *Annals of Iowa,* Emery's article is the second in this anthology.

Emery intended no revisionism. Entirely conventional in his approach, he made extensive use of local newspapers. Although he discusses the German-language press in general terms, he does not use it as a source; but he assumes that it was an accurate index of the political opinions of its readers. He observes few religions or social distinctions among the immigrants and accepts the standard assumptions regarding ethnic bloc voting and the political effectiveness of the German leaders. Yet Emery's effort is noteworthy for two reasons, one relating to issues, the other as a timid venture into quantitative methods.

Perhaps unintentionally, Emery demonstrates that, contrary to the accepted view, slavery was not an issue of major importance to the Iowa Germans. What loomed large in their minds, especially in 1859, were nativism, homestead legislation, and the protection of foreign-born citizens when they traveled abroad. However, since the traditional methods usually measure the salience of issues by their treatment in the newspapers, Emery was led to underestimate the vitality of issues such as prohibition that were related to the clash of cultural values between immigrant groups and the host or receiving society.

At the end of his rather discursive study, Emery asserts that the most accurate method of determining the political behavior of the Germans is to compare the election data of precincts with heavy German population with similar units having a constituency of largely native-born persons. His data, though treated in an unsystematic fashion, demonstrate that in the precincts selected the Germans voted much as did the native-born. Although Emery did not modify the major part of his study in the light of this discovery, he found that the Germans did not actually vote as a bloc—by no means did all of them prefer the Lincoln candidacy. He concludes that "while the German vote was important in Iowa in 1860, it was not essential to a Republican victory." Though inconsistent in conception and crude in its analysis of quantitative data, Emery's study represents something of a breakthrough. But since it was a graduate-student effort published in a minor journal, it went almost unnoticed by later historians, save those working with Iowa sources.

In the year following the publication of Emery's article, Joseph Schafer, superintendent of the State Historical Society of Wisconsin, drew upon his intimate knowledge of his state and its German immigrants to assess the importance of the ethnic vote in 1860.[3] By comparing manuscript census data with election records, he was led to conclude that "Lincoln would have won in Wisconsin if all German votes had been given to Douglas, as doubtless five-sixths of them were."

Schafer's attack, published in the *American Historical Review,* centers on the traditional assumption that the Germans were a homogeneous group who uniformly followed the leadership of their elite. The ordinary German immigrant, as Schafer points out, was conservative, religiously oriented in his values, loyal to his established attachments, and therefore thoroughly antipathetic to the goals and purposes of those articulate, politically active idealists, the so-called Forty-eighters, of whom the dynamic but "never overmodest" Carl Schurz was the best known. The adherence of these anticlerical, freethinking liberals to Republicanism was clear-cut, but their number was small and their ability to persuade the typical German immigrant was slight. Schafer shows that Catholic Germans, who experienced Know-Nothing enmity during the 1850s, could not support the Republican party because they perceived it as the heir of the nativist tradition. Moreover, he also demonstrates that townships dominated by the German Reformed or by German Lutherans preferred the Democratic candidate.

Though Schafer's argument is cogent and his style urbane, his analysis of voting data is unsophisticated. Highly selective in his choice of townships, he offers only a limited sampling of immigrant electoral data. Nor does he analyze changes over time. Yet his analysis is appropriately based on local sources; it distinguishes the interests of the elite from those of the masses; and it recognizes that ethnoreligious characteristics are important correlates of voting behavior.

Schafer's article brought a quick rebuttal from Jay Monaghan of the Illinois State Historical Library. In a brief essay he asserts

3. Among Joseph Schafer's major contributions to American immigration history are a biography, *Carl Schurz, Militant Liberal* (Madison, Wis.: State Historical Society of Wisconsin, 1930), and his translation and edition *Intimate Letter of Carl Schurz, 1841–1869* (Madison, Wis.: State Historical Society of Wisconson, 1928).

that Illinois data offer no reason to abandon the traditional interpretation of Republican voting among Germans in 1860. As if troubled by the implications of Schafer's attack for the political perspicacity of Lincoln and other national leaders, he asks, "Was Lincoln basing his appreciation of the German vote on a false assumption?" Indeed he was, we would reply today, if he assumed that the conservative Germans voted en bloc at the bidding of liberals like Carl Schurz, whose alleged boast that he could deliver 300,000 German votes to the Republican party should have been questioned by any astute politician.

In his defense of the traditonal view, Monaghan limits himself largely to evidence drawn from Saint Clair County, a center of German population immediately east of Saint Louis, Missouri. His association of demographic and electoral data suggests that Illinois Germans, in contrast to those of Wisconsin, preferred Lincoln to Douglas. He concludes with the observation that the liberal traditions of the Saint Clair Germans and the urban residence of Chicago Germans may account for their Republican proclivities.

In an article published in 1942 in the *Mississippi Valley Historical Review,* Andreas Dorpalen, now a professor of modern German history at Ohio State University, attacked the traditional notion that the Germans were highly motivated in their political behavior by the slavery issue. Drawing deeply from the well of economic "determinism," the dominant interpretive schema of the times, Dorpalen argued that vital political issues were only those with a capacity to affect the voter's economic well-being. His research convinced him that slavery was not an issue that impinged in any significant way upon the majority of German voters in the United States and that consequently they were indifferent to the institution and the debates that raged over it. Rather, they were influenced by conditions related to their residence in the South, Northeast, or Northwest, to urban or rural residence, or to occupation. Thus, the voting behavior of the immigrant was not shaped by moralistic ideologies but conformed instead to that of other persons in the same region, community, or occupation whose economic circumstances paralleled his own. Therefore, Dorpalen concludes, German voters could not be expected to have followed leaders who sought to unite them under Republican opposition to slavery and its extension. Rather, they voted strongly Democratic in some communities, and strongly Republican in others. Dorpalen asserts finally that Lincoln, indeed, required German support to win the election, but that "the Germans did no more to assure Lincoln's victory than did their American-born neighbors." In short, their voting behavior was not distinctive; consequently, ethnicity was not an important correlate of electoral decisions.

The importance of Dorpalen's article lies in its insistence on a comparative dimension. The politics of an immigrant group cannot be studied in isolation; it must be related to that of others, notably native Americans. If the majority of the voters in a given area voted strongly for Lincoln, one may expect Germans to have displayed similar tendencies; if a given occupational group perceived that their economic interests could be advanced by voting for Stephen A. Douglas, German members of that group are likely to have agreed. This view implicitly recognizes the force of social pressure felt by immigrant peoples to conform to the behavior patterns and value systems of the host society.

Ironically, Dorpalen's emphasis on the importance of economic issues, the central thrust of the article, is less convincing. He dismisses nativism in one paragraph and gives no attention whatever to the ethnocultural issues of prohibition, sabbatarianism, and education. He properly downgrades slavery as an issue for the ordinary German voter and he effectively challenges the idea that the leadership elite, specifically, Carl Schurz, could deliver the German vote en bloc to the Republican party. But his rigid adherence to an economic interpretation distorts his assessment of the issues affecting the German element in 1860.

It remained for a geographer skilled in demographic analysis to produce the finest of the early state studies of German voting in 1860. In an article published in 1947, Hildegard Binder Johnson, who is also a keen student of German immigration history,[4] examines Minnesota sources in much the same way Schafer studied Wisconsin data. Mrs. Johnson is not concerned with the question of whether the German vote was crucial to Lincoln's victory in Minnesota. The Republican margin there was so great that if every German-born voter in the state had cast his ballot for Douglas, Lincoln would still have won an easy victory. Rather she sought to determine partisanship: did a majority of the Minnesota Germans vote Republican? Her answer, unlike Schafer's, supports the traditional view.

Unlike the traditionalists, however, Mrs. Johnson avoids their assumptions regarding bloc voting and the efficacy of the campaign efforts of the elite. She surveys the press (including the German-language publications), the issues, the candidates, and the campaign of 1860 as a background for understanding German participation in the election. Thoroughly familiar with the varied character of the German immigrant voting population, she reveals that Democratic majorities occurred where Catholics prevailed and that Republican majorities were common in Lutheran settlements. Republican partisanship was most intense where German freethinkers and liberals dominated, as in the famous Turner settlement at New Ulm.

A special virtue of Mrs. Johnson's study is her analysis of voter turnout. She discovered no discernible tendencies that could be associated with ethnicity, place of residence, section, or party, indicating thereby that German participation was "at least as lively as that of the state's general population." In her examination of election data, Mrs. Johnson takes the first steps toward systematic analysis as she groups precincts according to percentage

4. Among Mrs. Johnson's other publications in German immigration history are "The Location of German Immigrants in the Middle West," *Association of American Geographers Annals* 41 (March 1951): 1–41; "The Distribution of the German Pioneer Population in Minnesota," *Rural Sociology* 6 (1941): 16–34; "Adjustment to the United States," in *The Forty-eighters: Political Refugees of the German Revolution of 1848,* ed. Adolf E. Zucker (New York: Columbia University Press, 1950), pp. 43–78; and "German Forty-eighters in Davenport," *Iowa Journal of History and Politics* 44 (January 1946): 3–60.

of German population. She does not, however, provide precise figures, since she is concerned mostly with simple majorities. Unfortunately, therefore, her interpretation of the data makes it difficult to compare German electoral preference with that of the total voting population. German voting in Minnesota should be compared to the standard of that state, which was nearly two Lincoln votes for each one Douglas received. Thus, while it is clear that a majority of Minnesota Germans voted for Lincoln, we should like to know if that proportion is larger or smaller than, or about the same as, that of the total voting population, for, as Dorpalen observes, the Germans may be expected to have conformed to behavior patterns of the host society.

In the decade following the publication of Mrs. Johnson's article, historians displayed slight interest in ethnic groups and their political behavior. It was the era of consensus history. Group differences tended to be ignored or minimized as common goals, similarities, and continuities were sought out. Studies touching on German ethnic politics frequently focused on the activities of prominent leaders and groups, such as the Forty-eighters.[5] Meanwhile, other students of American immigration history, less concerned about political history, endeavored to shift ethnic studies away from a filiopietistic orientation which stressed the contributions of immigrants to American greatness. This meant discovering the places of ethnic groups within the structure of American society.[6] By the late 1950s, other scholars influenced by the concepts and methods of the social sciences began to stress the need for reevaluating American political history. The careful use of quantitative evidence was introduced in preference to impressionistic sources, such as newspapers, speeches, letters, and docu-

5. The most important of these are the works of the distinguished historian of German America, Carl Wittke. They include his *Refugees of Revolution: The German Forty-eighters in America* (Philadelphia: University of Pennsylvania Press, 1952); *The German-Language Press in America* (Lexington, Ky.: University of Kentucky Press, 1957); *The Utopian Communist: A Biography of Wilhelm Weitling* (Baton Rouge, La.: Louisiana State University Press, 1950).

6. See especially Oscar Handlin's pioneering analysis, originally published in 1941, *Boston's Immigrants: A Study in Acculturation*, rev. and enlarged ed. (New York: Atheneum, 1968).

ments that usually reflected the activities, interests, and values of prominent persons. As a privileged stratum of society, the elite were seen to have had interests and goals different from those of the masses. National issues associated with presidential history and politics were increasingly distinguished from those that animated politics on the local level. Group conflicts and intragroup differences were explored as social, religious, and ethnocultural characteristics were investigated. Among the leaders of this movement were Lee Benson, Samuel P. Hays, Allan G. Bogue, and their students.[7] During the 1960s their number was swelled by many other historians who familiarized themselves with the mysteries of sociology and statistical analysis.

New studies treating ethnic political behavior have also been produced. Inevitably their point of view has tended to shift from the ethnic leaders to the common people—often impoverished, poorly educated, linguistically handicapped immigrants trying to succeed in a strange, new land. Instead of emphasizing the individual ethnic groups and their activities and accomplishments, the new studies seek to discover the place of these collectivities in the larger social structure, recognizing that each had its legitimate group interests. Among the questions reopened for fresh analysis was the role of the Germans in the election of Lincoln.

7. Lee Benson's extended essay, "Research Problems in American Political Historiography," has been especially influential. It appears in *Common Frontiers in the Social Sciences*, ed. Mirra Komarovsky (Glencoe, Ill.: Free Press, 1957), pp. 113–83. See also portions of his *Concept of Jacksonian Democracy: New York as a Test Case* (Princeton, N.J.: Princeton University Press, 1961). Samuel P. Hays's work in this field has appeared in the form of articles. See especially his "History as Human Behavior," *Iowa Journal of History* 58 (July 1960): 193–206; "The Social Analysis of American Political History," *Political Science Quarterly* 80 (September 1965): 373–94; "The Politics of Reform in Municipal Government in the Progressive Era," *Pacific Northwest Quarterly* 55 (October 1964): 157–69; "Political Parties and the Community-Society Continuum," in *The American Party Systems: Stages of Political Development,* ed. William Nisbet Chambers and Walter Dean Burnham (New York: Oxford University Press, 1967), pp. 152–81. Allan G. Bogue has produced an important historiographical essay, "United States: The 'New' Political History," *Journal of Contemporary History* 3 (January 1968): 5–27, and has sponsored much fruitful research in this field among his graduate students, including the Daniels and Swierenga contributions to this anthology.

The first of these studies was produced in 1962 by George H. Daniels, then a graduate student at the University of Iowa, now a professor of history at Northwestern University. Daniels's new orientation is immediately apparent. He is not interested in the Germans per se; they are merely the most numerous and most important of the several nativity groups whose political preferences he seeks to discover. Moreover, his quantitative approach permits meaningful comparisons between Germans and other native- and foreign-born groups. Thus, Daniels is able to show that Iowa voters born in the Middle Atlantic states were most consistently Republican, while Germans, Irish, and Southerners were clearly Democratic.

To support his contention that Iowa Germans voted Democratic, Daniels then turns to traditional sources on the local level to discover issues that may explain their preferences. These he finds in nativism and prohibition, both linked in the popular mind with the Republican party. Slavery, by contrast, was an issue that had salience chiefly for the intellectual elite among the Germans. The ordinary immigrant, he argues, was more concerned about his personal liberty than he was about the freedom of distant Negro slaves of whom he knew nothing. Daniels warns that "the masses do not necessarily vote the way their spokesmen are campaigning, and that contemporary opinion, including that of newspapers, is a poor guide." In an effort to explain the tendency of German voters in Dubuque and Davenport to vote Republican, he adapts Dorpalen's theory of conformity. Since rural Germans had minimal contact with other persons, they retained their traditional attachment to the Democratic party; urban Germans, by contrast, had the necessary interpersonal contacts necessary for them to discover the norms of the dominant Republican population.

Daniels's methodology is notably more sophisticated than that of his predecessors. He insists that only data of adult males (rather than of the total population) be used in connection with units no larger than the township or precinct if reliability is to be achieved.[8] Nevertheless, he is not as systematic as he might have been. Precise nativity data are not recorded for any of his groups; the reader is left to gather visual impressions from his appended tables, even though several simple correlational devices might have strengthened his case significantly. Yet Daniels's study represents a major step forward in the conceptualization and methodology used in the study of immigrant political behavior.

Robert P. Swierenga, another scholar trained at the University of Iowa, specifically attacks the traditional notion that immigrant voters adhered closely to the political counsel of their leaders. In an article published in 1965, he draws upon his intimate knowledge of the Dutch immigration and Dutch-language sources to explore the relationship between the Reverend Henry P. Scholte, a Dutch Reformed minister, and his followers in the Netherlands settlement at Pella, Iowa, during the 1850s and climaxing in the election of 1860.

Swierenga shows that at first the colonists were indeed largely dependent upon Scholte for guidance in political matters. Although he had been fundamentally in sympathy with the principles of the Whig party, the clergyman had led his Dutch followers into consistent voting for the Democracy because of the nativism and prohibitionism which he detected among the Whigs. In 1859, however, Scholte abandoned the party of Democratic President James Buchanan, whose stand on the slavery issue had become a major source of disillusionment, and supported the newly formed Republican party after it had tried to dissociate itself from Know-Nothingism and had endorsed measures favorable to immigrant farmers, such as homestead legislation. Yet, despite Scholte's well-known activity in behalf of the Republican cause, the Dutch voters of the Pella colony refused to follow his example. Swierenga's analysis of the election data reveals that they continued to vote Democratic in 1859 as strong-

---

8. Cf. George A. Boeck, "A Historical Note on the Uses of Census Returns," *Mid-America* 44 (January 1962): 46–50. Although they worked independently of each other, Daniels and Boeck arrived at similar conclusions regarding the use of census data.

ly as before. Moreover, the Democratic majority among these ethnic voters was only slightly diminished in 1860 when Lincoln was the Republican candidate. Swierenga concludes that the initial power of the ethnic leader to control immigrant ballots was clearly short-lived.

Although Swierenga makes use of quantitative methods elsewhere,[9] his analysis of demographic and electoral data in this study is of the simplest kind because the problem involved but one township. The article is significant rather for the way it illustrates the need for historians to stop guessing, as Schafer had warned a quarter century earlier, and to examine evidence from the lowest level—the township, ward, and precinct. Finally, Swierenga stresses that even issues burdened with implications for ethnocultural conflict may have minimal impact upon voters because of the tenacity with which most persons hold to their established habits of voting.

If immigrant voters, like the native-born, are frequently impervious to issues, including those that may impinge directly upon their personal interests, other, more basic conditioners of political behavior must be sought out and identified. Voter analyses, for example, have frequently indicated that Catholic Germans regularly voted more strongly Democratic than Protestant Germans; if similar patterns are discovered in the behavior of Catholics of other ethnic groups, such as the Irish or Bohemians, one might suspect that religious belief, rather than ethnicity, is the underlying factor in the formation of deeply rooted partisan attachments. Possibilities for such a religious polarization are explored by Paul Kleppner in his article on immigrant voting in Pittsburgh in the election of 1860.

Published in 1966, this essay is a model of cogent writing based on systematic research. The author, who studied with Samuel P. Hays at the University of Pittsburgh, introduces a comparative dimension, not in terms of time and space, but in the

9. See his *Pioneers and Profits: Land Speculation on the Iowa Frontier* (Ames, Iowa: Iowa State University Press, 1968); he is also editor of *Quantification in American History: Theory and Research* (New York: Atheneum, 1970).

statement of potentially verifiable hypotheses and in the sophisticated analysis of statistics. His basic purpose is simply to test
in a systematic fashion the traditional interpretation that the
German voters supported the Republican party in 1860.

Kleppner first establishes the fact that the Republican party
did indeed court German voters with a variety of campaign
issues and techniques that were assumed to be effective among
them. Next, he compares electoral and demographic data. His
first table reveals that the wards most heavily populated by German immigrants registered large majorities for Lincoln. Since
no other clear pattern emerges from a visual inspection of the
data, conventional research would have terminated at this point
and the traditional view would have been substantiated. Kleppner, however, recognizes that this interpretation of the data is
essentially superficial, since it establishes only the undisputed
fact that an unknown proportion of the Pittsburgh Germans
voted for Lincoln. It falsely assumes that the Germans voted Republican in roughly the same proportion as the total voting population. In order to clarify the relationship, Kleppner introduces
the Pearson coefficient of correlation. This device, common
enough among social and behavioral scientists but until recently
almost totally ignored by historians, may indicate (though not
prove) the degree of association between two variables, in this
case, German voters and Republican votes. Coefficients obtained
from the Pittsburgh data indicate a *negative* relationship between
the two variables, the reverse of the impression gained through
a visual examination of the data. This discovery implies that the
Republican majorities in the German wards were supplied largely
by the non-German residents and that, by comparison to other
voters, the Germans actually preferred the Democratic candidate.

Further examination of the data, however, led Kleppner to
suspect that a more significant variable than ethnicity lay hidden
within the ethnic data—one related to religious belief. Since reliable statistics of church membership are extraordinarily difficult to acquire, the systematic testing of this variable demanded
unusual research efforts. Ultimately, Kleppner assigned percentages to Catholic and Protestant German and Irish populations

in each of Pittsburgh's wards as well as to the total Catholic and Protestant population. These data, when associated with partisan preferences, produced coefficients of exceptional magnitude, and permitted the author to state an alternative hypothesis to describe the ethnic voting behavior in Pittsburgh in 1860: "German-American and Irish-American Protestants were more likely to vote for Lincoln than were their fellow countrymen of the Roman Catholic faith." Thus, what had appeared to be an ethnic response to political stimuli was in reality a reflection of religious attitudes.

The final portion of Kleppner's article explores possible explanations for a religious polarization. He finds them in the Know-Nothing movement in Pittsburgh during the 1850s. Its nativism was subsequently fused with temperance agitation, sabbatarianism, and abolitionism in the ideology of moral stewardship assumed by the Republican party. The anti-Catholic orientation of these consolidated movements encouraged Catholics of all ethnic groups to continue their habits of voting Democratic, while Protestants, who perceived no threat in the moralism of the Republicans, freely supported the candidacy of Abraham Lincoln.[10]

Two previously unpublished essays complete this anthology of articles on ethnic voting in the presidential election of 1860. The first is by Ronald P. Formisano, who has here adapted materials from a book on the formation of mass political parties in Michigan from 1829 to 1861.[11] As a social analyst of political

10. For a greatly expanded investigation into the ethnic, religious, social, and economic correlates of political behavior in Pittsburgh during the 1850s, see Michael F. Holt, *Forging a Majority: The Formation of the Republican Party in Pittsburgh, 1848–1860* (New Haven, Conn.: Yale University Press, 1969). Paul Kleppner has developed and extended his theories in his book *Cross of Culture: The Social Analysis of Midwestern Politics, 1850–1900* (New York: Free Press, 1970). Here he relates partisan preferences to contrasting religiously oriented value systems. The pietistic, evangelistic tradition with its emphasis on right behavior is associated with Republican voting, while the ritualistic orthodoxy of the Catholic church and certain Protestant denominations, chiefly German Lutheran, with their great stress on right belief, is associated with Democratic voting.

11. *The Forming of American Mass Parties: Michigan, 1829–1861* (Princeton, N.J.: Princeton University Press, forthcoming).

history, Formisano identifies a wide variety of variables that act in concert to influence voting decisions. Among these, he finds that religious heritage and ethnicity were among the most powerful shapers of party loyalty. Each of Michigan's ethnic groups that was numerous or concentrated enough for meaningful study is discussed, and party preferences are identified and explanations for central tendencies offered.

Formisano's findings correspond closely to those of other state studies. Both Lutheran and Catholic Germans in rural areas remained loyal to the Democracy in 1860, while other Protestants and the freethinking liberals were attracted to Republicanism. Irish Catholics were uniformly Democratic despite intraparty problems. The Dutch generally retained Democratic majorities, although there was a gradual erosion during the decade of the 1850s. Recent British immigrants displayed formidable anti-Democratic tendencies.

The methods of election analysis employed by Formisano are not systematic compared to the standard set by Kleppner. The required data are not always available and the problems connected with the acquisition of statistics for a statewide analysis of this kind are stupendous. Yet, whenever possible, Formisano identifies trends over time as he samples units across the state.

In his effort to discover reasons for the behavior revealed by the election data, Formisano repeatedly finds them related to religious belief. In this respect his study closely resembles Kleppner's. Both suggest, one explicitly, the other implicitly, that the religious factor ultimately conditioned political behavior in a more fundamental way than ethnicity did. Issues, such as nativism and temperance, assumed importance to the extent that they were related to ethnoreligious value systems. Thus, Formisano also finds that the importance of abolitionism as an issue for ethnic voters has been greatly exaggerated.

A special value of Formisano's essay is his warning that voting behavior is a vastly complicated phenomenon. Neither religion nor ethnicity works independently, he reminds us, nor do socioeconomic status, education, residential factors, or rate or degree of assimilation. Since few of these variables are subject to accurate measurement, historians must guard against the tendency to attribute importance only to those agents for which he has data.

The final contribution in this anthology is by James M. Bergquist, an associate professor at Villanova University whose specialty is American immigration history. Unlike those scholars who approach the problem from the point of view of the larger society of which ethnic groups were component parts, Bergquist concentrates on the experience of one group, the Germans, in the state of Illinois. Keenly aware of their heterogeneity and the diversity of their institutions, the author traces the changing character of the German community during the decade preceding the outbreak of the Civil War. He examines the political attitudes of the Germans, as revealed by their press, toward the Kansas-Nebraska Act, free soil, the leadership of Stephen A. Douglas, homestead legislation, nativism, temperance, and other issues that impinged upon German interests.

Bergquist's interest in German political involvement extends well beyond voting behavior. He describes the ways in which German immigrant leaders were able to influence the character of the political parties during a decade of flux and transition. His central thesis is that largely because of German influence, the Republican party of Illinois (unlike that of certain other states) developed without the stigmas of nativism and prohibitionism. Its platform was shaped to conform to German immigrant attitudes. The Germans of Illinois were thus free, according to Bergquist, to abandon the Democracy of Stephen A. Douglas for the new party of Abraham Lincoln.

Bergquist's examination of election data led him to conclude that, after the political realignment began in 1854, 60 to 65 percent of the Illinois Germans voted Republican. Moreover, their preferences in 1860 marked "no striking change" from their behavior in the previous election of 1858. Like other scholars, Bergquist finds diversity in political behavior among Germans to be related to religious belief. Catholics were the most strongly Democratic; Lutherans were somewhat more susceptible to Republican persuasion between 1856 and 1860; statistics for other religious groups do not permit generalizations. The author likewise suggests that there were regional differences within the state as he compares data from the Chicago area with those of Saint Clair County and vicinity. Throughout his analysis, he employs evidence drawn from the smallest possible local units. Bergquist concludes that the most significant effect the Illinois Germans had on the political process was not due to their distinctive voting habits but rather to their ability to influence the Republican party in its adoption of policies and nomination of candidates acceptable to them. In that way, he believes, the Germans influenced the "course of events far beyond what their numbers alone warranted."

This review has summarized the assumptions, concepts, and methods used by historians in their analyses of ethnic politics in the pre–Civil War years. In contrast to the earlier or traditional interpretations, recent studies have been based upon intensive analyses of local-level sources of both an impressionistic and a quantitative character. They have been skeptical of the assertions of ethnic leaders and their ability to persuade immigrant voters. They stress the importance of issues related to religious and cultural conflicts rather than of nationally oriented issues infused with an ideology which spoke chiefly to native-born citizens. They dismiss the old assumptions about ethnic bloc voting, especially among the Germans. Indeed, they question the importance of ethnicity itself as a correlate of political behavior, interpreting it rather as a cloak disguising more important religious and cultural variables.

Above all, contemporary scholars are insisting upon appropriate comparative dimensions to ethnopolitical studies: comparisons in time and space; comparisons with the larger society and with other groups within the larger society; comparisons with smaller religious, economic, social, and regional identities within the ethnic group. Such analyses, recent scholars have discovered, cannot be made without the systematic ordering of quantitative evidence.

More intensive studies of individual communities, both urban and rural, need to be undertaken if valid generalizations are to be made about ethnic voters in the election of Lincoln. Certainly immigrants must be analyzed as parts of the larger social context, as Merle Curti has done in his pioneering study of a frontier county in Wisconsin, and they must be placed solidly within the context of political history, as in Michael Holt's recent examination of party formation in Pittsburgh from 1848 to 1860.[12] Little systematic research has been done, for example, on the large German communities of the 1850s in New York, Philadelphia, and Cincinnati. Although the votes of Indiana Germans in 1860 have been recently analyzed on a township basis, data from Ohio, the oldest state of the Old Northwest, remain to be studied in a comprehensive fashion.[13] Moreover, little is known of the political behavior of the significant groups of Germans in the Southern states of Louisiana and Texas. How do they compare with the Germans of the border slave states of Missouri, Kentucky, and Maryland or of the Northern states of Pennsylvania and New York? Past research has revealed patterns of ethnic political behavior to be closely related to religious belief. Will similar patterns emerge from data about the class, occupation,

---

12. Merle Curti et al., *The Making of an American Community: A Case Study of Democracy in a Frontier County* (Stanford, Calif.: Stanford University Press, 1959); Holt, *Forging a Majority*.

For an early consideration of the urban-rural factor, see "Urban and Rural Voting in the Election of 1860," by Ollinger Crenshaw, in *Historiography and Urbanization: Essays in American History in Honor of W. Stull Holt*, ed. by Eric F. Goldman (Baltimore: Johns Hopkins University Press, 1941), pp. 43–66.

13. Thomas John Kelso, "The German-American Vote in the Election of 1860: The Case of Indiana with Supporting Data from Ohio" (Ph.D. diss., Ball State University, 1967). Like most of the other recent studies, Kelso's analysis shows that in 1860 an increase in the proportion of German voters on the township level paralleled higher percentages of votes cast for the Democratic candidate. He attributes the Democratic voting of the Indiana German to fears of nativism, temperance agitation, and abolitionism which they associated with the Republican party. A time dimension to comparable data is supplied by E. Duane Elbert, "Southern Indiana Politics on the Eve of the Civil War, 1858–1861" (Ph.D. diss., Indiana University, 1967). He finds that, while there was an extensive shift in the votes of Indiana Germans from the Democratic party in 1858 to the Republican party in 1860, the majority of them still remained with the Democracy, even though seven-eighths of the German-language newspapers of Indiana had switched to the Republican party. Thus both studies challenge the traditional thesis that the German vote was crucial to the election of Lincoln in 1860.

education, and mobility of immigrants? If these and similar questions are to be answered, immigration historians need to equip themselves with the conceptual and methodological tools of the social analysts, just as political historians must make new efforts to understand the language, the culture, the attitudes, and value systems of immigrant peoples.

ETHNIC VOTERS AND THE
ELECTION OF LINCOLN

For many years Donnal V. Smith (b. 1901) was president of the State University of New York College at Cortland. In 1961 he assumed a deanship at Bowling Green State University in Ohio. His article, originally published in the Mississippi Valley Historical Review *in 1932, is a summary of the traditional concepts, methods, and assumptions employed by historians in their analyses of ethnic political behavior. An extension of William E. Dodd's 1911 article, this interpretation is sometimes called the Dodd-Smith thesis.*

The Influence of the Foreign-Born of the Northwest in the Election of 1860

DONNAL V. SMITH

Historians have long recognized the influence of the Northwest in the election of 1860. As a section, it contained a large proportion of the two and a half million immigrants who came to our shores in the decade prior to 1860. As an electorate these foreign-born must have wielded a tremendous influence in a region where a change of one vote in twenty would have made Lincoln a defeated Republican candidate rather than a victorious president.[1]

Not all foreign-born who settled in the United States intended to make their residence permanent but of those who went into the Northwest practically all were home seekers. Usually they were in possession of a little money with which to gratify their desire to own land.[2] The Northwest offered them the best opportunities for investment. Ohio, Indiana, and Illinois had appealed to the newcomers for thirty years and in the four years before 1860 the Illinois Central Railroad, alone, sold over a million

1. William E. Dodd, "The Fight for the Northwest," *American Historical Review* 16 (July 1911): 788.
2. George M. Stephenson, *A History of American Immigration* (Boston, 1926), p. 99; *Eighth Census of the United States*, 1860, *Population*, xxiii–xxiv.

1

acres of land to them.[3] Michigan, Wisconsin, and Minnesota, all with unoccupied lands at their disposal, offered extra inducements and enacted special legislation to attract their share of the land hungry.

But the Northwest also appealed to deeper motive than the mere desire to own land. Many of the immigrants came from countries in which the revolutions of 1830 and 1848 had ended in reaction. Not a few of them were refugees and all had definite political notions unwelcome in the old country. Thus they arrived in the "Promised Land" with political concepts already formed. Of these, personal liberty and universal manhood suffrage were the clearest. As soon as the states of the Northwest learned of these fundamental political notions they endeavored to satisfy them. Indiana, Michigan, Wisconsin, and Minnesota enfranchised the foreign-born shortly after their declaration to become citizens, the interval ranging from four months in Minnesota to thirty in Michigan. According to the constitution of 1852, it was necessary to be a citizen of the United States and a resident of the state one year to vote in Ohio, but the state had been entirely settled under the constitution of 1802 which demanded only one year's residence and the payment of a property tax. Since most of the immigrants to the comparatively unpopulated Northwest were home seekers, eager to assume a place in the political life of their adopted country, it is logical to suppose that most of them took the necessary steps to secure the franchise shortly after their arrival, especially since it was offered to them as a special inducement.[4]

Once established in their own homes the foreign-born found their greatest contentment in the companionship of their own people, hence they settled in little communities where they could retain their own speech, press, schools, and most of their old customs. This social solidarity, translated into political solidarity by their speedy enfranchisement, made the foreign-born

3. Pamphlet reports of the Illinois Central Railroad for 1856–60, Chicago Historical Society Library.

4. Thomas J. McCormack, ed., *Memoirs of Gustave Koerner, 1809–96* (Cedar Rapids, 1909), I: 423.

vote pivotal.[5] Their political effectiveness was further enhanced by the control which a few leaders of their own nativity exerted. Because of his dependence on his own speech and press the immigrant experienced considerable difficulty in comprehending political issues until they were translated and explained in his own language. The leaders who were so trusted were in a splendid position to control the political strength of the foreign-born. Among such were the Ohioans, Judge John B. Stallo, Frederick Hassaurek, and the editor of the Cincinnati *Republican,* Colonel August Willich; Gustave Koerner of Illinois and Hoosier influence; Henry P. Scholte, editor of the Pella *Gazette,* and Nicholas J. Rusch, as well as several others of Iowa. More important, however, even than this group was the well-known Carl Schurz, whose influence extended throughout the entire nation.

Before 1854 many of the foreign-born had enrolled in the Democratic party, attracted by its name and the supposed ideals of its patron saint, Thomas Jefferson. Before long, however, they became aware of the close association of their adopted party with slavery. While they did not understand the plantation system of the South they remembered vividly the restrictions upon human freedom in Europe, and hence they viewed with aversion any form of slavery. A second reason why the Democratic party became impossible for the foreign-born was its supposed attitude toward homestead legislation. Douglas, said Republican heelers, would open the entire Northwest to planters and their slaves, thus depriving the small land owner of the chief thing that had drawn him westward. This sophistry was not without its success among the foreign-born. Out of a list of eighty-eight German papers, eighty actively opposed Douglas and the Kansas-Nebraska bill and the remainder said nothing in favor if it.[6]

The southern press did nothing to counteract the fallacious reasoning of the anti-Douglas propaganda; quite the contrary, it encouraged this belief. The celebrated and widely quoted

5. Frank I. Herriott, "Iowa and the First Nomination of Lincoln," *Annals of Iowa,* 3d ser. 8 (1907): 196.

6. Arthur C. Cole, *The Era of the Civil War* (Springfield, 1919), pp. 123–44. See also Stephenson, *History of American Immigration,* pp. 125, 130.

Charleston *Mercury* predicted that westbound trains "freighted with Germans and their plunder" could only mean the complete vitiation of the principles of the party. Their proof was that:

> Whole towns and counties are settled by these people, while they are scattered in every portion of the North in numbers sufficient to control the elections. The Homestead bill is a grand scheme to settle the Northwest and create new states. . . . We make bold to say that it is the most dangerous abolition bill which has ever been directly pressed in Congress.[7]

In similar vein Governor John Wise of Virginia admonished the Democrats of the Northwest to rule with an iron hand lest treason stalk too boldly there.[8] Such sentiment quickly reached the ears of the foreign-born by way of a Republican party anxious for converts. Buchanan, said to be under southern influence, added the last straw when he vetoed a homestead bill that had finally secured congressional approval. The foreign-born felt that their fears had materialized. It was now necessary to seek the cooperation of another party.

Ever since 1855, leaders of the embryonic Republican party in the Northwest had been endeavoring to win the foreign-born vote. Governor James W. Grimes of Iowa had written to Salmon P. Chase of Ohio, urging him to seek the German vote in his state, and Chase had not allowed the advice to go unheeded.[9] An Illinois Republican boasted a "well-drilled, 'Fritz' organized, educated, liberty-loving . . . broad and wide-a-wake, ready for the fight, shouting for man, liberty, justice, God and their complex duties and relations, now and forever."[10] The Republican party, however, was by no means entirely satisfactory to foreign-born leaders. The Know-Nothing element caused them much distress. In certain portions of the East the "beer-drinking, Sunday-despising German," as he was called, was just as unpopular as

7. March 17, 1860, triweekly edition.
8. Dodd, "Fight for the Northwest," p. 777.
9. Grimes to Chase, July 16, 1855; Maurice Jacobi to Chase, October 1, 1859, Chase MSS, Library of Congress. The Germans of Ohio claimed Chase as their champion in "these times that try men's souls."
10. Joseph F. Newton, *Lincoln and Herndon* (Cedar Rapids, 1910), p. 246, quoting letter of Herndon to Theodore Parker, November 27, 1858.

he was with southern Democrats. Thus, was the foreigner placed in a dilemma; to remain a Democrat meant the sacrifice of political principles and economic interest, while the threat of Know-Nothingism among eastern Republicans caused him to view that party with the gravest misgiving. In their uncertainty foreign-born leaders and voters drew closer together, thus accentuating an already marked solidarity. Republican leaders in the Northwest did their best to destroy the feeling that their party espoused the tenets of the waning Know-Nothing party but whatever hope of success they might have entertained was diminished by two events of April, 1859.

The first factor to confound the situation was Horace Greeley's announcement in the New York *Tribune* that he would support John Bell, Edward Bates, or John M. Botts for president in 1860.[11] All three had been closely associated with the American party in the Fillmore campaign and were, therefore, equally undesirable to the foreign element.[12] The large circulation which the weekly edition of the *Tribune* enjoyed in the Northwest served to disseminate the announcement widely, and the foreign-born, seeing few other papers of national circulation, attached more importance to Greeley's influence in national politics than the facts warranted. Moreover, this popular paper was so involved in eastern politics that its columns never once espoused the cause of the immigrant.[13] They no doubt rightly felt that Greeley did not consider them at all.

Before Greeley's announcement could be properly protested, there occurred a second event to confirm the worst suspicions. That was a proposal of the Republican legislature of Massachusetts to amend its constitution so that naturalized citizens could not vote for two years after they had attained citizenship. This

11. New York *Tribune*, April 26, 1859.
12. Frank I. Herriott, "Iowa and Abraham Lincoln" (Des Moines, 1911), p. 51.
13. Herriott, "Iowa and the First Nomination of Lincoln," *Annals of Iowa*, 3d ser. 9: 47–48, 59–60. After the furore caused by the proposed Massachusetts amendment Greeley wrote his first lines on naturalization and these were far from satisfactory from the standpoint of the naturalized citizen (ibid., 8: 206).

was at once accepted by the foreign-born as unmistakable discrimination, which, unless withdrawn by the national organization, would effectively bar their entrance into the Republican party. This was the opinion expressed by Schurz in a letter to Edward L. Pierce, a prominent lawyer and reformer of considerable repute in the Bay State.[14] Probably Schurz's letter had no influence in shaping opinion in Massachusetts but in the Northwest his, and similar other protests, were not without results. In Illinois the opposition of a radical German paper, the *Belleviller Zeitung,* so impressed Norman B. Judd of the national Republican committee, that he publicly repudiated the action of Massachusetts, denying that it in any way reflected the opinion of the party.[15] Just as active in its opposition was the Pella *Gazette,* edited by Henry P. Scholte, a recent Republican convert whose influence among his Dutch countrymen and other foreign-born, not only in Iowa but all over the Northwest, was generally conceded.[16] As a result of the efforts of Scholte and other editors, a committee of German voters was delegated to wait upon Governor Grimes as the spokesman of the Republican party in Iowa, to request a statement regarding the conduct of the party in Massachusetts. Grimes, admitting the local character of the proposed amendment and the right of the people to enact it, nevertheless believed such action "to be based upon a false and dangerous principle, fraught with evil to the whole country." Hence he felt called upon to "condemn and deplore it, without equivocation or reserve."[17]

From Minnesota, H. C. Wheeler, chairman of the state Republican committee, sought to allay the mounting fear by demanding that "the great Know-Nothing lobby must be silenced," adding that it had already "decidedly damaged . . . prospects of success" and was "now on every tongue as a stigma of the Re-

14. Schurz to Pierce, March 26, 1859, Frederic Bancroft, ed., *Speeches, Correspondence and Political Papers of Carl Schurz* (New York, 1913), 1: 41–44.
15. Koerner, *Memoirs,* 2: 74–76.
16. Stephenson, *American Immigration,* p. 130.
17. Grimes to the committee, April 30, 1859, William Salter, *Life of James W. Grimes* (New York, 1876), pp. 119–20.

publican party—foreigners here all understand it and many, I fear, that have been with us will leave us in disgust. Some palliation should be made and it will require the strongest kind of argument to convince them that it is not the principle of the Republican party."[18]

In Ohio, Colonel Willich called a meeting of German voters which resolved to issue a manifesto, setting forth the principles of the German Republicans against discrimination between native and naturalized citizens. Prominent among the out-of-state leaders at this meeting were Schurz of Wisconsin, Nicholas J. Rusch of Iowa, George Schneider, editor of the Illinois *Staats Zeitung,* Koerner of Illinois, and Frederich Kapp of New York.[19] The militant feeling of the German voters was graphically expressed by one of their number from Iowa who recalled that the legions of the mighty Caesar went to smash in the woods of Germany.[20]

By the spring of 1860 the Illinois management decided that Lincoln had better set forth his position upon the Massachusetts enactment. His word of reassurance, published in the *Staats Anzeiger,* reads:

> I am against its adoption, not only in Illinois, but in every other place in which I have the right to oppose it. . . . It is well known that I deplore the oppressed condition of the blacks, and it would, therefore, be very inconsistent for me to look with approval upon any measure that infringes upon the inalienable rights of white men, whether or not they are born in another land or speak a different language from our own.[21]

The whole discussion in the Northwest served to do two things. First, to use a favorite boast of Carl Schurz, it revealed a "solid column of German and Scandinavian anti-slavery men

18. H. C. Wheeler to Chase, May 18, 1859, Chase MSS.
19. Koerner, *Memoirs,* 2: 75.
20. Herriott, "Iowa and the First Nomination of Lincoln," 8: 207. One disappointed office seeker was led to comment that all that was now necessary to secure office in Iowa "was to be born in Germany, by G——!" (Herriott, "Iowa and Lincoln," p. 117).
21. *National Intelligencer,* May 28, 1860, quoting *Staats Anzeiger,* which made public a letter from Lincoln, dated May 17, 1859.

who know how to handle a gun and who will fight too";[22] a group of voters that would be practically certain to vote as a unit. Secondly, it was made very clear that to win this vote it would be necessary for the Republican party to give absolute assurance on the two vital questions at issue; one pledge that there would be no proscription of foreign birth in the Republican party and another promising homesteads to all. Thus on the eve of the national convention the foreign-born vote of the Northwest stood outside of the Democratic party but not yet satisfied with the prospects of action with the Republican party.

The selection of Chicago as the Republican convention site was a victory of the Illinois managers for their none-too-certain candidate. For the foreign-born it was an opportunity to press their demands and they were not slow to follow up their advantage. Every one of the seven Northwestern states had representatives of its foreign element in their delegations, thus furnishing, said the Pella *Gazette*, "renewed and indubitable proof" that there was no proscription of foreign birth there.[23] Scholte, Stallo, Hassaurek, Koerner, Schurz—all had credentials from their respective states. In addition the Missouri delegation included such supporters of the immigrant cause as Henry Boernstein, the able and well known editor of *Der Anzeiger des Westens,* Judge Arnold Krekel, and Frederick Muench.

Secure in the knowledge that the Republican party needed their support to win, these leaders called a meeting of their own for the day preceding the opening of the convention. The aim was to consolidate their strength and unify, as well as simplify, a statement of their demands. For this reason the meeting wisely refrained from taking any official action whatsoever with reference to candidates, thus leaving the delegates free to support whoever offered most. The next day Schurz placed the work of this meeting before the convention, not forgetting to emphasize for publication the fact that he spoke for 300,000 voters.

22. *Speeches of Carl Schurz* (Philadelphia, 1865), pp. 32–33.
23. Herriot, "Iowa and Lincoln," pp. 184–85.

So far as accomplishment on the floor of the convention is concerned it does not seem that the foreign-born exerted much influence. That appearance, however, is deceptive. In organizing the convention both Schurz and Koerner were included on the platform committee. Already prepared, they produced two planks which were approved by the convention and immediately dubbed the "Dutch planks."[24] One, the thirteenth of the platform, demanded the much desired homestead law and the other, the fourteenth, expressed unequivocal opposition to any change in naturalization laws or discrimination against the foreign-born in the award of franchise. These planks were at once hailed as satisfactory by the immigrants and the press in half a dozen languages began predicting the size of the Republican foreign-born vote.[25]

Over the selection of a candidate there was but little difference among the naturalized delegates. The Germans of Missouri would have liked Bates to be the man but were easily reconciled to the impossibility of their desire. The Ohio delegates early asserted that they would support Chase, Seward, or Lincoln. Schurz was personally in favor of Seward but Koerner was sure that Lincoln would be more concerned with the welfare of the Northwest. He finally had his way, Schurz agreeing that Lincoln was "not only the best and purest but also . . . the most available candidate."[26]

Lincoln was no sooner officially notified of his nomination than the foreign-born leaders began an active campaign for his election. Hassaurek and Schurz, both members of the notification committee, addressed a large crowd at Springfield, thus sounding the opening gun of the campaign. Both were very optimistic and predicted that Lincoln would get the immigrant vote.[27] Hamlin joined Lincoln in unqualified approval of the "Dutch planks"[28] and in the Northwest, the Chicago *Press and Tribune*

24. Koerner, *Memoirs,* 2: 87; *The Reminiscences of Carl Schurz* (New York, 1907), 2: 180.
25. *Illinois State Journal,* June 20, 1860.
26. Koerner, *Memoirs,* 2: 85.
27. Springfield *Republican,* May 23, 1860.
28. *National Intelligencer,* May 22, 1860.

began a series of special articles for the foreign-born voters of
the nation, stressing Lincoln's ideals of liberty and democracy
and his support of the "Dutch planks."[29] In July, the New Ulm
Pioneer reported a list of seventy-three German papers which
supported the Republican cause.[30]

Important as was the work of the press it was a distant second
to the work of a few foreign-born leaders. Schurz, as a member
of the national committee, had charge of a specially created
"foreign department" which employed speakers of every tongue
to go among the immigrants of the Northwest and campaign for
Lincoln. They presented him as the opponent of slavery and the
protector of the natural rights of man, whether native or foreign-
born. This they could do without alienating the more conservative element of the party in older sections of the country.[31] They
explained away the fear of Know-Nothingism by pointing to
the two "Dutch planks" which Schurz and Koerner, their respected leaders, had written into the platform.[32] The absence
of similar pledges in the Democrat platform was pointed out and
the continued opposition of the Democrats to homestead legislation was recalled. Slavery was mentioned in the campaign
among the foreign-born but the real issues to them were more
personal and immediate. To the naturalized voter the contest
appeared to be a continuation of the old continental struggle of
the people versus an aristocracy—a landed interest opposing the
landless. To them the platform had only two real planks, the
thirteenth and fourteenth. These they reprinted in several languages and scattered broadcast.[33]

Schurz spoke everywhere he could. In village or in county
seat the people assembled from miles around to hear him;
"packed like sardines" they "trembled with excitement" at his
words.[34] Indiana begged for his aid, her leaders saying, "One
week's work from you is worth more than all the [other] German

29. May 15 and after.
30. Stephenson, *History of American Immigration,* p. 130.
31. Dodd, "Fight for the Northwest," p. 786.
32. Koerner, *Memoirs,* 2: 87.
33. Stephenson, *History of American Immigration,* p. 129.
34. Bancroft, *Papers of Schurz,* 1: 110; *Reminiscences of Carl Schurz,* 2: 197.

help we have in the State."[35] While there he estimated that more than ten thousand German votes would be converted to the Republican cause.[36] Michigan offered to pay him twenty-five dollars a day and expenses for his services for ten days. Ohio leaders, despite numerous able German speakers of their own, felt it imperative that they have Schurz.[37] Pennsylvania Germans replied, when they were solicited to vote for Lincoln, "Wait until we hear Carl Schurz." After visiting the state Schurz wrote to his wife, "The old 'Pennsylvania Dutch' follow me like little children."[38] Everywhere he spoke Schurz made votes and all things considered, it is not strange that the "boss of the German vote" should feel that he had earned more than a post at Madrid.

Just as active as Schurz, and quite as important was Gustave Koerner. Even lowly "Egypt," pro-Douglas if not pro-Southern, listened to his speeches with avid interest.[39] Iowa leaders felt sure that many Yankees, as well as the entire German population, could be influenced by a visit.[40] All over the Northwest he was received by bands and Wide Awake Clubs displaying the most active enthusiasm.[41] His home paper, ably edited by the radical Franz Grimm, wielded even more than its usual influence. The *Staats Zeitung*, published in Chicago, but enjoying a national circulation among the Germans, featured his speeches along with those of Schurz.[42] Koerner, Schurz, and the other speakers of the "Foreign Department" succeeded in lending a charm to Lincoln's name that was well nigh irresistible to the foreign-born. In many places entire German Democratic clubs went over to the Republicans with noisy acclaim.[43] The Scandinavians were so solidly Republican that one who did not openly indicate

35. Ibid., pp. 161–62, n. 2.
36. Ibid., p. 108.
37. Ibid., pp. 161–62, n. 2.
38. Ibid., p 160.
39. W. A. Myers, "The Presidential Campaign of 1860 in Illinois" (Ph.D. diss., University of Chicago, 1913), p. 4; Koerner, *Memoirs*, 2: 98–102.
40. Koerner letters in Illinois State Historical Society, *Transactions*, 1907, pp. 222–46, passim.
41. *Illinois State Journal*, August 5, 1860.
42. July–August, passim.
43. Stephenson, *History of American Immigration*, p. 130.

his support of Lincoln was a rarity. The *Hemlandet*, a Swedish paper published in Chicago, and the *Emigranten*, a Norwegian paper published at Madison, were in the van for Lincoln and both were influential.[44] To even the casual observer it must appear that by election time the foreign-born leaders had overcome their fear of Know-Nothingism in the Republican party and had accepted its platform as a satisfactory reply to their demands.

Thus the foreign-born went to the polls. By the nature of their social life in a new land and the uniformity of their political demands they were solidly united. Because of their eagerness to participate in the political government of their adopted land and the ease with which they could obtain the franchise in the northwestern states it is only logical to think of them as voters. Because of the vital nature of the issues involved in this campaign it is also logical to consider them preponderatingly Republican. Unfortunately, it is impossible to tell from exact statistics precisely how many voted for Lincoln but conjecture can be convincingly substantiated. None of the states enumerated the naturalized population of voting age nor did the *Eighth Census of the United States* do so, but the latter report does furnish figures which serve as a basis for a close approximation. The report of Illinois, for example, shows that 49% of the total male population was over twenty years of age in 1859, that is, 439,304 males were qualified by age to vote. The same report enumerates the total foreign-born male population of the state as 181,629. Granting, for the sake of argument, that the proportion of foreign-born males over voting age was no greater than the proportion of the total male population, that is, 49%, their number would have been 88,998. So far as this percentage is concerned, it is distinctly low. The superintendent of the census stated in his report that of the foreign-born who arrived in this country in the decade prior to 1860, 63%, rather than the estimated 49%, were over twenty years of age.[45]

44. Ibid., p. 131.

45. *Eighth Census of the United States, 1860, Population,* p. xx. All of the population figures are found in this volume.

The election returns for Illinois show that 339,693 votes were cast for president in this election. This means that of the 439,304 males of voting age, 77% voted. It would seem from the account given in these pages that a still larger proportion of the eligible foreign-born males voted, due to the fact that proscription and homestead legislation were made vital issues to them. But again, to be safely conservative, it will be assumed that of the 88,998 foreign-born of voting age only 77% exercised their right. This would mean that 68,528 foreign-born votes were cast. The real significance of this figure is revealed when it is noted that Lincoln's majority over Douglas was less than 12,000 votes. If the 68,000 foreign-born Republican votes, arrived at in the above calculation, be reduced two-thirds, the result would still be impressive; as it is, it is overwhelming.[46]

By following the same method of determining the foreign-born Republican vote in Indiana it will be found that 26,000 foreign-born voted. Lincoln's plurality there is considerably less than 24,000. Over the entire field Lincoln's lead was less than

46. Undoubtedly there were minorities among the foreign-born of the Northwest which did not support the Republican party in this election. Judging by the press and the memoirs of foreign-born leaders these minorities were small and merely qualify, rather than disprove, the conclusion that the foreign-born of the Northwest elected Lincoln.

In Chicago the Irish vote was undoubtedly Democratic but it was neither so large nor so influential as it was to become a decade later. Even though the total Irish vote of the state be counted anti-Lincoln, the conclusion drawn would stand, for by liberal computation it could not have been over 18,800 votes, a number insufficient to destroy Lincoln's majority among the foreign-born. In other states the influence of the Irish must have been less, for Illinois had not only the largest Irish population but also the largest proportion of Irish in comparison with other nationalities.

The Irish of the Northwest, however, were not always Democrats in 1860, nor were they generally city dwellers, a difference from later conditions which must be kept in mind. Professor Herriott, in his study published in the *Annals of Iowa*, 8: 196, concludes that the Irish of Iowa helped to swell Lincoln's majority in 1860.

In both Wisconsin and Minnesota there were settlements of German Catholics which, in some instances at least, were solidly Democratic. Their numbers, however, were not large and their vote, even though counted as Democratic, is not large enough to overcome the undoubted power of the Republican party among the other foreign-born voters in 1860. (Koerner, *Memoirs*, 1: 21).

6,000. For Ohio, this calculation gives 65,900 foreign-born Republican votes while Lincoln's majority over his nearest rival is less than 45,000. Wisconsin, the home of Schurz, gave Lincoln a majority of 21,000, but the foreign-born vote for the state was over 56,000. In Michigan, the foreign-born vote exceeded Lincoln's majority over Douglas by 10,000.

Minnesota entered her first national campaign as a Republican state by giving Lincoln a 10,000 majority. Her foreign-born vote was over 12,000. This margin is relatively small but it must be remembered that the population of the two-year-old state was still well under 200,000, much less than the population of any of her sister states in the Northwest. Iowa, with the next smallest aggregate population, registered over 21,000 foreign-born votes to give Lincoln his majority of 15,298 over Douglas.

For the seven northwestern states as a whole, Lincoln's majority over Douglas was 149,807, while this method of computation shows the foreign-born vote to be 283,748. Schurz had claimed 300,000 in the Chicago convention.

Thus it has been established that the foreign-born settled in the Northwest in large numbers, with the definite intention of permanent residence. Because of their social solidarity and their eagerness to avail themselves of the easy means offered by the states of the section to secure the franchise, they immediately assumed a position of political importance. Their solidarity was further enhanced by their dependence upon a few capable leaders of their own nativity to translate and explain political questions to them.

Due to their aversion for slavery the foreign-born quickly perceived the impossibility of acting with the Democratic party. They stated their demands for homestead legislation and freedom from proscription with unmistakable clearness. After the Republican party met these demands by specific party pledges, the foreign-born press and leaders expressed complete satisfaction.

Despite the fact that the census does not specify exactly how many of the foreign-born voters were Republican, it seems reasonable from the above proof to deduce that a very large proportion acted with that party. By using the most conservative estimates the result reveals that without the vote of the foreign-born, Lincoln could not have carried the Northwest, and without the Northwest, or with its vote divided in any other way, he would have been defeated.

Reprinted from the *Mississippi Valley Historical Review* 19 (September 1932): 192–204.

Originally written as a master's thesis in history at the State University of Iowa, this article by Charles Wilson Emery is interesting because it was conceived in entirely traditional terms and yet its evidence suggests conclusions at considerable variance with what the author expected; hence he offers them timidly and tentatively.

The Iowa Germans in the Election of 1860

CHARLES WILSON EMERY

THE GERMAN-AMERICANS IN NATIONAL POLITICS IN 1860

In the stormy period of the 1850s the young American nation was trying by democratic processes to determine its future way of life. Many of its statesmen had come to realize that the agrarian civilization of the South based upon slavery and the new industrial civilization of the North were incompatible. They saw that if the nation was to endure, one of these opposed cultures must predominate. It was a critical choice which the Americans were forced to make in that trying decade, and the problem was only resolved by a bitter civil war.

Strangely enough, circumstances transpired which gave the new German-American citizens, largely untrained in American ideas and ideals, an importance in deciding this question which was all out of proportion to their numerical strength. The presidential election contest was closely fought in 1860, and the winner, Abraham Lincoln, received fewer popular votes than his combined opponents, becoming the fourth minority President of the United States. In so close an election a small minority group without strong allegiance to either party could, if well led and united, wield tremendous influence.

The German-born Americans comprised such a group. Although only 1,301,136, or 4.73%, of the entire population of the United States in 1860 were of German birth, the fact that

16

the great majority of these immigrants had settled in those states west of the Appalachians and north of the Ohio gave them great political significance. Professor A. B. Faust says that in 1860 "the Germans clearly held the balance of power at the polls in Missouri, Iowa, and Minnesota, in Illinois and Wisconsin, in Indiana, Ohio and Michigan, in Maryland, Pennsylvania, New Jersey, New York, and Connecticut."[1]

The unity of the German-Americans was another element in their political strength. Like other foreign-language groups, the German immigrants were clannish. They lived in settlements and certain cities—Cincinnati, Milwaukee, St. Louis, and Davenport—came to be known as German cities. The German-language press was large and active. According to the Cincinnati *Gazette* of 1854, it consisted of eighty-eight papers in that year. Devotedly following their able leaders, the German-Americans presented a nearly solid political front in 1860.

Until 1850 the great majority of German-Americans were Jacksonian Democrats, largely because the Democratic party had always been the party of the immigrants and the "common people." After the Mexican War, however, the increased agitation of the slavery question and the arrival of the émigrés from the German revolutions of 1848 led many Germans to renounce their ties to the Democracy. The "Forty-eighters," who soon assumed the leadership of the German-Americans, hated slavery as another form of the oppression from which they had fled. Therefore, when in 1853 Stephen A. Douglas introduced in the United States Senate a bill to repeal the Missouri Compromise, his German followers deserted the Democratic party by the thousands.

The problem of finding a party which stood for political principles to which they could subscribe confronted those who had left the Democracy. The great opposition party, the Whigs, was decadent, ineffectual, and in the process of disintegration. No major party appeared to take its place as an opponent of the Democratic measures which the Germans had found so distaste-

1. Albert Bernhardt Faust, *The German Element in the United States,* 2 vols. (New York, 1909), 1: 462.

ful. Some of the German voters did ally themselves with the Whig party. Others supported the Free Soil party, newly organized by those opposed to the extension of slavery into the territories. *Der Bund Freier Männer,* an independent anti-slavery party, was organized by German radicals in Louisville in 1853, and spread through most of the Western states. Needless to say, the American, or "Know-Nothing," party, which was definitely anti-foreign and anti-Catholic, gained no German adherents.

When the Republican party was organized in 1854 and 1855 to prevent the extension of slavery and to succeed the party of Clay as a proponent of internal improvements, a protective tariff, and a strong central government thousands of Germans attached themselves to it. Among the German leaders who took an active part in early Republican councils were Gustave Koerner and George Schneider of Illinois, Philip Dorheimer of Buffalo, and Carl Schurz of Wisconsin.

Nineteen of the delegates to the first Republican convention in Philadelphia on June 17, 1856, were German-Americans. George Schneider composed the tenth plank in the platform adopted by this convention. This resolution, which was an assurance to German voters that the party had their interest at heart, condemned all proscriptive legislation. It was an open challenge to the nativistic element within the party. During the campaign that followed, the "Forty-eighters" worked strenuously for Frémont, the Republican nominee. Although the Republicans lost the election, the labor of these German leaders bore fruit. Schurz estimated that 300,000 German votes were cast for Frémont in 1856 in Illinois, Indiana, Iowa, Wisconsin, Michigan, and Ohio.

Although these Germans gave the Republican cause strong support in 1856, there were elements within the party organization that antagonized the new citizens. In addition to the nativistic element, there was a puritanical group within the party which attempted to regulate Sunday observance and prohibit the use of alcoholic drinks. This ran counter to the Germans' interpretation of individual liberty and separation of church and state. Naturally the Democrats were quick to point out to the Germans the harshness of these elements.

The activities of Know-Nothings under the cover of Republicanism made the German-Americans particularly anxious. Less than two months after the election of President Buchanan, a bill was sponsored in Congress by Republican representatives which would have required a foreigner to reside twenty-one years in this country before he should be allowed to vote. The bill was defeated by a Democratic majority. Further evidence of the existence of nativism within the Republican party appeared in 1857 when Carl Schurz was defeated for lieutenant-governor of Wisconsin by the same Republicans who had used his name to decoy German votes for the Republican ticket.

There was, however, no organized movement among the German Republicans to protest against nativism within the party until 1859. In that year the General Court of Massachusetts, in which the Republicans were in a large majority, passed what was known as the "two year" amendment to the state constitution. This provided that

> No person of foreign birth shall be allowed to vote, nor shall he be eligible for office, unless he shall have resided within the jurisdiction of the state for two years subsequent to his naturalization and shall be otherwise qualified according to the Constitution and laws of the Commonwealth.[2]

The amendment was submitted to the voters of the state whose affirmative vote made it a law. So evident was the activity of the Massachusetts Republicans in behalf of this proscription that Republicans in other states could not disavow the action although they did condemn it.

Immediately a storm of protest arose from the German Republicans. Although the German press was angered, it was not united in either its conclusions or its recommendations. A movement was initiated to call a national convention of German Republicans during the summer of 1859, but it failed. The assurances of friendship given the adopted citizens by the western Republicans undoubtedly helped to hold their allegiance to the new party.

2. *Iowa Democratic Enquirer* (Muscatine, Iowa), September 29, 1859.

Had nativism seemed to the Germans to be the greatest issue facing the Republican party in 1859 they would probably have left the organization without even making an attempt to alter party policy. But by this time they were thoroughly aroused over the slavery question and were bent upon forcing the nomination for President of a man whose anti-slavery attitude was strong and sure. William Henry Seward of New York was the German Republicans' first choice for President; Lincoln had also made himself acceptable to the German element by his clear statements on slavery and Know-Nothingism.

The desires of the German Republicans in regard to the platform of 1860 were as definite as was their choice of candidate.

> A minimum of demands of the German radicals embraced the following: 1. Repeal of the infamous Fugitive Slave law; 2. Protection of citizens of free states sojourning within the slave states; 3. Freedom of speech, press, and of assembling in the southern states as well as in the northern; and, 4. Abolishing slavery in the District of Columbia, which depends solely upon Congress.[3]

Some within the Republican councils in 1859 and 1860 felt only a moderate candidate who was not unfavorable to slavery and Americanism could be elected President. This group, led by Horace Greeley and his New York *Tribune,* inaugurated a movement for the candidacy of Judge Edward O. Bates, of St. Louis, many months before the national convention. Because of Judge Bates's pro-slavery and nativistic views he was unacceptable to the German Republicans; and as his campaign gained momentum, it met stiff opposition from the Germans.

On March 7, 1860, the Germans of Davenport, Iowa, called together by Henry Ramming, associate editor of *Der Demokrat* of that city, held a mass meeting to discuss the proper attitude for the Germans to maintain in the coming contest for the Republican presidential nomination. The result of the meeting was a series of resolutions denouncing the conservative element in

---

3. Theodor Olshausen, in *New York Abendzeitung,* January, 1860, quoted in Frank I. Herriott, "The Conference of German Republicans in the Deutsches Haus, Chicago, May 14–15, 1860," reprinted in *Transactions of the Illinois State Historical Society for 1928,* pp. 11–12.

the party and Judge Bates in particular. The resolutions concluded with the statement that "we therefore under no circumstances will vote for the Hon. Edward Bates."

The German Republicans of New York City, probably influenced by the Davenport meeting of March 7, adopted seven resolutions on March 13, denouncing the Massachusetts amendment and demanding a presidential candidate who was unequivocally opposed to Know-Nothingism and the perpetuation of slavery. Ten days later the same committee sent out a call to "all similar organizations" urging them to send delegates to a meeting to be held in Chicago on May 14, to influence the Republican platform and to control the German delegates to the Republican national convention to be held in Chicago on May 16.

The conference of the German Republicans was held at the Deutsches Haus, in Chicago, as scheduled, William Kopp, editor of the *New Yorker Demokrat,* presiding. The resolutions adopted at this meeting were really an "ultimatum that the German Republicans would bolt the ticket if their demands as to the platform were not complied with and their general wishes as to the character of the Candidate were not met."

There can be no doubt that the Deutsches Haus conference greatly influenced the actions of the Wigwam convention. The platform adopted at the convention complied with the demands of the German Republican committee of New York of March 13, 1860. While Seward, the German choice, did not receive the nomination for the presidency, Lincoln, an entirely acceptable candidate did. The German Republicans had defeated the conservative elements of the party by preventing the nomination of Judge Bates for President.

While addressing the convention on behalf of the naturalization plank, Schurz promised the party 300,000 votes in Illinois, Indiana, Iowa, Wisconsin, Michigan, and Ohio. Schrader estimates the German Republican vote in those states in 1860 to be nearly 450,000.[4] A vote of 450,000 could easily have swung those

4. Frederick F. Schrader, *The Germans in the Making of America* (Boston, 1924), p. 194.

states into the Democratic line. If Schrader's estimate is at all reasonable, the Germans of the Northwest tipped the scales for Lincoln; for, without the Northwestern states, Lincoln would have only secured 114 electoral votes to his nearest opponent's 138 electoral votes.

THE GERMANS IN IOWA:
THEIR LEADERS AND PRESS

Although it has been asserted that the Iowa Germans seemed to have little genius for pioneering or frontier life, many of them were to be found among the early settlers of Iowa. They had been drawn from Missouri, Illinois, and the eastern states, along with the native Americans, toward new homes and brighter prospects in the new territory. Most of their settlements were along the Mississippi River or in the country immediately west of it. Dubuque, the largest city in the state in 1860, had, at one time, a population that was over half German. The two other leading cities, Des Moines, the state capital, and Davenport, also had large German populations. From the nucleus at Davenport, other German communities sprang, such as Avoca, Minden, Walcott, Wheatland, and Dewitt. Many of the Germans in these communities were from Schleswig-Holstein and Denmark. German Catholics settled the town of New-Wien, northwest of Dubuque; and Guttenberg, north of Dubuque on the Mississippi, was founded by Germans from Cincinnati.

Several communistic and mystical religious groups of Germans migrated to Iowa before 1860. The Amana settlement in Johnson County was well established by this time. It was a group bound by religious ties. Another communistic society, the "Icarians," moved from Nauvoo, Illinois, to Corning, Adams County, Iowa, in 1856. They had bought the property from the Mormons in Nauvoo, in 1850, when the Latter Day Saints fled to the west under Brigham Young. These communists, upon the death of their leader, Etienne Cabet, settled at Corning and named the community they founded the "Icaria Commune" in honor of Cabet's book *Icarie*. Most of the members of this society were French, "but the most influential of them after Cabet's death were Germans." On "Potato Prairie," in Clayton County, Heinrich Koch, after his return from the Mexican War in 1847, founded another colony of German communists.

Much greater in number were the Amish Mennonites, a mystical religious sect composed largely of Germans. The vanguard of this group settled in West Point township, in Lee County, in 1831. They next founded a community in Henry County, in 1843. The Johnson County settlement, from which was destined to grow the largest Amish district in the state, was made in 1846. The Mennonites in Davis County came to Iowa in 1854.

The early Germans in Iowa were mostly of the peasant type. They were content to work their farms or conduct their little businesses. Proud of their new nationality, they attempted, without complete success, to become Americanized. To their leaders, who were sometimes incapable and short-sighted, they gave blind obedience. Their record of political leadership in Iowa is not brilliant. In the history of the state there has never been a candidate for either governor or United States senator with a German name. What political strength they possessed was due, largely, to their numbers and unity.

Less than one-third of the early Iowa Germans were Catholics. A small minority were members of various mystical sects and the remainder were Protestant. There were 38,555 native Germans living in Iowa in 1860. They formed 5.79% of the entire state population of 674,913 and 36.34% of the total foreign population of the state, which was 106,081.

The Germans in Iowa, as in other parts of the United States, had turned, during the fifties, for leadership to the refugees of the German and Austrian revolutions. Henry Ramming, of Davenport, was such a leader. A native of Hungary, he had once been an officer in the Austrian army. From 1856 to 1860 he served as associate editor of *Der Demokrat,* and was editor of that newspaper in 1860 and 1861. During the Civil War he served on General Frémont's staff and later as colonel of the 3rd Missouri Infantry.

Carl Rotteck, a leader of the German radical thought in the state, was also a refugee of the Revolution of 1848. Educated as a lawyer in Germany, he attempted farming in America. Like many another "Latin farmer" he was unsuccessful in this enterprise. After a second failure, this time as a shoe merchant, he founded the Muscatine (Iowa) *Zeitung* in 1857. Because of Rotteck's outspoken comment in this paper, readers were alienated and he was forced to stop publishing the *Zeitung*. In 1859 he moved to Burlington, Iowa. From there to went to Keokuk, where in 1862 he published the *Beobachter des Westens.*

Dr. William Hoffbauer of Guttenberg and Dubuque, Iowa, was a leading Republican and a close friend of Carl Schurz. He had been educated at the University of Berlin, from which he had received the M.D. degree. Dr. Hoffbauer had lost an arm, supposedly in a duel, before coming to America. As a member of the Frankfort Parliament, he was on the extreme left, and upon collapse of the Revolution he fled to Switzerland, from where he had come to the United States in 1850.

Another prominent leader of the Iowa Germans in 1860 was Nicholas J. Rusch, who served as lieutenant-governor of Iowa in 1859 and 1860. Rusch was born in Marne, Holstein, in February, 1822. He received his education at the gymnasium in Meddorf, a seminar of Segeberg, and later at the University of Kiel. Because of political disturbances in Schleswig-Holstein he emigrated to Scott County, Iowa, near Davenport, where he farmed very successfully. He was elected to the state senate of Iowa in 1857 where he served until his election as lieutenant-governor of the state. In 1860 Governor Kirkwood appointed Rusch immigration commissioner for Iowa. He resigned this position when Civil War broke out and gave his services to the Union cause. When he died at Vicksburg, Mississippi, he was serving as a colonel in the Union army.

Hans R. Claussen and Theodor Olshausen were also leaders of great authority among the Germans of Iowa. The latter acquired a national reputation as an editor and writer. For years he edited *Der Demokrat,* a German Republican newspaper in Davenport, Iowa. "Olshausen was of a famous family and had a notable career in letters and politics" in Germany. Claussen had been an advocate in the Holstein courts, and a member of the Frankfort, Holstein, and Stuttgart congresses. These two men had been imprisoned in Denmark, because they had protested against the treatment of the Holsteiners by the Danish king. Upon their release from prison they had migrated to America and had eventually settled in Iowa.

In 1860 only five German newspapers were being published in Iowa. The oldest of these, the *Iowa Staats Zeitung,* had been founded in Dubuque in 1849, as the *Northwest Demokrat.* Its first editor was B. Hauf, who published the paper until 1855. In that year D. A. Mahoney became editor, but in a short while John Bittman took over the publishing of the *Northwest Demokrat* and changed its name to the *Iowa Staats Zeitung.* At the same time Dr. George Hillgartner became the editor. The *Zeitung,* originally Democratic, became Republican in 1856.

The Burlington, Des Moines County, *Volksblatt* was established in 1852 by Metz and Loeber. It changed editors several times, and in 1855 the name of the paper became the *Freie Presse.* In 1860 it was being edited by a Mr. Vanzelow.

Der Demokrat, an important Republican newspaper, was founded in Davenport as a Whig organ in 1851. Henry Lischer and Company owned *Der Demokrat* in 1860, and Theodor Olshausen was its editor.

The Democratic German-American newspaper *Beobachter des Westens* was located in Keokuk. It was begun in 1855 by William Kopp, but was managed by Leopold Mader in 1860.

When the *Northwest Demokrat* changed its political affiliations in 1856, a demand arose in Dubuque for a Democratic German newspaper. In answer to this demand, Frederick A. Giuffke founded *Der National Demokrat.* This paper was published as a daily in 1857, but reverted to a weekly about a year later.

The political sympathies of the German newspapers in Iowa in 1860 were, no doubt, reflections of the attitudes of their constituents. The fact that these papers were so evenly divided on party ties leads one to suspect that neither political party in Iowa could claim the entire German vote in 1860.

THE POLITICAL SCENE IN IOWA BEFORE 1860

The decade of the 1850s was a period of political revolution in Iowa. Sentiment in the Territory of Iowa had been strongly Democratic. Only once, in the "hard cider" year of 1840, did the Whigs win control of the territorial legislature. During the first eight years of statehood, from 1846 to 1854, the state government remained in the hands of the Democracy. In that year, however, under the dynamic leadership of James W. Grimes, their candidate for governor, the Whig party won a foothold in the government at Iowa City. Although the Democrats secured a majority of one in the state senate, the Whigs had won the governorship and a majority in the house.

Several factors probably entered into this unexpected political turn. The source of immigration to Iowa had shifted from the southern and border states to the strongly Whig states of New England, New York, and Pennsylvania. The pro-slavery leanings of the Democratic senators from Iowa, Augustus C. Dodge and George W. Jones, as demonstrated by their votes for the Kansas-Nebraska bill and against the Wilmot Proviso, also had an unfavorable effect upon the Iowa Democracy. No doubt the personal popularity of Grimes was an added factor in the Whig victory of 1854.

Governor Grimes, who had parted with the Whig party before he took office, was instrumental in the formation of the Republican party in Iowa. On February 22, 1856, a meeting was held at Iowa City, at which the state party organization was established. The Republicans gained strength so rapidly that twenty-one of the thirty-six delegates elected to the constitutional convention in August 1856 were listed as Republicans.

This first Republican administration of Iowa was one of reform. During its tenure of office the state constitution was revised, a state bank founded, and a prohibitory liquor law, similar to the famous "Maine Law," was passed. The latter measure proved to be very unpopular with the Germans in the state and was modified in 1857 and again in 1858.

When Governor Grimes refused the renomination which the Republicans offered him in 1857, Ralph P. Lowe of Muscatine was chosen instead and elected governor. Grimes succeeded George W. Jones to the United States Senate on March 4, 1859.

In the election of 1858 the Republican ticket swept the state. For the first time in the history of Iowa there was an overwhelming representation of one party in the state government. The Republicans controlled both houses of the General Assembly by substantial majorities and elected a complete slate of Republican state officers. In addition both United States senators and the entire delegation to Congress were Republicans. The political revolution was complete.

While the Republican party had entrenched itself in the state capitol in 1858, its chances for success in the elections of 1859 and 1860 were not assured. There was criticism of state taxes and expenditures which had been raised to carry out the Republican reforms. The Democrats were demanding a revision of existing banking laws and of the state constitution. Attacks were being made on the Republican attempt to amend the Iowa school law which barred Negro children from schools unless unanimous consent of the white parents of the district was given. Democratic papers were accusing the Republicans of being a prohibition party, on the one hand, and of amending the prohibition law on the other. Among the more serious worries of the Republicans was the restlessness of the Germans, who suspected Iowa Republicans of sympathy with the Know-Nothings.

THE STRUGGLE FOR GERMAN VOTES IN THE CAMPAIGNS OF 1859 AND 1860

The Iowa Republicans were put on the defensive in their dealing with the naturalized citizens by the passage of the proscriptive "two year" amendment which was submitted to the people of Massachusetts in March, 1859. As soon as this measure had passed the Republican Massachusetts legislature, the Democratic press of Iowa featured it in their editorials as an evidence of Know-Nothingism within the Republican ranks. These papers warned the Germans that the only reason such a measure had not been introduced by the Iowa Republicans was that the party in Iowa needed the German vote, but that as soon as the Republicans could, with the aid of the German voters, split the nation in two and get control of the government, they would turn on their German friends. Not only had the Massachusetts Republicans debased the foreigner, but by enfranchising the Negro had placed the adopted citizen in an even more unworthy position. The editor of the *Iowa Weekly Democrat,* of Sigourney, sarcastically remarked:

> But Massachusetts has made . . . progress; she has extended to the African the immunities of the elective franchise, and repealed all laws that stigmatized the negro, and in her love for humanity, has adopted State laws in conflct with the Constitution of the United States, and now she is endeavoring to disenfranchise the white foreign citizens by extending the period allowed them by the federal constitution to become voters and citizens of the American Union.

The Democratic party, they said, "places the adopted citizen, wherever he may have been born, or at whatever altar he may worship on a basis of perfect and entire equality with the native." Several of the Democratic papers printed a clipping from the Quincy (Massachusetts) *Herald* of the proclamation of the Germans of Massachusetts that they would never again support the Republican party.

The Republican papers of the state were equally emphatic in condemnation of the Massachusetts amendment, but pointed out that the entire Republican party could not be censured for the actions of its partisans of one state. They said that the Republican party the country over condemned the "two year" amendment, and went so far as to hope that the Republicans of Massachusetts would lose the coming election. No doubt this wish was sincere for it was felt that many Germans would be driven from the party by the amendment, and as one paper said, "Without the German vote, Illinois and Wisconsin would today be in the hands of the black Democracy."

When on May 9, 1859, the people of Massachusetts ratified the "two year" amendment, the discussion of the question became even more agitated in Iowa. Many of the Democratic papers in the latter state carried several articles on the subject in one issue. The *Weekly Independence* (Iowa) *Civilian* prophesied that if the Republicans of Iowa

> were strong enough to do without foreign votes, they would soon be walking in the steps of Massachusetts. But the Democratic party has never had but one creed and one record on this question. The Democratic party has never proscribed any portion of the white race, and has claims upon the support of naturalized citizens that we believe will not be forgotten. Old friends are the best, provided they have been tried and found true,—new friends may prove treacherous.

By this time, the Republicans had organized a rebuttal, which, however, was very weak. The *Gate City* (Keosauqua) *Republican,* and Davenport *Gazette,* following the lead of Horace Greeley's *Tribune,* charged that the Massachusetts amendment was passed by a secret vote of the Democrats, in an effort to discredit the Republicans. The Democratic press, in refutation, pointed out that the Boston *Bee,* a Republican paper, boasted that the amendment was a Republican victory, that the Springfield (Massachusetts) *Republican,* though opposing it, admitted it was a Republican measure, and that the Massachusetts Germans themselves blamed the Republicans of that state for the law. The Sioux City (Iowa) *Register* said:

> It is useless for the Republicans of two or three Western States to excuse or repudiate the purpose foreshadowed by the action of Massachusetts. Adopted citizens simply ask the enjoyment of all the political rights and equality guaranteed them by the constitution—no more or less. These they begin to see will be secured to them by the Democracy only, a party that has never wavered in its fidelity to the constitution.

In answer to the Republican defense that the nativist attitude in the party was purely local, the Democrats showed the Germans that a proscriptive amendment was pending at the time in Connecticut, sponsored by the Republican party, and that the Republican state convention in New York had recommended a similar law for that state. The union of the American and Republican parties in Hamilton, Ohio, was also pointed to as proof that Know-Nothingism was not a local element in the Republican party.

The best defensive argument that the Iowa Republicans could present was that the vote on the Massachusetts amendment was very small, very close, and from the city districts, indicating it was an American rather than a Republican vote.

The nativist Republican press of the East caused the Iowa Republicans more worry than did the Massachusetts amendment. Their editorials were freely clipped by Democratic papers in Iowa to offer proof of the American tendencies of the Republicans. Two eastern Republican papers so used by the Democratic press were the Cleveland (Ohio) *Herald* and the Boston (Massachusetts) *Bee,* which denounced all foreigners and Catholics in very insulting terms.

The Germans of Iowa were thoroughly aroused by the Massachusetts amendment and seemed to fear that the Republicans of the West were sympathetic to the nativist activities of the eastern party members. Nicholas Schade, a German-American of Burlington, Iowa, on May 20, 1859, wrote a public letter of nearly five columns' length to the press of Iowa, urging the Germans not to vote the Republican ticket because the Republicans were the party of nativism and prohibition. The Republicans were to hear more of Schade before the end of the campaign. An association of Germans known as the "Schulverein" met at Le Claire, Scott County, to draw up a set of resolutions denunciatory of Massachusetts Republicanism. In April a committee of German political leaders, among whom were Hillgartner, Bittman, Freund, Olshausen, and Gulich, submitted a questionnaire to the congressional delegation from Iowa, in which they asked them:

> 1st. Are you in favor of the Naturalization Laws as they now stand, and particularly against all and every extension of the probation time?
> 2nd. Do you regard it as a duty of the Republican party, as the party of equal rights, to oppose and war upon each and every

discrimination that may be attempted to be made between the Native born and Adopted citizens as to the right of suffrage?

3rd. Do you condemn the late action of the Republicans in the Massachusetts legislature, for attempting to exclude the Adopted citizens for two years from the ballot box, as unwise, unjust, and uncalled for?[5]

Senator James W. Grimes, in an open letter from Burlington, Iowa, on April 30, replied to this inquiry:

To each of these interrogations I respond unhesitatingly in the affirmative.

In regard to the recent action of the Massachusetts Legislature in relation to the right of suffrage, I have this to say: That while I admit that the regulation sought to be adopted is purely of a local character, with which we of Iowa have nothing *directly* to do, and while I would be one of the last men in the world to interfere in the local affairs of a sovereign State, or with the action of any party in that State upon local matters, yet I claim the right to condemn, as my judgement may dictate, such a State or party action, when, in my conviction, it is based upon a false and dangerous principle.

I believe the action of the Massachusetts Legislature alluded to, to be based upon such a principle, and to be fraught with evil and only evil, continually, to the whole country and not to Massachusetts alone. Hence I condemn and deplore it without equivocation or reserve.

Knowing how much the adoption of the proposed constitutional provision will offend their brethren elsewhere, the Republicans of Massachusetts owe it to their party, that this amendment should be overwhelmingly voted down.[6]

In reply to the same letter Senator James Harlan answered:

I am compelled as a Republican, to say in reply to your first interrogatory, that I am not an advocate for any material change in the naturalization laws; to the second I do not approve any discrimination whatever against the rights of naturalized citizens; to the third, that I would not, if I were a citizen of Massachusetts, advocate the adoption of the proposed amendement to her Constitution.

Representatives Curtis and Vandever answered the inquiry in terms equally clear. Because of his letter Grimes was accused

5. *Weekly Maquoketa* (Iowa) *Excelsior*, May 17, 1859.
6. Ibid.

of hypocrisy by the Democrats who charged that he had been a Know-Nothing in 1854–55 and had supported the belief that all foreigners should wait twenty-one years after naturalization before voting.

It was necessary in the face of these charges of nativism that the Republican party of Iowa, if it was to win the German vote, take a definite stand against proscriptive legislation. Such a step was taken even before the "two year" amendment went to the people of Massachusetts for their approval. In the spring of 1859 the Republican state central committee of Iowa issued a public denunciation of the recent action of the Massachusetts legislature. This proclamation did not meet the approval of all of the Iowa Republicans. There were those who felt that though the action of the Massachusetts legislature was impolitic, it could not affect the party elsewhere. "It is their affair, and not ours," they said. "Our policy is to let the Republicans of each state take care of themselves." The Democrats, of course, cried again, "Hypocrisy!"

Many of the county conventions of both parties, who were choosing delegates to the coming state conventions, passed strong resolutions denouncing the "two year" amendment of Massachusetts. Prejudice, though, appeared in the ranks of both parties in spite of their professions of friendliness to the naturalized citizens. In the Johnson County convention, Edward Zitschke, a German-American, asked to represent the German element of the county at the state convention, and his name was placed on the ballot list by a friend. Without reason his name was erased. In the Davenport city election the editor of the Davenport *News*, who was a candidate for office, offered a ballot to a German citizen. When the German refused it, the candidate called him "a d——d Dutchman." In the next issue of his paper, June 11, 1859, the editor admitted that he used the phrase and reserved the right to use it against any German who gave him provocation.

Many Republicans, however, thought that mere denunciations were not enough to hold the vote of the Germans of the party. They felt that more tangible proof of friendship was needed. This group recommended that the Republican state convention nominate a German for lieutenant-governor. Such a move had a precedent, for in two neighboring states the Republican party had chosen German leaders as standard bearers. Illinois, where the German vote was important, had honored Gustave Koerner with the lieutenant-governorship in 1852 and again in 1854. The Republicans in Wisconsin, to hold the German vote, had nominated Carl Schurz for lieutenant-governor in 1857, but he had been defeated.

This suggestion was fruitful, and at the state Republican convention at Des Moines on June 22, 1859, the name of Nicholas J. Rusch, a German, was placed as lieutenant-governor on the ticket headed by Samuel J. Kirkwood. Rusch, who had been educated in Germany, came to Scott County, Iowa, in 1847. He had been elected to the state senate in 1857 and was prominent in that body as a liberal. At the Republican state convention at Iowa City on June 17, 1858, he was chosen for the state Republican central committee, and at the moment he was in the political limelight because of a powerful letter he had written to the New York *Tribune* on April 11, 1859, severely criticizing the action of the Massachusetts Republicans for sponsoring the "two year" amendment.

In appearance Mr. Rusch was a typical German. He smoked a long-stemmed pipe, the bowl of which was porcelain and had pictures painted on it. His English was so poor that he felt it to be a handicap. When Rusch learned that he had been mentioned as a possible candidate for lieutenant-governor, he wrote to Kirkwood that he felt his "broken English and little experience are not proper qualifications for an office of that nature."

No doubt Senator Rusch's estimate of himself was too modest. As might be expected, the Republican papers spoke very favorably of his ability. But a leading Democratic organ paid him a high compliment, the sincerity of which cannot be doubted. Before the Republican nominating convention was held, the Davenport (Iowa) *News* prophesied that if "Iowa remains a Republican State, and Rusch's countrymen continue to exercise so important an influence over the destinies of the Republican party here, he will have, with his fine natural abilities, a glorious future before him. He will undoubtedly go eventually to the arena of the United States Senate to display them."

Among the planks of the Republican platform adopted at the Des Moines convention in June, 1859, was one claiming "for citizens, native and naturalized, liberty of conscience, equality of rights, and the free exercise of the right of Suffrage." This plank cordially approved "of the action taken by the Republican State Committee in regard to the amendment proposed by the Massachusetts Legislature to its Constitution."

The platform contained two other planks of special interest to the Germans of the state. One was a resolution denouncing the Democratic party for defeating, in the United States Senate, "the Homestead Bill, which was designed to secure free homes for free people, whether native or foreign birth." The other of these two planks resolved:

> That the rights of citizens are equal, and they are equally entitled to protection at home and abroad, without regard to nativity or duration of domicil [sic], and that the late refusal by the federal government as expressed in the late official communication of Lewis Cass, Secretary of State, to guarantee against arrest and detention abroad of naturalized citizens on the ground of their allegiance to a foreign power, is a cowardly abandonment of the true and noble position hitherto occupied by our government.

The latter resolution referred to the difficulty being encountered by the State Department in attempting to protect naturalized American citizens who had visited their homelands from being forced into military service abroad against their wills. France, Austria, Prussia, and some other foreign countries denied the right of expatriation. This problem, always a trying one to the United States, had increased in difficulty with the breaking out of the Austro-Sardinian War in the winter of 1859. In May of that year Mr. Felix Le Clerc, of Memphis, Tennessee, a naturalized American who was a refugee from France for refusing military service, asked the United States government to protect him if he should return to France. In a letter of May 17, 1859, Secretary Cass informed Le Clerc that his naturalization in this country would not exempt him from military service that the French government claimed from him.

Another naturalized citizen, Lieutenant-Colonel Charles Ernst of Cincinnati, an officer of the Ohio militia, wished to observe the European War zone. Although he had been an American citizen for thirty years, Secretary Cass would not guarantee his protection from impressment. The government gave a similar warning to a German, Mr. A. V. Hofer, in June, 1859.

The seeming weakness of the Buchanan administration in protecting naturalized Americans abroad greatly alarmed the Germans and gave the Republican party a backfire against the Democratic attack on nativism. "If a 'naturalized' citizen cannot claim the protection of his government in a foreign country," they said, "then it is clear that no citizen can, unless there is a distinction between the native and foreign born; and if there is a distinction, it will not be forgotten that a Democratic administration was the first to find it out and make it operative." Compared to this ruling of the State Department, the restrictive action of Massachusetts was as nothing, the Republicans claimed. "If one ten times more stringent were enacted in every State in the Union, it could not affect the foreign born citizen so disastrously" as the Cass ruling. The Iowa Democrats contended that this policy of the government in regard to naturalized citizens abroad had been adhered to for years and quoted past incidents similar to those of Le Clerc's to prove their contention.

These two issues, the Massachusetts restrictive amendment and Cass's "Le Clerc ruling," were the major points of argument in the struggle for the Iowa German vote in 1859. They were hotly debated in the newspapers of the state from March until well after the October election.

On June 23, the day after the Republican state convention in Des Moines, the Democrats convened in the same city to choose a state ticket and construct a platform. Augustus C. Dodge, United States minister to Spain, was nominated for governor and Lysander W. Babbitt for lieutenant-governor. The lengthy platform adopted included a plank assuring naturalized citizens that the doctrine of the Democratic party was equal rights and protection for adopted and native-born citizens at home and abroad. It also favored a homestead law.

The Democratic platform attempted to revive the question of the Iowa prohibition law, which it said was "inconsistant with the genius of free people, and unjust and burdensome in its operation." It declared that it had "vexed and harassed the citizen, burdened the counties with expense and litigation, and proven wholly useless in the suppression of intemperance." Although the Democratic papers occasionally referred to the "Maine Law" during the campaign, the question of prohibition did not become a major issue. The Republicans had modified the law twice, largely at the instance of the Germans, and it is doubtful whether the temperance question greatly influenced the German vote in Iowa in 1859.

From the moment Rusch was nominated he was under fire from Democratic speakers and newspapers. They charged that he had been nominated only as a matter of policy and that even the Republicans hoped that he would be defeated, as Schurz had been in Wisconsin. Unless he had been nominated, the Democrats said, the German Republicans, disgruntled over the nominations of "Know-Nothings Vandever, Harlan, Grimes, Thorington, and others" would have left the party. It was prophesied that because of Rusch's nomination there would be disaffection in the Republican party, for "the lager and Dark Lantern elements rest in uneasy companionship."

Many of the Democrats, who had been pleading their friendliness for the adopted citizens before the nominating convention, now turned on the Germans a scorn as biting as that for which they had previously condemned the Republicans of Massachusetts. They declared that the Germans were "busy bodies, and mischief makers in every community where they reside. They were driven out of Germany in '48 for their clannishness and meddlesomeness. They ignore the Bible, and all revealed religion, believe in no future state of rewards and punishment, and act on an infidel motto, 'live while we live.' They aim at anarchy in politics, morals and religion, and are a curse to any country or community."

Mr. Rusch was attacked because of his activities in attempting to change the school law to make it easier for Negro children to attend public schools in Iowa, and for his opposition to the state prohibition law. His opponents denounced him as a "Red, alias Black, alias Free Thinking, alias anti-Sunday, alias anti-Bible, alias anti-Maine Law, alias pro-Lager Beer Republican."

It was charged that he was not intelligent and spoke English so poorly that it would be impossible for him to preside over the senate. The prediction was made that if elected he would either resign the office or get sick, requiring his absence from the senate, so that he could not preside. A prominent Democrat was heard to say at the state convention that the Germans would do very well for " 'Voting Stock,' but he hoped the state would never be disgraced by having a German to preside in the Senate."

The only criticism voiced against Rusch in the Republican party was from prohibitionists who opposed the candidate's efforts to amend the "dry" law. The Reverend Jocelyn, a Methodist minister, said that he would never vote for Nicholas J. Rusch, "who had been instrumental in modifying the prohibitory law of 1855." Senator Harlan, a prominent Methodist, was soon to be a candidate for reelection; so Rusch men declared that if the Methodists voted against Rusch, Harlan would never be reelected.

The fact that Kirkwood and Rusch were both farmers caused the *Democratic Clarion,* published in Bloomfield, to deride the Republican candidates as the "Plough-handle ticket." This proved to be a costly error, for the Republicans took up the catchy phrase and, comparing Kirkwood to Cincinnatus, went into the campaign marked as the friends of the farmer.

Mr. Kirkwood and General Dodge "took the stump" shortly after the nominating conventions had selected them. The extension of slavery was the most important issue of the campaign, but the whole reform program of the Republicans was under fire.

Neither Rusch nor Babbitt was able to do any active campaigning until late in the summer. Mr. Rusch, being a farmer, could not leave during the harvest season, and was further detained by what a friendly newspaper announced as the arrival of "another little Rusch light to illuminate his domestic pathway."

He was booked, generally, to deliver German addresses in German communities, but he also spoke English at times. On these occasions the Democrats mercilessly ridiculed his accent. To counteract Senator Rusch's influence with the Germans, the Democrats employed Colonel Louis Schade, of Burlington, Iowa, to debate with him in the German language. There seemed to be no organized "stump" campaign. Schade followed Rusch from town to town and disturbed his addresses by argument and, if possible, by leading part of the crowd to another meeting place. Senator Rusch also met Van Antwerp and Clagget in debate during this campaign. All in all, the German candidate seems to have carried out a successful speaking tour and to have gained many friends for himself and the party.

It was freely predicted by the Democrats that even though Samuel Kirkwood should be elected governor, Nicholas J. Rusch would be badly defeated. Some prophets guessed that Rusch would fall 5,000 votes behind Kirkwood. The defeat of Carl Schurz for lieutenant-governor in Wisconsin was pointed to as proof of the treatment a German Republican candidate would receive. Their predictions that Rusch would fall behind Kirkwood were correct, for although the German candidate received 55,142 votes, a clear majority of 2,279 over his opponent, he fell 1,363 votes short of Kirkwood.

Before the furor of the election of 1859 had died away, the national campaign of 1860 was shaping itself in Iowa. The German Republicans who had so recently gained political prestige in the state, through the election of one of their leaders as lieutenant-governor, were a bloc with which the party had to reckon. They were radically opposed to slavery and certainly would not approve of a compromise attitude on that question by the party organization. When John Brown was hanged on December 2, 1859, many German citizens of Davenport wore crepe, and many business houses displayed signs of mourning. A German theater flew its flag at half mast, and *Der Demokrat* shrouded its editorial on the hanging in black lines of mourning.

In state politics the only issue of particular interest to the Germans in 1860 was the attempt of the Democratic members of the house in March to repeal the "Lager beer amendment" to the prohibition law. The Republicans supported the amendment, and it remained in force. The attention of the Germans, therefore, was focused on the national scene.

There was strong sentiment among Iowa Republicans for the nomination of Judge Edward Bates, of St. Louis, for President. Mr. John Mahin, editor of the Muscatine *Journal,* a liberal leader, said on December 3, 1859, that Bates "would doubtless receive the united support of the Republican party." On January 17, 1860, Mr. Clark Dunham, editor of the *Hawkeye,* of Burlington, Iowa, announced that he also favored the St. Louisan. Mr. John A. Kasson, chairman of the Republican state central committee of Iowa, had practiced law in the same courts with Judge Bates in St. Louis before coming to Iowa and favored him as a candidate. The fact that the New York *Tribune,* which sponsored Bates's candidacy, was the most widely read Republican paper in Iowa kept his name alive in the state as a prospective nominee.

The German Republicans the nation over were opposed to Judge Bates as a nominee for President because of his conservative stand on slavery and the taint of nativism which they felt he possessed. The first organized move that was made by the Germans against the Bates candidacy was the meeting of Germans held in Davenport, Iowa, on March 7, 1860. As previously mentioned, this meeting started a movement which culminated in the conference of German-Americans in the Deutsches Haus in Chicago on May 15 and 16 where the Bates campaign was effectually stopped. The Davenport meeting presented resolutions to the congressional delegation from Iowa declaring that under no circumstances would the Germans vote for Edward Bates. Hans R. Claussen accompanied these resolutions to Senator James Harlan by a letter written March 31, 1860, informing him that "those who think Bates still available must not count upon the German vote."

Mr. Add. H. Sanders, the editor of the *Daily Gazette* of Davenport, criticized the Germans in his March 10 issue for the stand they had taken. He felt that if the Germans did not want Bates for a candidate, they should work to see that he wasn't nominated; but if the national Republican convention should, in its wisdom, decide that he was the correct nominee, every Republican should support him. Theodor Olshausen, of *Der Demokrat,* replied to him that "no matter what course the majority of the republican party may pursue, we for our part shall always and immutably remain true to the principles of liberty and humanity which we heretofore have considered identical with those of the republican party."

The Republican state convention held at Des Moines, January 18, 1860, to choose a delegation to the Republican national convention of May 16 at Chicago was uninstructed. Iowa had eight votes at the national convention. On the first ballot Iowa voted: Lincoln, two; Seward, two; Cameron, one; Bates, one; Chase, one; McLean, one. On the final ballot the vote was: Lincoln, five and one-half; Seward, two; Chase, one-half. Something had happened to the Bates "boom" in Iowa between March and May. No doubt the German attitude had much to do with it.

While the German Democrats in Iowa did not play a leading role in forming the policy of their party, as did their Republican fellows, some of them were active in support of the Democracy. At a Douglas ratification meeting held in Independence, Iowa, on June 25, 1860, three of the addresses were delivered in German by Messrs. Cummings, Bitnes, and Hegee, and several Germans were mentioned as converts to the Democratic party.

In the campaign of 1860 there was less effort made by both parties in Iowa to win the German vote by arguments directed to them than there was in 1859. The bitter attitude that Douglas was taking toward the Germans was pointed out by the Republicans, but there were no other issues specifically presented for them. It is only through the analysis of their vote that any conclusion can be reached as to their sympathies in the election campaign of 1860.

HOW THE IOWA GERMANS VOTED IN 1860

There are four possible methods of estimating the political leanings of the Germans in 1860. One obvious way is to compare the strength and activity of the Germans in the political organizations of the time. Another method of estimating their vote is by ascertaining the opinions of contemporary politicians, A third way is to analyze the political leanings of the German press. A more accurate method than any of these is to compare the election returns of a considerable number of voting precincts with a heavy German population with the same number of townships of largely native composition.

As related above, the German-Americans took an active and influential part in the councils of the Iowa Republican party in 1860. Their vote was considered so valuable that one of their leaders was honored with election as lieutenant-governor of the state in 1859. Acting as a pressure group, they killed the campaign of Edward O. Bates for the Republican nomination for President. On the other hand, there seems to have been little German activity in the Democratic party compared to that in the Republican organization. This would lead to the belief that the Germans in Iowa were preponderantly Republican in 1860.

The opinions of contemporary politicians would lead to the same conclusion. When Carl Schurz estimated that 300,000 Germans in Illinois, Indiana, Iowa, Wisconsin, Michigan, and Ohio voted for Frémont in 1856, he spoke as a trained political leader and observer of his countrymen. His prophecy that the same number of Germans from those states would vote for Lincoln in 1860 was also based upon an intimate knowledge of his followers. The opinion that the German vote was essential to the Republican party in Iowa was held by the leaders of both parties in the state. It was generally predicted by the newspapers that without the Germans the Republican party would be in the minority in 1860. The *Weekly Independence* (Iowa) *Civilian* said, "Well they [the Iowa Republicans] know that without their [the German] votes, Republicanism would be in the minority." The Sioux City (Iowa) *Register* predicted that "if they [the Republicans] refuse to accede to the demand of their German allies [in the Massachusetts amendment repeal] they will be defeated in every state west and north of the Ohio."

The Iowa Republicans considered the German voters "the chief cornerstone of their political fabric" according to the *Iowa Weekly Democrat* of Sigourney. These opinions may signify that the majority of the Iowa Germans were Republicans in that year, but it is untrue that they could have given Douglas a majority over Lincoln by shifting to the Democratic party en masse. Lincoln received 70,118 votes in Iowa in 1860, or 54.54% of the entire state ballots. Douglas secured 55,639 votes, or 43.28% of the total. This gave Lincoln a majority of 11.26% of the entire vote over his strongest opponent.

German-born inhabitants formed only 5.71% of the population of Iowa in 1860. Many of these Germans could not vote in that year because the Iowa election law made naturalization a prerequisite to suffrage. It can be taken for granted, then, that in relation to their whole population a much smaller proportion of Germans voted in 1860 than did native citizens.

If the German inhabitants of the state had voted in the same proportion that the native-born citizens did, and if they had all voted for Lincoln, they would have been responsible for only 5.71% of his 11.26% lead over Douglas. If these Germans had voted for Douglas instead of the Republican candidate, Douglas would have had a majority of only .16% of the entire state over Lincoln. However, the campaign activities showed that there was some German support of Douglas, and that part of his vote in Iowa came from the German element. The additional fact that a considerable proportion of the Germans were prevented from voting by the election laws would doubtless have entirely eliminated the Douglas majority in case of a bolt of the German Republicans. The conclusion is that while the German vote was important in Iowa in 1860, it was not essential to a Republican victory.

Of the five German newspapers in Iowa, three were Republican organs and two had Democratic leanings. This would indicate that a majority of the Germans of the state were Republican, but that a strong Democratic opposition existed among their countrymen.

The election returns of a large number of the townships in Iowa in 1860 are not in existence. It is impossible, therefore, to compare the vote of townships settled by Germans with that of precincts with a large majority of native-born citizens. Tabulation of the population and election returns of twenty-three selected Iowa townships will be found at the end of this chapter. Returns are available for only four townships with very heavy German populations. In one of these, Jefferson township, in Clayton County, 86.87% of the heads of families were born in Germany. This precinct gave Lincoln 55.24% of the total vote, while Douglas received 44.75%. Another strongly German precinct which delivered a Republican majority was the city of Davenport, where the heads of 43.55% of the families were German natives. The percentage of vote in this city was: Lincoln, 64.52%; Douglas, 31.41%; Breckenridge, 1.77%; and Bell, 2.28%. 41.87% of the heads of families in Buffalo township, near Davenport, in Scott County, were of German nativity. This precinct gave Lincoln 52.54% of its vote; Douglas, 46.89%; and Bell, .56%. Although all of these election precincts gave the Republican candidate a comfortable majority, the township of Franklin in Lee County, where 66.89% of the heads of families were born in Germany, voted strongly Democratic. In this precinct Lincoln received only 43.56% of the vote, while Douglas secured 55.77% of the ballots. The other .66% of the vote went to Bell.

It would be impossible to estimate the German vote from a study of these few precincts. Such an examination merely tends to confirm the conclusion that, while a majority of the Germans in Iowa in 1860 were Republicans, neither party could claim the entire German vote, and that, while the vote of the Germans in Iowa was important in 1860, it could not, of itself, decide the issue between Lincoln and Douglas in that state.

Reprinted from *Annals of Iowa,* 3d ser. 22 (October 1940): 421–52. Original footnotes have been omitted except when necessary for clarity.

TABLE I

NATIVITY OF HEADS OF FAMILIES IN
SELECTED IOWA TOWNSHIPS IN 1860

	NATIVE-BORN		GERMAN		OTHERS	
COUNTY AND TOWNSHIP	No.	Per cent	No.	Per cent	No.	Per cent
Allamakee						
Center	21	19.09	19	17.27	70	63.63
Hanover	15	20.54	20	27.39	38	52.05
Boone						
Yell	56	100.00	0	0.00	0	0.00
Clayton						
Jefferson	17	6.02	245	86.87	20	7.09
Crawford						
Denison	19	79.16	1	4.16	4	16.66
Union	13	68.42	0	0.00	6	31.57
Davis						
Marion	121	90.20	4	2.98	9	6.71
Decatur						
Center	157	98.12	0	0.00	3	1.88
Johnson						
Monroe	77	81.05	1	1.05	17	17.78
Lee						
Franklin	74	25.00	198	66.89	24	8.10
Linn						
Bertram	107	83.59	3	2.34	18	14.06
Putnam	65	67.81	10	10.41	21	20.83
Mahaska						
Union	99	90.00	6	4.45	5	4.54
Poweshiek						
Bear Creek	39	88.63	2	4.54	3	6.82
Deep River	63	92.64	1	1.47	4	5.88
Scott						
Davenport City	651	28.64	990	43.55	632	27.80
Buffalo	92	45.32	85	41.87	26	12.80
Washington						
English River	192	76.49	50	19.92	9	2.58
Iowa	91	65.46	36	25.89	12	8.63
Jackson	113	91.86	3	2.43	7	5.69
Webster						
Wahkonsah	103	58.52	23	13.06	50	28.40
Woodbury						
Sioux City Twp.	98	61.63	21	13.20	40	25.15
Sargeant's Bluffs	21	91.30	0	0.00	2	8.69

SOURCE: Manuscript reports for Iowa and the Eighth Census, 1860, Department of History and Archives, Des Moines, Iowa.

TABLE II

ELECTION RETURNS OF
SELECTED IOWA TOWNSHIPS IN 1860

COUNTY AND TOWNSHIP	Lincoln No.	Per cent	Douglas No.	Per cent	Breckenridge No.	Per cent	Bell No.	Per cent
Allamakee								
Center	82	82.00	18	18.00	....	....	....	....
Hanover	41	62.12	25	37.87	....	....	....	....
Boone								
Yell	27	40.90	39	59.09	....	....	....	....
Clayton								
Jefferson	237	55.24	192	44.75	....	....	....	....
Crawford								
Denison	17	51.51	16	48.48	....	....	....	....
Union	17	73.91	6	26.08	....	....	....	....
Davis								
Marion	38	25.50	77	51.00	15	10.06	19	12.75
Decatur								
Center	124	48.81	130	51.18	....	....	....	....
Johnson								
Monroe	64	69.75	28	30.43	....	....	....	....
Lee								
Franklin	132	43.56	169	55.77	....	....	2	.66
Poweshiek								
Bear Creek	131	49.80	128	48.66	2	.75	2	.75
Deep River	60	65.93	31	34.07	....	....	....	....
Linn								
Bertram	48	40.33	71	59.66	....	....	....	....
Putnam	53	63.09	31	36.90	....	....	....	....
Mahaska								
Union	61	49.59	62	50.40	....	....	....	....
Scott								
Davenport City	1493	64.52	727	31.41	41	1.77	53	2.88
Buffalo	93	52.54	83	46.89	....	....	1	.56
Washington								
English River	108	42.04	125	48.63	14	5.44	10	2.89
Iowa	63	39.13	97	60.24	....	....	1	.62
Jackson	87	70.73	32	26.01	....	....	4	3.25
Webster								
Wahkonsah	83	41.91	72	36.36	43	21.72	....	....
Woodbury								
Sioux City Township	68	38.62	97	55.11	7	3.97	4	2.27
Sargeant's Bluffs	19	76.00	6	24.00	....	....	....	....

SOURCES: County Election Boards' abstracts of returns of the national and state elections held in Iowa on November 6, 1860, Department of History and Archives, Des Moines, Iowa; Wahkonsah data are from the *Mississippi Valley Register* (Guttenberg, Iowa), November 8, 1860; Sioux City data are from the Fort Dodge (Iowa) *Republican*, November 14, 1860; Sargeant's Bluff data are from the Sioux City (Iowa) *Register*, November 10, 1860.

A student of Frederick Jackson Turner, Joseph Schafer (1867–1941) is best known for his regional and agricultural histories and for his five-volume Wisconsin Domesday Book, *a microscopic historical analysis of selected townships in which political data are related to ethnocultural, geographic, social, and economic data. Written shortly before his death, this article was the first full-scale attack on the traditional interpretation of Republican preferences among German voters. Schafer argues that they were neither numerous nor unified enough to have been the decisive element in the election of Lincoln in 1860.*

Who Elected Lincoln?

JOSEPH SCHAFER

On November 7, 1860, the day after Lincoln's election, a New York *Times* reporter "searched in vain for someone that could tell us the feelings of the defeated. Everyone declared himself a Lincoln man or else said nothing." Today, fourscore years later, the descendants of those who then kept silent, or most of them, in New York and throughout the North, boast of their forebears' attachment to the "rail-splitter's" cause. And as with individuals, so with groups. Lincoln's election was accomplished, each major element representing that day's citizenship would have the world know, largely if not absolutely because of the prescience of its group in pinning faith upon the homely Illinois statesman.

The honest pride and satisfaction of the Norwegians in the thought that their people, though not then numerous, nearly all "voted right" in 1860 is to this day a vital element in that people's public morale. The same can be said of the Welsh, English, and Scotch, but the Irish, being then as now Catholics and in that era bedeviled by animosities peculiar to the adherents of that religion, are perhaps the only English-speaking contingent which has never claimed credit for sending Lincoln to the White House. This is due not to the inherent modesty of the race but rather to the persistence of its Democracy and reluctance to acknowledge an early error.

On the other hand, by a queer distortion of both logic and history it has often been sought to include the Catholic Germans among the hosts of Lincoln electors. And taken as a body, the Germans have so skillfully and persistently pressed their claims that historians of all shades of opinion as to Lincoln and of the most diverse traditions have seemed eager to endorse the German contention without analysis or criticism. Thus we read in staunch Republican writers of Yankee lineage that the Germans in 1860 rushed to the aid of antislavery forces, while at the same time Southern "revisionists," seeking a scapegoat, find it in the fact that the black Republicans won success only with the aid of a multitude of alien, especially German, voters.

Carl Schurz is universally acknowledged to have been the leading German campaigner for Lincoln. As a member of the Republican National Committee from Wisconsin he was given charge of the "foreign department" and promptly analyzed the problem confronting him, which was to secure speakers and arrange meetings in all the non-English-speaking communities. He was the logical man for the function to be performed, for it was Schurz who—more than any other Republican—had shown himself the foreigners' defender against the onslaught of nativism, hateful to all foreigners and doubly repellent to Catholics in the alien groups.

In the spring of 1859 he had given out a brilliant utterance on that theme from the sacred precincts of Faneuil Hall. Again, at the Chicago National Republican Convention, Schurz, as a member of the resolutions committee, insisted on a clean-cut antinativist declaration in the platform on which the Republican candidate was to appeal to the electorate. He was determined to omit nothing that could in any measure offset the serious handicap of the acknowledged infestation of the Republican party by Know-Nothings.

Having made all preparations, he sallied forth as the most ubiquitous as well as the ablest speaker in the German language, if not as the ablest Republican campaigner in English also. He invaded the "October" states—Pennsylvania, Ohio, and Indiana—and they gave an encouraging account of themselves. He then campaigned in those states once more to guarantee the result and also spoke famously in English at St. Louis to the slaveholders, while at Cooper Union he castigated Douglas, also in English; then he traversed New York State, visited Illinois, and wound up his Herculean labors with a series of speeches in Milwaukee and throughout the German communities along Lake Michigan.

Schurz was never overmodest about telling what he thought of his own achievements, and some of the letters he wrote during the campaign, had they not been intimate recitals of his prowess to his wife, could be criticized by faultfinders as unblushingly boastful. It would hardly be fair to quote them as representative of his considered opinion. On September 24, 1863, however, he wrote to Theodore Petrasch, whom he had not seen or heard from since their university days in 1848, telling about his part in American political affairs:

> My activities were very extended and had a large and direct influence upon the political development of the country. I have been told that I made Lincoln president. That is, of course, not true, but that people say so indicates that I contributed something toward raising the breeze which carried Lincoln into the presidential chair and thereby shook slavery in its foundations.[1]

The idea that he made Lincoln president, which, though he seemingly waved it from him after giving it utterance, he obviously delighted to entertain, could rest only on the theory that he had been instrumental in converting to Republicanism a large, and in some states a controlling, proportion of German Democrats, for with few exceptions his speeches were made in German to audiences made up of Germans. The argument is, therefore, that it was the Germans who elected Lincoln and that Schurz, as the leading campaigner in their language, was respon-

---

1. Joseph Schafer, tr. and ed., *Intimate Letters of Carl Schurz, 1841–1869*, Publications of the State Historical Society of Wisconsin Collections 30 (Madison, 1928), p. 284.

sible for the dominantly Republican German vote. Hence he was the man who made Lincoln president.

A sample of the reasoning on which extravagant Germanists rely is seen in the book called *Wisconsin's Deutsch Amerikaner,* published at Milwaukee in 1900 and written by a versatile German named Wilhelm Hense-Jensen. "The breach in the national Democratic party," he says, "which before the election divided into two factions, and more yet, the support of the immigrant vote, led in the year 1860 to the election of Abraham Lincoln." He followed the generalization with what he considered proof of the Germans' agency in giving Lincoln a better than 20,000 majority in Wisconsin:

> In Wisconsin 86,113 votes were cast for Lincoln. The percentage of inhabitants in the state who were of German derivation (born in Germany or of German-born parents) was at that time the highest it was ever to show. It amounted, according to careful and credible compilation, to 69 per cent of the entire population. Accepting this percentage and assuming further that only two thirds of the voters of German derivation voted the Republican ticket, the conclusion is reached that at least 40,000 German voters in Wisconsin voted for Lincoln.

If 40,000 voted for Lincoln and that was two thirds of the German voting strength, then the Germans were of course responsible for the Lincoln majority over Douglas of a few more than 20,000 votes. Naturally, Hense-Jensen glories in his people's supposed noble achievement. "The German population," he proclaims, "had once more fulfilled its original mission. For, whithersoever the German directed his steps, everywhere it appeared to be his function to open the way for freedom."

His conclusions, however, were reached with such suspicious facility as to challenge a careful scrutiny and analysis. The result is a very different picture from that which is here presented in that author's own language turned into English.

In the first place, we would like to be clear on how he discovered that Germans constituted 69 per cent of the state's population in 1860, particularly since by reading forward to the chapter describing the participation of Germans in the Civil War, he is caught using an entirely different yardstick for measuring, from the very same census returns, the German element of the population. Instead of 69 per cent, for military purposes that element mysteriously shrinks to about 16 per cent. This enables him to prove that his countrymen exceeded their quota in the military effort made by the state.

In view of this showing it is not imperatively necessary to pay much attention to the figures given above, either for German Lincoln voters or for German Lincoln soldiers. We believe that Germans of Wisconsin did their full duty in the war and that their number was approximately one sixth of all the men sent to the front by the state.

It is not remarkable, therefore, to discover from the census that the German-born citizens in 1860 constituted almost exactly one sixth of the state's total population. If we had to deal only with the German born, our task would be simple, for the number of those is clearly set forth in the census. A good argument could be made for disregarding their native-born children, on two grounds: first, that there were few if any voters, at least among those born in Wisconsin; second, if in some states like Ohio there were native-born voters of German parentage, they would be quite as apt to vote against as with the older generation of Germans, for they had lost much of the racial feeling. However, for convenience in computing the total number of German voters, under the well-established rule of one to every five of the population, some approximation to the number of natives of German parentage should be found. For Wisconsin, as stated, we find the German born to be one sixth of the aggregate population.

Were we to assign to that group one sixth of the natives born in Wisconsin, that would add a third to the number of Germans. The proportion would manifestly be overgenerous because the majority of the German born whose numbers are definitely ascertained by the census entered the country only a few years prior to 1860, while other population groups, like the Yankees, had been present in force for many years and contributed much more heavily to the aggregate of the native born. Nevertheless, since it is practically impossible to determine how many native-born children any given group was responsible for, let us assume, for convenience, that in the case of the Germans the native children equaled one third of the German born, which would be one sixth of all Wisconsin native born. The same one third rule may be applied when we come to consider the German element in other states, though it cannot be regarded as other than an estimate, sometimes too large, as in Wisconsin, occasionally perhaps a bit too small.

Wisconsin in 1860 had 123,879 German born in her population. Adding 41,196, which equals one sixth of the entire native group and is about 100 less than one third of the German born, we have 165,075. Since one in five could be a voter, the potential voting strength of the German aggregation was 33,015 instead of 60,000, as Hense-Jensen estimated it. If, with him, we assign to Lincoln two thirds of that vote, he would have received 22,010 votes. But, in that case, 11,005 must have voted the Democratic ticket, leaving the Germans far short of providing Lincoln's 20,000 majority. The extent of the Republican majority can by no stretch of the facts be attributed to German votes even under the assumption that two thirds of them went to Lincoln.

Our crucial question now is: Did two thirds of the German voters in 1860 cast their ballots for Abraham Lincoln? We are arrived at the point where the "grass roots" population studies carried out under the Wisconsin Domesday Book project, a superior "Gallup poll" covering the time in question, begin to apply in significant ways to the consideration of a problem of nation-wide import which hitherto has always been treated as a subject for vague speculation or sheer guesswork. Several of the most "German" counties in Wisconsin have been studied socially by townships, which were also the election precincts, in order to discover how the several social groups voted in the two presidential elections of 1856 and 1860.

What can the speculative historian oppose to facts like these: The town of Marshfield, in Fond du Lac County, in 1860, by careful hand count of the manuscript census entries, had 239 family heads, of whom 229 were German and 10 non-German. The vote, as recorded for that precinct in the Wisconsin *Blue Book,* is Lincoln 6, Douglas 193. Another case: The town of

Cedarburg, in Ozaukee County, had 229 German family heads and 111 Irish. There were only 7 who did not belong to those two groups. In that town the vote was Lincoln 7, Douglas 299! Can there be any question as to what groups were voting against Lincoln?

Now contrast the following case. In the town of Rosendale, Fond du Lac County, were 211 family heads, of whom 140 were native American, 15 English, 1 Scotch, 15 Welsh, and 12 British American. There were only 12 Irish family heads and 16 German. That town recorded a vote of 215 for Lincoln, 22 for Douglas. Can there be much doubt as to what groups in that town were casting votes in Lincoln's favor? Nearly, if not quite all, must have been given by the American and British family heads and their connections, such as the superannuated men of the households, hired men, et al. It is known that a good many Germans were still shy about voting, though the Irish were not. The town of Emmet, in Dodge County, had 180 Irish and German family heads, practically an equal number of each, against 34 Americans, 9 English, 13 Welsh, and 1 British American—total 57. The vote was Lincoln 55, Douglas 155.

Marshfield, Cedarburg, and Emmet were in large part Catholic towns, though the bulk of Cedarburg's Germans were Protestants, and the voting records suggest that Catholic Germans and Catholic Irish were very nearly if not quite unanimous in their opposition to Lincoln. In fact, from the above and many other test cases it can be affirmed that the Irish of Wisconsin could be counted solidly for the Democratic candidates. The German Catholics were also practically unanimous on the same side. Catholics had not forgotten their ancient enemy, the nativists or "Know-Nothings," who had now been absorbed by the Republican party. Though that party had adopted a vigorous platform plank denouncing nativism, Catholics could not trust a party which harbored Know-Nothings. Besides, the Democratic party had always been hospitable to foreigners; they felt that the slavery issue should be left to the slave states to settle, and they would not desert the party in its time of obvious distress.

Non-Catholic Germans present a more complex problem, and we shall see that some precincts in which such persons dominated reported many German votes for Lincoln. The town of Mequon, Ozaukee County, is an example. It had 561 family heads, of whom 459 were German and 30 Irish; that is, 489 of the two groups combined. Americans and British at the census date, June 1, were but 31 all told. Yet the vote of that town stood Lincoln 141, Douglas 314. Inasmuch as the Irish are sure to have voted for Douglas, this means that probably as many as 110 Germans, out of 459, voted for Lincoln. The proportion was not two thirds, nor yet one third, but it may have approximated one fourth.

Other non-Catholic German towns show varying proportions of Lincoln votes. The town of Herman in Dodge County had 401 family heads, 337 German and 11 Irish. Other groups totaled 53. The vote was 65 for Lincoln, 282 for Douglas. Here we can only say that some—not many—Lincoln votes might have been cast by Germans; although it is not impossible that the 53 non-Germans, reenforced by a few hired men, could have accounted for the entire Lincoln vote.

A better test of Protestant German voting is afforded by another town of Herman, this one in Sheboygan County. That precinct had 355 family heads, all, without a single exception, born in Germany. It was a colony of German Reformed religionists, most of them from the petty state of Lippe-Detmold. It had a vigorous church life and was about to establish a mission school of some reputation. Evidently the moral aspect of the slavery question had made some impression on those people. Four years earlier the town had voted 201 for Buchanan to 27 for Frémont. Now, however, they gave Lincoln 122 and Douglas 210, practically 36 per cent to 64 per cent.

A fairly comprehensive sampling of the Wisconsin election vote of 1860 shows few German communities that were more favorable to Lincoln than the one just discussed. Moreover, it gives convincing evidence that the American born of New England and New York lineage were prevailingly Republican, those of Kentucky, Tennessee, and Missouri derivation largely, though not always mainly, Democratic. Wherever the population was English, Scotch, or Welsh, the vote was preponderantly Republican; and the same was true as respects most of the as yet small Norwegian communities, though some were influenced by Norwegian Democratic leaders to vote for Douglas. But so surely as the tally of the family head count in a precinct comes out as German, Irish, or a combination of those two groups, the majority vote was Democratic.

While some Germans, especially the Forty-eighters and some part of the Lutherans, voted the Republican ticket, that vote in 1860, while larger than in 1856, was still very light. When we recall that Catholics seem to have been nearly unanimous for Douglas, that German people of that faith in Wisconsin were at least as numerous as Lutherans and Reformed combined, and that the German Lutherans, so far as we have canvassed the matter, always showed a strong partiality for Douglas, it would be quite unsafe to assume that the proportion of· the German voters who preferred Lincoln was more than one sixth of the whole, which would be considerably less than 6,000. The estimate of 40,000 so confidently published by Hense-Jensen is fantastic.

Looking at the election of 1860 from the national standpoint, the first item one can generalize about with safety is that the canvass for Lincoln involved a moral crusade. Opposition to the institution of slavery on moral grounds had been gradually making itself felt among the nonslaveholders of the North for the better part of a century, and from the time of the Mexican War the sentiment against the further extension of the institution had been growing ever more relentless. Quite naturally, it was the older Americans, especially those of the Puritan tradition, who were most deeply affected by the agelong propaganda against slavery on moral principles, and who were now—when an opportunity seemed to offer in the fateful Democratic split—determined to erect a permanent barrier against its further spread.

The historian Rhodes tersely remarks: "Because slavery was wrong, the great majority of northern people had declared against its extension." He had discussed in the preceding chapter the morals of that period, which, he contended with reason, were better than those of the years following the Civil War. And Carl Schurz, in his *Reminiscences,* asserts:

> There has never been in the history of this Republic a political movement in which the moral motive was so strong—indeed, so dominant and decisive. . . . I have been active in many political campaigns, but none in which the best impulses of human nature were so forceful and effective and aroused the masses to so high a pitch of almost religious fervor.

These testimonies are typical and cannot be disregarded or minimized. They are witnesses to a crusade which had been long coming to a head through the gradual indoctrination of those most susceptible to moral appeals. Of course, the weight of the antislavery propaganda fell upon those who could receive it unhindered by linguistic and other obstacles, which meant the English-speaking-and-reading portion of the population, or at least that dominant fraction of the English-speakers who were not conditioned against it by religious partisanship.

The Irish, being Catholics and having experienced the enmity of the Know-Nothings, now masquerading as Republicans, were effectually prevented from embracing Republican dogmas or supporting Republican candidates, deeply sensitive as that people normally was to the claims of freedom and humanity. The Germans in part were hindered by their adherence to the Catholic Church, and upon the great majority of both Protestants and Catholics the impact of the campaign of education, carried on almost exclusively in English, fell in a mitigated, mangled, and partly ineffectual form. There were some Republican German newspapers, but their influence was slight as compared with the vastly larger number and greater popularity of the Democratic German papers. It would have been a marvel if, under these circumstances, the Germans could have caught up and kept pace with the psychological movement among American and other English-speaking citizens.

The group of Germans currently described as Forty-eighters, many of whom came to the United States as political refugees after the failure of the '48 revolution, mostly, it is thought, allied themselves with the antislavery forces; at least many of the leaders did so. They were, in the main, educated men, they learned English readily, and they quickly grasped the fundamentals of the antislavery problem as affecting American politics. In the campaign of 1860 men of that group performed yeoman service in propagandizing the German element. Carl Schurz, Gustave Koerner, Franz Hoffmann, Hecker, Stallo, and others threw themselves unreservedly into the campaign to elect Lincoln.

Their work bore fruit, but not nearly as large a harvest as has generally been supposed, and for this there were several reasons. The first is the extreme conservatism of the average German and his loyalty to personal, party, and religious attachments once faithfully established. The second is the skepticism with which German religionists of both groups, Catholic and Protestant, looked upon the revolutionary group, who were not only considered radicals in politics but also, for the most part, anticlericals or outright freethinkers in religion. In a word, the Forty-eighters were in some measure insulated from their religious fellow countrymen and had first to build up among their fellows confidence in themselves before they could hope to detach the mass of the German immigrants from their old political moorings in the friendly Democratic party.

Religion affected the large Lutheran body in still another way. Among Wisconsin churchmen and also those of neighbor states, the powerful intellectual leaders of the Missouri Synod, with whom the doctrine that slavery was a biblically justified institution was almost an article of faith, were a strong influence. This proved to be one ground of opposition to that synod's control among Norwegian Lutherans, fierce and eager haters of slavery, but to the Germans it was a stone of stumbling and a cause of intellectual confusion. Time and struggle, especially the Civil War, would bring clarity upon the slavery issue. Then, however, other issues were destined to divide the two parties, and so instead of the Wisconsin Germans having "nearly all" attached themselves to the Republican party by 1856, as one historian unwarily affirms, the majority could not be safely counted for the Republicans until forty years later than the date indicated. To be sure, there were flurries and oscillations during the intervening years, and so far as the cities, especially Milwaukee, were concerned, Republicanism gained a firm control by 1880. Unfortunately for the German claimants, however, probably most Germans were farmers, who were far less amenable to propaganda than the city dwellers. To take a single example, the county of Ozaukee, a few miles north of Milwaukee, a rural county with a heavy preponderance of Germans, gave no Republican presidential candidate a majority prior to the election of 1916; and even then Hughes received only 33 more votes than Wilson.

The campaign directed to the German voters in the hope of bringing them into the Lincoln camp in 1860 was a strenuous one, as anybody can see by reading Carl Schurz's letters written almost day by day during those hectic weeks. The flying squadron of Republican Forty-eighters saved, as brands from the burning, enough Wisconsin German votes to make Lincoln's clear majority about 20,000. But Lincoln would have won in Wisconsin if all German votes had been given to Douglas, as doubtless five sixths of them were.

Where then, it may be asked, did the shift in party allegiance occur which brought success so promptly to the Republican party? The election in 1860 occurred on November 6. From Milwaukee a participant in the Lincoln campaign wrote next day:

> When the voting was over, we gathered in the Chamber of Commerce at Spring Street bridge to receive the telegraphed returns. The hall was crowded. As the dispatches arrived the excitement mounted; and when Lincoln's majority appeared ever to be growing the cheering was tremendous. Finally, came New York, the actual battle ground of the campaign. Early dispatches spoke of a majority of 40,000 in the city against us. The stillness of dread among the Republicans! Then the telegrams came, stroke after stroke, and the formidable count melted away, first to 35,000, then 28,000, and, finally, 25,000. Everyone breathed freely once more. Then, like a veritable hailstorm, the Republicans reported majorities from the western portion of the state. The crowd went wild with shouts and cheering; hats were flying to the ceiling, against the walls, and to the floor as if they were worth nothing at all. Finally at about two

o'clock the telegraph announced: "According to reports received, New York is good for a majority of 50,000." The cannon was now dragged out and we woke up the Democrats, they having withdrawn from the streets pretty early in the evening.

Just as, in Wisconsin, Republican gains between 1856 and 1860 were much more rapid in the Yankee counties than in the counties settled largely by Irish and Germans, so in New York the greatest gains had been in the upstate region settled mainly from New England. The counties of northeastern Ohio, the old Connecticut reserve, likewise showed distinctly larger gains for free soil than did the counties along the Ohio River, not excluding Hamilton, Cincinnati's county, with its very large German population. Hamilton, indeed, in 1860 gave Lincoln 750 votes more than Douglas but 2,934 less than the combined votes of Douglas and Bell. The 366 votes for Breckinridge have been disregarded in this computation.

A writer in Volume III of the Centennial History of Illinois tells us: "The German vote of Illinois and neighboring states was so powerful in 1860 that without its assistance Lincoln and his party would have been decisively defeated."[2] He obviously takes it for granted that majorities of the Germans in those states supported Lincoln. As already shown, that was not true of the neighbor state of Wisconsin, where it is so certain that a large majority of Germans voted for Douglas as to make the Lincoln majority of 20,000 a sure proof of the Germans' inability to alter the result. If all Germans had voted for Douglas, Lincoln would, nevertheless, have won that state.

Let us consider another of the neighbor states, Indiana. Foreign immigration had affected that commonwealth far less than either Illinois or Wisconsin; and the number of those born in Germany was reported in 1860 at 67,000. Applying the test used in our Wisconsin study, which calls for the addition of one third to the German born by reason of the interest of that element in the state's natives of German parentage, we have an aggregate

2. Arthur Charles Cole, *The Era of the Civil War* (Springfield, 1919), pp. 341–42. Cf. William F. Dodd, "The Fight for the Northwest, 1860," *American Historical Review* 16 (July 1911): 774–88.

body of 89,000 Germans, who would be represented by 17,800 voters. But the Lincoln majority over Douglas was 24,000, which would have much more than canceled the entire German vote had it been thrown solidly for Douglas.

Ohio's German contingent was much larger, 168,000; adding a third to that number to represent the native-born children, we have a body of 224,000 Germans and a possible 44,800 German voters. But the Lincoln majority over Douglas was 44,378, which doubtless exceeded the entire German vote actually polled. Breckinridge and Bell received a combined vote of 21,600, showing the importance in that state of the Democratic party split.

The case of Michigan is yet more striking. Her small contingent of Germans, not more than 53,500, including the German born and the American born, could have contained not over 10,700 voters. The Lincoln majority over Douglas, however, was 22,500 and over all Democratic candidates better than 21,000.

We have left one other neighbor state of Illinois which proved to be in the Lincoln column after his election—Iowa. There the German contingent was almost precisely equal to that of Michigan—only 38,555, which, corrected to include American-born Germans, yields the aggregate of 51,400, or a body of 10,280 potential German voters. The Lincoln majority in Iowa was over 15,000.

It appears, then, that so far as the neighbor states of Illinois were concerned, the generalization with which this discussion began has no facts to sustain it. The case of Illinois itself may be quite different, depending on what detailed research as to group voting by precincts may show with reference to the disposition of Germans to favor Lincoln over Douglas.

If Illinois's German element, in round numbers 131,000 in 1860 and with their American-born children possibly capable of providing a voting strength of nearly 35,000, had voted for Lincoln in two out of three instances, they could have provided the 12,000 majority for him which the final count showed.

It will now be the duty of historical researchers to exhibit the probabilities in this connection. If the number voting for Douglas turns out to equal the number voting for Lincoln, the result of the German vote was, of course, nil. We do not know, as yet, whether Lincoln or Douglas captured the majority of the large German vote of Illinois. But even assuming that the majority, to an extent exceeding 12,000, went to Lincoln—an extremely doubtful assumption in view of the way Germans are known to have voted in Wisconsin—that would merely prove that the German vote was effective in Lincoln's favor in Illinois. The neighbors were certainly in the category of states in which the net result was unaffected by the German vote.

It is not known how far, if at all, studies of group preferences, like those included in the Wisconsin Domesday Book series, have been made for the other states. Until such studies will have been made for Illinois, Indiana, Michigan, Pennsylvania, and New York, we shall not be in a position either to generalize with complete confidence from the results of the Wisconsin studies or, on the other hand, to refute those findings. But if it should be found, as seems likely to be the case, that Germans elsewhere in the North behaved as did those in the badger state, then we should be able to affirm that so far from the Germans producing Republican success, it was such success which produced German Republican voters.

If one cared to speculate, there is a possible approach to the question which, while no substitute for the security of the Domesday Book method, may, nevertheless, yield probabilities. The census of 1860 lists the number of churches under the names of the several denominations and gives the estimate of their individual and collective "accommodation." The accommodation would bear a definite relation to the actual customary attendance or those who were subjected to the influence of the spirit of the given sect.

Now in Illinois there were in 1860 churches of the Lutheran denomination which provided accommodation for 33,000 and of the Catholic which provided for 91,000, making together 124,000. But the aggregate accommodation of Presbyterian, Congregational, Methodist, Christian (or Campbellite), Episcopal, and Baptist churches was 534,000. The Presbyterian alone was 128,000, the Baptist 130,000, and the Methodist 267,000. Since the moral leaven of antislavery was working with peculiar activity within some of the American Protestant churches, notwithstanding Lincoln's supposed complaint to Dr. Bateman about the preachers, this affords at least a hint as to where the cauldron may have been in which Republican principles were being brewed.

In any event, it appears all but certain that the assignment of a dominant influence to the foreign born in the election of 1860 is 100 per cent wrong; that Lincoln was elected through an upsurge of moral enthusiasm and determination on the part of the distinctly American folk; and that the foreign-born contingents participated, but in no sense as determinative factors.

The author's chief reason for calling sharp attention to the futility of the speculative method hitherto commonly used by historians in dealing with subjects of this kind is to protest against an outworn methodology. The "guessing game" is no longer permissible to those who claim the right to be called historians, in the American field at least. Like Hamlet, we demand "proofs more relative" than those supplied by ghosts.

Reprinted from the *American Historical Review* 47 (October 1941): 51–63.

Jay Monaghan (b. 1891) was Illinois state historian before he moved to Santa Barbara, California, where he is now consultant for the Wyles Collection of Lincolniana and Western Americana at the University of California at Santa Barbara. A widely known Lincoln scholar, Monaghan supports the traditional view that, at least in Illinois, Lincoln won the support of German voters. He suggests reasons why the electoral behavior of the Illinois Germans may have diverged from that of Germans elsewhere.

Did Abraham Lincoln Receive the Illinois German Vote?

JAY MONAGHAN

In a recent article in the *American Historical Review* the late Dr. Joseph Schafer, superintendent of the State Historical Society of Wisconsin, analyzed the presidential vote of 1860 and came to the conclusion that the Wisconsin Germans were not an important factor in the election of Abraham Lincoln. Indeed, most of them seem to have voted against the Emancipator, due, Dr. Schafer believed, to the violent anti-foreign, anti-Catholic principles of the American or Know-Nothing Party which the Republicans had allegedly absorbed. Dr. Schafer assumed further that the German vote was of small importance in Illinois as well as in other states, and intimated that the time had come to rewrite the history of the election which precipitated our Civil War.

Historians may have erred in their interpretation of the election of 1860. If they have, they were led astray by the voluminous contemporary documents which relate the enthusiasm of German liberals for Abraham Lincoln, by the active part taken by prominent German speakers and writers like Carl Schurz, Gustave Koerner, George Schneider,[1] editor of the *Illinois Staats-*

1. Bessie Louise Pierce, *A History of Chicago* (New York, 1940), 2: 233.

Zeitung, and by the numerous resolutions passed by Turnvereins and the military displays indulged in by these gymnastic societies. This activity may have been only the noisy demonstration of a small minority, but certainly the contemporary newspapers are filled with notices which give the impression that the Germans were vitally interested in the election. Democratic vituperation against the "lop-eared Dutch" has helped strengthen the assumption that German sympathies were Republican.

In 1860 the German-born residents of the northern states amounted to 5.74% of the population[2]—a small percentage but sufficient to be a deciding factor in doubtful elections. Republican politicians saw to it that their newspapers constantly wrote "leaders" to flatter the Germans, who were presumed to be a liberty-loving people escaped from the tyranny of European monarchies. This impression was cultivated in the minds of contemporary Republican politicians—as well as later historians—by the German-American press. When the execution of John Brown was announced with mourning borders by *Der Demokrat*[3] in Davenport, Iowa, it is easy to understand how party managers might have inferred that the German population was inclined toward abolitionism. So too, when the German-American politicians convened in Chicago immediately before the national Republican convention it is not surprising that the Republicans adopted the Germans' resolutions as planks of the Republican Party.[4] The German vote was considered of such great importance that the party distributed thousands of political pamphlets printed in German type, the most notable being the Republican tract, *Die Heimstätte-Bill—"Land für die Landlosen,"* which quoted the political pronouncements of Lincoln and Douglas. At the same time campaign managers translated and distributed addresses by G. A. Grow, John Hickman, James

2. Joseph C. G. Kennedy, comp., *Population of the U.S. in 1860; Compiled from the Original Returns of the Eighth Census* (Washington, 1864), pp. 103, 104.

3. Frank I. Herriott, "The Conference in the Deutsches Haus, Chicago, May 14–15, 1860," *Transactions of the Illinois State Historical Society, 1928,* pp. 101–91.

4. Ibid., p. 108.

Harlan, Owen Lovejoy, and William H. Seward, to mention only a few. If all these men erred in judgment, Dr. Schafer's thesis is an arresting commentary on the perspicacity of many national leaders on the eve of the Civil War.

A re-evaluation of the importance of the German vote in 1860 will also entail a reappraisal of the political vision of Abraham Lincoln, who, both before and after the election, considered the Germans an important part of his constituency. For campaign purposes, Lincoln secretly purchased the *Illinois Staats Anzeiger*,[5] Springfield's German newspaper, and shortly after the election rewarded the editor with a consular post. Lincoln's German appointments were characteristic of his administration. In the army Carl Schurz and Franz Sigel were commissioned major generals. German brigadiers were legion.[6] The State Department relied on Francis Lieber, author of numerous Republican tracts, for interpretations of involved questions of international law. In the diplomatic field, when Secretary Seward attempted to fill his ministerial posts with American politicians, Lincoln asked, "What about our German friends?"[7] Was Lincoln, like his colleagues, basing his appreciation of the German vote on a false assumption?

When Lincoln made up his mind about the importance of the German vote, records were available that have since disappeared. In neighboring states he probably took the word of committee chairmen who may have deceived him, but in Illinois he knew the poll book. The state had a population of 1,711,951, of whom 324,643 were listed as foreign-born. Of these the census shows that 130,804 were German.[8] This is roughly 8% of the population of the state, and Lincoln won by a plurality of only 3%. It is interesting to note that the number of Illinois residents born in slave states was 179,426, or slightly more than the Ger-

5. Paul M. Angle, *New Letters and Papers of Lincoln* (Boston, 1930), pp. 204–5.

6. Albert B. Faust, *The German Element in the United States* (Boston, 1909), 1: 522–72.

7. Letter of March 18, 1861. John G. Nicolay and John Hay, *Complete Works of Abraham Lincoln*, Gettysburg ed. (New York, 1905), 6: 223–24.

8. Kennedy, comp., *Population in 1860*, pp. 103, 104.

man-born residents. If the two groups voted in blocs each might have neutralized the other. The only foreigners who approached the Germans in number were the 87,573 Irish immigrants, generally conceded to have been Democrats. As Lincoln studied the state vote another thing must have been evident to him. Two counties, Cook and St. Clair, led all the rest in the number of foreign residents, and both these counties returned Republican majorities. Such evidence must have made Lincoln susceptible to the arguments of German politicians who claimed that their nationals had voted en masse, thus assuring his election. Cook County, in the North, might have been expected to contain a native-born population with Republican principles. However, 50% of the residents were foreign-born, half of them German, and Lincoln polled 58% of the votes. Obviously his majority contained more than the native-born vote.

St. Clair County presents a less complicated problem. Unlike Cook, it had a foreign population almost exclusively German. Bordering on a slave state, it also had intimate steamboat connections with the deep South, and its native population was assumed to be anti-Lincoln.

St. Clair County had a population of 37,694 with 43% foreign-born, but this number does not adequately represent the German vote as it does not include the adult descendants of early German settlers, some of whom had been in the region over forty years.[9] A better indication of the total German population can be obtained from another source. In 1855 the state conducted a census by counties.[10] Although the nativity of the residents was not recorded, an actual count of the St. Clair County roster shows that 55% of the population had German names. Is it a coincidence or is it significant that the vote for Lincoln in this county amounted to 54.8%?

Two objections may be raised to any conclusion drawn from these figures. In the first place, personal names may seem to be

9. Ferdinand Ernst, "Travels in Illinois in 1819," *Transactions of the Illinois State Historical Society, 1903*, pp. 150–65. See also John A. Hawgood, *The Tragedy of German-America* (New York, 1940), p. 125.

10. State census, 1855, MS, Archives Division, Illinois State Library, Springfield.

uncertain criteria of nationality. In the second place, what proof is there that the Lincoln vote was not made up of 45% native American votes and only 9.84% German? The first objection is not serious. There can be little question about the national derivation of Schoff, Buchholtz, Snider, Schmidt, Hartman, Eckert, Scott, Cox, McCoy, McDonald, and Jones. The names of early French settlers, J. Cartoe, G. Baptiste, C. Thucoits, J. Marchal, L. Chartrand, and L. Lamieux, are also easily distinguished. Some few like Miller, Fisher, Jacobs, Buck, Baker, and Wagoner are questionable, but such names do not constitute 2% of the whole. This objection, then, is not material. But how about the second one? Is there any way to prove that the Lincoln majorities were German votes? Yes, by at least two lines of reasoning. The Democratic faction is known to have been sympathetic towards the South. The county became a recruiting ground for Confederate irregulars, and at the same time, in adjacent Missouri, men were flogged and occasionally hanged for no other offense than the possession of a German name. This inference should be sufficient, but let us try a second test. The vote and census were both taken by precincts, and a comparision of the figures broken down into these divisions may serve as another clue. The oldest precinct was Cahokia, center of the early French settlement. This precinct had the smallest German population and it cast the largest anti-Lincoln vote. Fayetteville, with a population of 66% non-Germans, also cast a majority for Douglas. Athens precinct, with a population of 54% Germans, gave Lincoln a vote of 53%. Centerville, with a population of 61% Germans, gave Lincoln a vote of 64%. So in precinct after precinct a preponderance of Germans is always associated with a Lincoln majority.[11] Once more the figures indicate the soundness of contemporary politicians' judgment.

This analysis of the vote in St. Clair County, Illinois, shows a condition exactly the reverse of the one found by Dr. Schafer in Wisconsin. Nevertheless, the precision with which the ratio holds in case after case indicates its validity. One qualifying factor, however, must not be ignored—and the Wisconsin study,

11. *Belleviller Zeitung*, November 8, 1860.

it seems, did not take this into consideration. St. Clair County had approximately 10,000 potential voters and only 6,866 votes were cast.[12] In other words almost a third of the electorate did not appear at the polls—a margin sufficient to invalidate any of our conclusions. In Lincoln's day one more test was possible that cannot be repeated today. Then the names in the poll books could be checked against the vote. These records have disappeared, so the most that can be said is that every test available has confirmed the opinions of both the Illinois politicians and the contemporary press. There is no warrant for a serious revision of the accepted interpretation of the importance of the Illinois German vote in the election of 1860.

It is not difficult to explain the difference between the voting habits of the Germans in Illinois and those studied by Dr. Schafer. The Wisconsin Germans seem to have lived in small, rural communities with little admixture of other nationals. The Illinois Germans lived in or near large urban centers where they were constantly in contact with people of diverse convictions. Many Chicago Germans were organized into strong labor unions, socialistic in philosophy, pink in shade. Their life had little in common with the parochial prairie communities and it is unwise to assume that their voting habits were the same. The St. Clair Germans conform to a third pattern. Led by men of culture and intellect like Gustave Koerner and Friedrich Hecker, their political principles might be expected to differ from Germans with narrower backgrounds. "Latin farmers," they were called by their catfish American neighbors. Urbanization and liberal education may account for the German vote in Illinois. It will be interesting to see dissections of the vote in other states. Perhaps Dr. Schafer's thesis may yet be upheld, but if not, he deserves high tribute for his provocative investigation. As the French would say, *"mais c'est une idée."*

Reprinted from *Journal of the Illinois State Historical Society* 35 (June 1942): 133–39.

12. 1860 Election Returns by Counties, MS, Archives Division, Illinois State Library, Springfield.

Andreas Dorpalen was born in Berlin, Germany, in 1911. Educated in German universities, he has lived in the United States since 1939 and has retained a natural interest in the history of German immigrants in America. He is now professor of modern German history at Ohio State University. Published in 1942, Dorpalen's article sharply criticizes the idea that ethnicity caused German voters to respond to issues differently than did the native-born persons among whom they lived. Dorpalen's insistence on appropriate comparisons makes his article an important contribution to the methodology of research in ethnic political history.

The German Element and the Issues of the Civil War

ANDREAS DORPALEN

To German-American historians the attitude of the German element in the United States toward the issues of the Civil War has never been much of a problem. "The achievement of the Germans in this great crisis," said Professor A. B. Faust, "was that they, holding the balance of power, threw their entire weight into the scale of justice, humanity, and national union."[1] Others agreed with him. "It was Germans," wrote Julius Goebel, "who can claim the honor of having been responsible for the abolition of this shame."[2] And Georg von Bosse likewise found that "though Germans may generally have differed in their views and principles—in this question they were firmly united."[3]

All three authors, writing in the first decade of this century, still saw slavery as the main issue of the Civil War. No later

1. Albert B. Faust, *The German Element in the United States,* 2 vols. (Boston and New York, 1909), 2: 137.

2. Julius Goebel, *Das Deutschtum in den Vereinigten Staaten von Nord-Amerika* (Munich, 1904), p. 59.

3. Georg von Bosse, *Das deutsche Element in den Vereinigten Staaten* (Stuttgart, 1908), p. 255.

author, as far as can be ascertained, has attempted to reexamine the attitude of the German element toward the "irrepressible conflict" in the light of more recent findings on the war causes. Nor has Professor Faust seen fit to change his viewpoint in the new edition of his book.[4] A reexamination of the German-American attitude toward those issues that finally had to be settled by armed force needs therefore no further justification.

From the earliest colonial times the German element in this country had shown itself particularly susceptible to environmental pressure. It accepted, and adopted, conditions as it found them. While zealous German Mennonites in Pennsylvania clamored against the "vicious" institution of slavery, Germans in the Carolinas and Georgia found nothing objectionable in the use of slave labor. Their attitude toward the American Revolution was likewise determined by sectional considerations, and similar motives led them into the Federalist and anti-Federalist camps, respectively, after the Revolutionary War.[5] Nor could the young German national movement of the eighteen-thirties change this attitude. Any attempt to unite the German-American element in anything that went beyond loose social organizations failed from the beginning, and ambitious schemes to establish a German republic in one of the western states found their first insurmountable obstacle in German disunion.[6] The overwhelming majority of the German immigrants of the eighteen-thirties, forties, and fifties had come over for economic reasons. Their material welfare, not nationalist designs, determined the course of their actions.

Yet faced with an issue that divided the American nation into two bitterly hostile factions, the Germans in America are said to have overcome all other considerations and suddenly to have found themselves solidly united. Were they really?

To Germans in the South the slave issue was of minor importance. Comparatively few Germans had settled in the south-

4. *The German Element in the United States* (New York, 1927), 2: 652.
5. Andreas Dorpalen, "The Political Influence of the German Element in Colonial America," *Pennsylvania History* 6 (1939): 147 ff., 221 ff.
6. Heinrich H. Maurer, "The earlier German Nationalism in America," *American Journal of Sociology* 22 (1917): 519 ff.

ern states since the War of Independence. The North, more easily reached and with a healthier climate, offered much better economic opportunities to the immigrant, especially if he had no, or but limited, means. Some, however, did go south. In the Old South, these new arrivals were mostly traders and artisans, who established themselves in the coastal cities of Baltimore, Charleston, Mobile, and New Orleans and in certain inland centers such as Richmond and Memphis.[7] A few farmers settled in Virginia. They devoted themselves to fruit culture, market gardening, dairy farming, and cattle raising, all pursuits that required no slave labor.[8] German workers came south in still smaller numbers, for their status as free laborers gave them no social standing in the South, where common labor was considered degrading and unworthy of a white man.[9] Moreover, since Negro slaves were considered too valuable to be risked in dangerous jobs, southern employers preferred to hire white laborers only for perilous work.[10]

Owning no slaves, these Germans in the South were affected only indirectly by the slave problem. Some of them might condemn slavery privately on moral or religious grounds; in public, they refrained from opposing it. They seemed satisfied with the existing order of things, and many of them feared that abolitionist propaganda could only lead to the disruption of the Union.[11] Moreover, living in a section where nativism was particularly strong, they were naturally inclined to side with their American neighbors rather than to risk social ostracism. Economic con-

7. Ella Lonn, *Foreigners in the Confederacy* (Chapel Hill, 1940), pp. 2 ff.

8. Hermann Schuricht, *History of the German Element in Virginia*, 2 vols. in 1 (Baltimore, 1898–1900), II: 27; Frederick Law Olmsted, *Journey in the Seaboard Slave States* (New York, 1856), pp. 510–11, 587 ff.

9. Olmsted, *Journey in Slave States*, p. 211.

10. Frederick Law Olmsted, *Journeys and Explorations in the Cotton Kingdom*, 2 vols. (London, 1861), 1: 276; Charles Nordhoff, "America for Free Workingmen," *Loyal Publication Society No. 80* (New York, 1865), pp. 7–8.

11. New York *Staats-Zeitung* (weekly ed.), June 7, 1862; Hermann Schlüter, *Die Internationale in Amerika* (Chicago, 1918?), p. 8; Louis P. Hennighausen, "Reminiscences of the Political Life of the German-Americans in Baltimore during 1850–60," *Seventh Annual Report of the Society for the History of the Germans in Maryland* (Baltimore, 1892–93), p. 55.

siderations, also, kept them in the southern camp. While not owning slaves themselves, many depended in one way or another on the proceeds from slave labor. Above all, however, they too believed that the tariff policy of the North placed the South at the mercy of the Yankee merchant. The tariff wall with which the latter had surrounded the country enabled him in their eyes to share in the profits of every pound of cotton, tobacco, and sugar that the southern planter produced.[12] Thus to give in to northern demands meant economic ruin to them. Any moral objections against slavery must necessarily yield to this consideration.

Finally, also, to uphold their own social prestige, the Germans wanted slavery preserved. "No native even can exceed, in idolatry to Slavery, the mass of the ignorant foreign-born laborers," wrote Olmsted.[13] "Their hatred of the Negro is proportionate to the equality of their intellect and character to his: and their regard for Slavery to their disinclination to compete with him in a fair field." Social outcasts themselves, the Germans still felt infinitely superior to the slaves. Yet once the Negro was no longer branded with the stigma of slavery, there was nothing, they were afraid, that would distinguish them socially from the black man.

Only in Baltimore did the North have more than just a handful of sympathizers among the Germans. Baltimore, like St. Louis, was one of those borderline cities where northern and southern interests crossed. It had long been a center of German immigration. There the slave offered serious competition to German artisans and mechanics. Moreover, one of the mainstays of German social life, the gymnastic Turner associations, had one of their strongest organizations in that city. Under the influence of liberal leaders still imbued with the democratic spirit of the revolutionary uprising of 1848, the Turners saw in abolition not only a way to eliminating an economic competitor, but also a means of realizing those ideals of freedom and equality for

12. Schuricht, *German Element,* 2: 60.
13. Olmsted, *Journey in Slave States,* p. 512; Hermann Schlüter, *Lincoln, Labor and Slavery* (New York, 1913), pp. 89–90.

which they had been fighting in the Fatherland. They were encouraged in all their abolitionist activities by the three local German papers, all staunch advocates of the antislavery cause.[14] Most likely, therefore, the majority of the 1,083 votes that Lincoln polled in Baltimore in 1860, almost half of his Maryland total,[15] were German votes.

In Texas, again, the Germans proved entirely indifferent toward the slave problem. Most of them had settled in the southwestern part of the state, which lent itself well to small-scale farming. Slave labor constituted no competition there, since soil conditions made cotton growing unprofitable. The proximity of the Mexican border over which slaves could easily escape served as a further deterrent to their use in that section. Besides, even at that time Mexican labor was cheaper.[16]

Few of the Texas Germans owned slaves. Most of them were too poor to employ any help at all. If they could, they generally hired newcomers from Germany who worked until they were able to buy a small farm themselves.[17] It was not moral or religious reasons that kept them from acquiring slaves, but rather, aside from financial difficulties, an aversion to working in close contact with Negroes. They preferred tilling their fields in the same intensive way in which they had cultivated them in the Fatherland, and would rather do everything themselves than have it done by slaves who were less thorough and reliable.[18] To be sure, the *Neu Braunfelser Zeitung* professed that the question of acquiring slaves was merely a matter of money: "At the cheap price of from $100 to $200 for a Negro many a German farmer

14. Henninghausen, "Reminiscences," p. 55. None of these papers achieved more than local success. However, by their blunt and often tactless aggressiveness they unfailingly antagonized former southern sympathizers. Their defiant editorials were mainly responsible for repeated nativist acts of violence against Baltimore Germans.

15. *Tribune Almanac for 1861* (New York), p. 49.

16. Charles W. Ramsdell, "The Natural Limits of Slavery Expansion," *Southwestern Historical Quarterly* 33 (1929): 98–99.

17. Frederick Law Olmsted, *A Journey through Texas* (New York, 1860), pp. 133, 140, 432.

18. Ibid., p. 235.

would procure one or more of those every ready laborers."[19] Yet it is doubtful whether this view really reflected the general German attitude or was only a well-meant attempt to appease a growing opposition to the German element, which, because of its personal dislike of slave labor, was constantly suspected of abolitionist sympathies.

Thus in Texas the slave issue again affected the German element only indirectly. There, slave labor was not even a competitor of free labor. Rather, the latter became a serious threat to the slave owner. By superior skill the free laborer crowded Negroes out of many places and employments. Germans soon monopolized almost all local industries and workshops in Galveston, Houston, and San Antonio.[20] Where Germans planted cotton, it was generally cleaner and of better quality than plantation-grown cotton and consequently brought better prices.[21] Nor was manual labor considered degrading and below a white man. In fact, German laborers were much in demand as cotton pickers because of their greater efficiency. "I was told," Olmsted reported, "that some mechanics made more in a day, by going into the field of a slave-owner and picking side by side with his slaves, being paid by measure, than they could earn at their regular work in a week."[22]

Texas Germans, consequently, saw no threat to free labor in an extension of the slavery system to the territories. And although they advocated the free distribution of public lands, they had no objection to the introduction of slavery into these lands. On the contrary, well aware of the antagonism of native Americans toward them because they threatened to undermine the profitability of slave labor, they were overwhelmingly opposed to all abolitionist activities. "The Germans in the South," the *Neu*

19. Reprinted in *Southern Intelligencer* (Austin), April 6, 1859, and quoted in Gilbert G. Benjamin, *The Germans in Texas* (Philadelphia, 1909), p. 107.
20. Olmsted, *Journey through Texas*, p. 160; Moritz P. G. Tiling, *History of the German Element in Texas from 1820–1850* (Houston, 1913), pp. 128–29.
21. Olmsted, *Journey through Texas*, p. 141; Hinton R. Helper, *The Impending Crisis* (New York, 1860), p. 301.
22. Olmsted, *Journeys and Explorations*, 2: 263.

Braunfelser Zeitung assured native Americans, "have an identity of interests with the slaveowners."[23]

For the same reason, the majority of the Germans bitterly denounced the platform of the first German state convention in Texas in 1854, whch bluntly declared that "slavery is an evil the removal of which is absolutely necessary according to the principles of democracy." For months the *Neu Braunfelser Zeitung* editorialized against these efforts "which would endanger the free institutions of the United States and bring ruin to the richest section in the country." The paper likewise opposed the Kansas-Nebraska Bill on the ground that Congress had no right to exclude slave property from the territories, and applauded the Supreme Court decision in the Dred Scott case, which had been nothing but "another instance of wanton provocation of the South by the North."[24]

That Lincoln would find but few supporters among the Texas Germans in the election of 1860 was therefore to be expected. In New Braunfels, the most important of the German settlements, he did not get a single vote.[25] Moreover, after his election the Germans in Texas joined in the general demand for secession. A German convention in that state recommended that in the event of violation of southern rights and institutions, Texas should "peacefully or by force . . . demand a return of all the powers and rights delegated to the United States"; in addition, the state should organize "the whole population in defense of those rights."[26] In the special session of the legislature the German delegates likewise voted for secession. Apparently they considered this attitude most likely to preserve the Federal Union, hoping, presumably, that an uncompromising attitude on the part of the South would induce the North to compromise. When it actually came to voting the state out of the Union, however,

23. Rudolph L. Biesele, *The History of the German Settlements in Texas, 1831–1861* (Austin, 1930), p. 200; Boston *Pionier,* December 13, 1860.

24. Biesele, *German Settlements,* pp. 199 ff.

25. *Neu Braunfelser Zeitung,* November 16, 1860, quoted in Biesele, *German Settlements,* p. 204.

26. *Neu Braunfelser Zeitung,* December 14, 1860, quoted in ibid., p. 205.

the Germans reversed their former stand and voted against secession.[27] They realized from their knowledge of the Fatherland what the disruption of the Union into petty states would mean. Moreover, they abhorred the war that secession might bring. After years of hard toil they did not care to see their fields trampled by marching armies and their homes go up in flames. They had crossed the Atlantic to find peace, not to take up arms again.

Of all the southern states, Missouri (at that time considered part of the South) attracted the most German immigrants. Its fertile soil permitted small-scale farming, and St. Louis, a rapidly expanding center of commercial and industrial enterprise, proved attractive to laborers, mechanics, and tradespeople. Besides, it was easily accessible by boat and wagon and, beginning with the fifties, by rail. Although the state had first been settled almost exclusively by southern immigrants, it had never become a typical plantation state. The cultivation of cotton proved unprofitable there, and of staple crops common to the South, only hemp and tobacco could be grown successfully. Both lent themselves to small-scale production. Thus Missouri was settled by log cabin folk and small farmers rather than by wealthy planters and slaveowners. It became a region of small farms, small slaveholdings, and, in comparison with other southern states, of few slaves. In 1860 each slaveholder owned, on the average, less than four slaves.

Under these conditions, German farmers as well as German laborers found Missouri particularly attractive for settlement. There the slavery issue presented no problem to them. In the cities they soon supplanted the slaves as domestics and laborers. Prince Maximilian of Wied, who visited St. Louis in 1832, had noted that "the greater part of the workmen in the port, and all the servants in St. Louis, are Negroes."[28] Yet thirty years later, in 1862, Anthony Trollope found that "slaves are not generally

27. Ibid., p. 206.
28. Maximilian, Prince of Wied, *Travels in the Interior of North America,* in Reuben G. Thwaites, ed., *Early Western Travels: 1748–1846,* 33 vols. (Cleveland, 1904–1907), 22: 216.

employed in St. Louis for domestic service. . . . This work is chiefly in the hands of Irish and Germans."[29]

In the German-settled rural areas of Missouri few Negroes, free or slave, could be found. As in Texas the German system of intensive cultivation left no room for the use of slave labor, and to use Negroes as domestics was repulsive to most of the German settlers. Thus only a few among them, in the country as well as in St. Louis, owned Negroes.[30]

Even though Negro slaves could offer no serious competition to the German immigrant in that section, the latter, nevertheless, soon showed signs of abolitionist inclinations. "The tremendous majority of the citizens of our State are tired of the improper influence of the Slavocratic interest," warned the *Anzeiger des Westens* as early as 1854.[31] "They are not willing any longer to be tyrannized by a few thousand slaveholders." However, no immediate unqualified emancipation was advocated. "We are for the abolition of slavery in Missouri," the paper added, "but only constitutionally and in a manner to pay due respect to the just claims of the citizens of the State."

That Missouri Germans took this stand was only natural. Though geographically belonging to the South, Missouri was economically and socially a western state. Surrounded on three sides by free states, it has been aptly compared to a "peninsula of slavery extending out into a sea of freedom."[32] St. Louis, where Germans were particularly numerous (more than half its population was foreign-born in 1860), depended on the markets of the East for its continued commercial progress. And the proximity of valuable raw materials, of lead, iron, coal, copper, manganese, and nickel deposits, and its situation at the confluence

29. Anthony Trollope, *North America,* 2 vols. (London, 1862), 2: 125; see also Edward Dicey, *Six Months in the Federal States,* 2 vols. (London, 1863), 2: 105.

30. William G. Bek, "The Followers of Duden," *Missouri Historical Review* 14 (1919–20): 66, 441.

31. *Anzeiger des Westens* (St. Louis), July 21, 1854, quoted in *Missouri Republican* (St. Louis), July 24, 1854.

32. Sceva B. Laughlin, *Missouri Politics During the Civil War* (Salem, Ore., 1930), p. 1.

of the Missouri and Mississippi promised a bright future for the young city.[33]

Secession of the South threatened to destroy these hopes. As for the Germans, moreover, they feared that it would deal not only a severe blow to merchants and manufacturers, but would hit laborers just as much. For both extension of slavery into the territories and secession would immensely undermine the power of free labor. After having superseded slaves in many jobs and fields, the German laborer was not willing to lose again the monopoly he held in certain lines of work. Less from sympathy for the Negro, therefore, than from the desire to preserve the Union, the Germans sided with the abolitionists. Under the leadership of some of the political refugees who had settled in Missouri after the abortive German revolution of 1848, they joined the young Republican party.

Rural Germans, on the other hand, economically much more self-sufficient than those in St. Louis, were inclined to take a less radical stand. They were willing to tolerate slavery in the states, but opposed its extension into the territories because such an extension might endanger the fulfillment of their fondest wish, the distribution of public lands.

For this reason, in the presidential election of 1860 Lincoln received most of his Missouri votes in St. Louis. Of the 17,028 votes he polled throughout the state, St. Louis gave him 9,945. However, not even in St. Louis did he get a total majority. He carried that city because both Douglas and Bell obtained less votes than he. Yet the combined vote received by Douglas and Bell surpassed Lincoln's by almost 50 per cent. As a matter of fact, Douglas received only 681 votes less than Lincoln.[34] The other county which Lincoln carried in Missouri was Gasconade, whose population was predominantly German. In other German-settled counties, however, the German vote went to Bell and Douglas, so that Lincoln received less votes in Missouri than

33. *Missouri Republican,* January 10, 1854, Supplement, "Annual Review," p. 12.

34. The exact figures were: Lincoln 9,945; Douglas 9,264; Bell 4,931; Breckinridge 610 *(Tribune Almanac for 1861,* pp. 54–55).

any other candidate. Douglas polled 58,801 votes, Bell 58,372, and Breckinridge 31,317, while Lincoln trailed far behind with only 17,028 votes.[35]

Yet this did not mean that Missouri wished to secede. The strong support the Douglas and Bell tickets received proves rather that the state desired to compromise. Strongly pro-Union, it opposed both the radical abolitionists of the North and the stubborn secessionists of the South. And when a special convention was to determine the future relations between Missouri and the Union early in 1861, it adjourned after several weeks of deliberation without coming to any decision, again indicating, if only indirectly, that Missouri favored the preservation of the status quo. "I have been from the beginning in favor of decided and prompt action on the part of the Southern states," Governor C. F. Jackson admitted as late as April, 1861, "but the majority of the people up to the present time have differed with me."[36] If nothing else, the state's exposure to Federal troops from three sides virtually forced it to remain in the Union.

With an overwhelming majority of the people of Missouri unwilling to secede, the frequently heard assertion that the state would never have stayed in the Union but for its German element is not supported by the facts.[37] Those who share this erroneous view generally point to the capture of Camp Jackson, an encampment of the pro-secession state militia near St. Louis, by Union forces—four fifths of them of German stock[38]—as the decisive victory of the North in the state. Actually, however, this incident drove many Union sympathizers into the secessionist camp; for the blood shed on that occasion, though probably

35. Ibid., p. 55.

36. Letter of April 19, 1861, Missouri State Convention, *Journal*, July, 1861, p. 28.

37. "Their preparedness and eagerness to enter the conflict saved Missouri for the Union" (Faust, *German Element*, 2: 136). See also Frederick F. Schrader, *The Germans in the Making of America* (Boston, 1924), p. 203; Robert S. Douglass, *History of Southeast Missouri*, 2 vols. (Chicago and New York, 1912), 1: 249.

38. Report of Adjutant General John B. Gray, December 31, 1863, Missouri Senate, *Journal, Adjourned Session*, 22nd General Assembly, 1863–64, Appendix, p. 133.

through no fault of the Union men, was not easily forgotten.[39] This particular action of German troops was certainly not responsible for Missouri's remaining in the Union. In fact, it would have been one of history's major miracles if a few thousand untrained recruits could have forced a state of more than a million people to act against its own sovereign will.[40]

In the North the attitude of the Germans corresponded more or less with that of their native neighbors. German commercial and financial circles were, on the whole, bitterly opposed to the growing Republican party and its exponent, Lincoln. To them a Republican victory implied secession, and secession meant loss of the vast southern market. "Whatever the Republican leaders may say to the contrary," warned August Belmont, the New York representative of the Rothschilds, "I fear that the election of Mr. Lincoln to the Presidential chair must prove the forerunner of a dissolution of this confederacy amid all the horrors of civil strife and bloodshed."[41] Belmont was elected chairman of the National Committee of the Douglas Democrats in Baltimore in 1860. He contributed heavily to Douglas' campaign fund, particularly in Pennsylvania, where his fellow countryman, Carl Schurz, sought to rally the German farmers to the Republican flag. The New York *Staatszeitung*, edited by Oswald Ottendörfer, another leading Douglas Democrat, gave him its fullhearted support.[42]

Yet, in keeping with their desire to see the Union preserved, the German Democrats of the North rallied to the northern cause as soon as the South threatened to secede. "Nobody can regret more than I do the election of Lincoln," wrote Belmont to a southern editor in November, 1860, "and I certainly need

39. J. Thomas Scharf, *History of St. Louis City and County*, 2 vols. (Philadelphia, 1883), 2: 1485.

40. Raymond D. Thomas, "A Study in Missouri Politics, 1840–1870," *Missouri Historical Review* 21 (1927): 453.

41. August Belmont, *Letters, Speeches and Addresses* (New York, 1890), p. 130. Belmont had come to the United States from Frankfort-on-the-Main in 1837.

42. Gustav P. Körner, *Das deutsche Element in den Vereinigten Staaten von Nord-amerika, 1818–1848* (New York, 1884), pp. 112 ff.; Adolf Douai, *Land und Leute in der Union* (Berlin, 1864), p. 224.

not tell you how earnestly I strove to prevent that calamity; but . . . I hope and trust that the disunionists *per se* stand alone in their conspiracy against the Union."[43] And a few weeks later:

> I know that the disunionists at the South taunt those who counsel the more wise, efficient and patriotic course of seeking redress *within* the Union, by calling them *"submissionists"*; but I, for one, would most certainly rather submit to the constitutional election of an opponent than to the terrorism evoked by a faction whose treasonable designs my best efforts had been exerted to defeat.[44]

When hostilities actually broke out, Belmont took a leading part in attempts to obtain German money for the Union cause.

The attitude of the German farmers in this crisis was less clear. While probably antislavery in their attitude, they were too little concerned with the outcome of the conflict one way or the other to side with any party. All they wanted was peace and security. "Our own children are closer to our heart than the children of the Negroes," a German pamphleteer had written during the presidential campaign of 1856.[45] These words still held good in 1860. The Republican party was, moreover, suspected of nativist sympathies, since many former Know-Nothings had joined up with the new movement. Above all, the Massachusetts "Two-Years" Amendment, although directed mainly against the Irish-Catholic element in that state,[46] had aroused widespread indignation among the Germans against the Republicans in 1859.[47] It took months of untiring effort on the part of the Republicans to allay German fears, and Lincoln had to come out openly against the law. In a letter to Dr. Theodore Canisius, editor of the Illinois *Staats-Zeitung*, he denounced the

43. Belmont, *Speeches and Addresses*, p. 23.
44. Ibid., p. 37.
45. *Was erheischt das deutsche Interesse bei der nächsten Präsidentenwahl und wie sollen die Deutschen stimmen?* (N.p., 1856), p. 7.
46. According to the *Eighth Census of the United States*, 1860, *Population* (Washington, 1864), p. 227, there were 9,961 Germans in Massachusetts as against 185,434 Irishmen. The Irish amounted to 15.07 per cent of Massachusetts' population, the Germans to only 0.81 per cent (ibid., p. xxxi).
47. Boston *Pionier*, February 19, 1859. The amendment provided that naturalized citizens were not to vote until two years after they had become citizens.

measure as "strangely inconsistent" with the ideals and program of the Republican party.[48]

In Carl Schurz the Republican party found a valuable ally who was particularly active in New England and Pennsylvania. But it was not the slavery issue with which Schurz sought to rally the Germans of the Northeast to the Lincolnian cause. Equal rights to all citizens, whether native or foreign-born, free homesteads in the West, adequate compensation to all laborers-- these were the questions closest to the hearts of the Germans in that section. Schurz pledged the Republicans to the solution of these problems when he spoke to the German farmers, mechanics, and laborers in New York, Pennsylvania, and Massachusetts; for they cared little about the emancipation of faraway Negro slaves. In fact, anxious to avoid any controversy that might lead to internal strife and secession, many opposed the abolitionist program. Lincoln polled a majority of 50,000 over the Fusion ticket of Douglas, Bell, and Breckinridge in New York, but the proposed constitutional amendment to introduce Negro suffrage in that state was defeated by 140,481 votes.[49]

While German businessmen and farmers in the Northeast thus remained indifferent to the question of slavery as such, German workers in that section had long watched the abolitionist movement with open hostility. For the abolitionists, while storming against Negro slavery, failed to show any interest in the misery of the working class. "White slavery" met with little concern on their part. In fact, Garrison never tired of repudiating attempts to organize workers in order to fight their ruthless exploitation. "It is a miserable characteristic of human nature," he said, "to look with an envious eye upon those who are more fortunate in their pursuits, or more exalted in their station."[50] Under these circumstances workers naturally were opposed to the antislavery movement. By focusing public attention on the lot of the slaves it detracted from their own hardships, which

48. The letter is reprinted in *Deutsch-Amerikanische Geschichtsblätter* (Chicago) 15 (1915): 219.

49. *Tribune Almanac for 1861*, p. 41.

50. *Liberator* (Boston), January 29, 1831.

were much closer to their hearts. Between the fight against wage slavery and that against Negro slavery, German laborers, of course, chose the former.

Only gradually did a change become noticeable. The Kansas-Nebraska Act which threatened to open the western territories to slavery may have been partly responsible for this development, since some workers probably feared—erroneously—that the slave might become a serious competitor of the white laborer in the West. Thus in 1859 a convention of the *Arbeiterbund* finally came out openly against "all slavery, in whatever form it may appear," and pledged itself to combat it "with all the means at our disposal."[51]

Still, a good many workers remained lukewarm toward the question of abolition, and the Democrats took care to arouse their anxiety concerning the consequences of an antislavery victory. They pictured the Negro as a serious economic rival who would come north as soon as he was freed and compete with white mechanics and laborers. Fears of a complete disruption of the economic system as a result of the Negro emancipation, with the closing of factories and widespread unemployment as its inevitable consequences, also kept many workers from joining the Republicans. Besides, workers' organizations had to be careful lest they antagonize their southern branches by the adoption of too vigorous an antislavery policy.[52] The demand for free homesteads, on the other hand, incorporated in the Republican platform, could hold but little attraction for the industrial worker, for few laborers and mechanics ever became farmers.[53]

Only in the western part of New York did the German element support the Republican ticket. Erie, Monroe, Onondaga, and Rensselaer, all strongly German-settled, gave Lincoln com-

51. Schlüter, *Lincoln, Labor and Slavery,* p. 82.
52. Hermann Schlüter, *Die Anfänge der deutschen Arbeiterbewegung in Amerika* (Stuttgart, 1907), p. 213.
53. Murray Kane, "Some Considerations on the Safety Valve Doctrine," *Mississippi Valley Historical Review* 23 (1936): 169 ff.; Carter Goodrich and Sol Davison, "The Wage-Earner in the Westward Movement," *Political Science Quarterly* 50 (1935): 161 ff.

fortable majorities.[54] Doubtless the Republican pledge to enact a homestead law won the solid support of these districts.

From the outset it was evident that neither North nor South would be able to secure victory without the support of the Northwest. The vote of that section, therefore, would decide the outcome of the conflict.

The Northwest was more or less unconcerned about the slavery issue. If the South meant to keep its "peculiar institution," it would not object. Western individualism rather objected to the efforts of northern abolitionists to intervene in southern affairs.[55] The argument that an opening of the territories to slavery would deprive white workers and farmers of their livelihood likewise failed to make an impression in the Northwest; for by 1860 it had become evident that climate and soil conditions closed the West more effectively to slavery than any law could have done.

Economically the Mississippi Valley, and with it the Northwest, had long been bound equally to North and South. After 1850 the construction of railroads began to bring the East into closer contact with this part of the country, but at the same time the South still absorbed a considerable part of western produce. In fact, southern consumption of western goods increased continuously up to 1860.[56] Thus both North and South were important markets for the Northwest, which could ill afford to lose either one.

For this reason only one issue mattered to this section—preservation of the Union. Once the Union broke up, the Northwest was doomed to the sterile fate of a backward agricultural province ringed by tariff barriers. In consequence, for the Westerner, the problem of for whom to vote resolved itself into the question of with whom the Union was better safeguarded.

For businessmen the answer was camparatively simple. By nature conservative, they shied away from any reform movement

54. *Tribune Almanac for 1861,* pp. 44–45.
55. Louis F. Frank, *Pionierjahre der deutsch-amerikanischen Familien Frank-Kerler in Wisconsin und Michigan, 1849–64* (Milwaukee, 1911), p. 409.
56. Cincinnati *Daily Gazette,* June 27, 1861; Charles Cist, *Sketches and Statistics of Cincinnati in 1859* (Cincinnati, 1859), p. 345.

that might endanger the status quo. Maintenance of the Union in their eyes depended therefore upon the election of a Democratic President.

With business circles opposed to them, the Republicans had thus to concentrate their main efforts on farmers and laborers in the western states. The latter's votes, however, were not at all assured to the Republican party. Wisconsin, Michigan, Indiana, and Iowa had been settled during the two preceding decades by a great number of foreigners who were by no means *a priori* Republicans. Among them the German-born voters, who greatly outnumbered all other foreign elements, presented a special problem to the Republicans.

Once solidly Democratic, the Germans were now torn between their desire to see their personal liberties and political rights safeguarded and their hope to carve free homesteads out of the public lands of the western territories.[57] While the Democrats seemed more likely to protect the former, only the Republicans appeared willing to grant the latter. Thus neither party offered an entirely satisfactory alternative.

German Republican leaders saw their chance in this impasse. Knowing that the party needed their support, they demanded a price for it. Open letters were sent to Republican candidates to ascertain their stand on the questions of naturalization and homesteads. To give their demands adequate expression, moreover, a meeting of representative Germans convened at Chicago a few days before the Republican national convention opened, and adopted several resolutions.[58] Of these, two deserve particular attention, for they found their way into the Republican party platform. As so-called "Dutch planks" they were intended to reassure the German voter on two issues that were particularly close to his heart. One demanded equal rights for all citizens, whether native or foreign-born, and the other asked for the

---

57. Carl Schurz, *Reminiscences,* 3 vols. (New York, 1907–1908), 2: 66; Gustave P. Koerner, *Memoirs,* 2 vols. (Cedar Rapids, 1909), 2: 21.

58. The complete resolutions are reprinted in Frank I. Herriott, "The Conference in the Deutsches Haus, Chicago, May 14–15, 1860," *Transactions of the Illinois State Historical Society* 35 (1928): 189; Cincinnati *Daily Gazette,* May 16 and 17, 1860.

"immediate passage by Congress of a Homestead law by which the public lands of the Union may be secured for homesteads of the people and secured from the greed of speculators."

At the party convention Carl Schurz chose an opportune moment to bring fully home to his fellow delegates the weight of the German vote, and the vital importance consequently of including the two planks in the Republican platform. "The German Republicans of the Northern states have given you 300,000 votes," he implored them, "and I wish that they should find it consistent with their honor and their safety to give you 300,000 more." And his fellow delegate, Friedrich Hassaurek, made the vote of 20,000 German Republicans in Ohio likewise dependent on the adoption of these two planks.[59] Both were thereupon accepted unanimously by the convention—not, however, without the active assistance of Gustave Koerner, a German delegate from Illinois, who kept one of the Massachusetts representatives from voting against it by getting hold of his coat tails and holding him down in his chair until the resolution had been passed.[60]

Having thus placed themselves on record for equal political rights to foreign-born citizens and the free distribution of public lands, the Republicans entered the election campaign confident of their ability to win the German vote. Untiringly they pointed to their stand on both issues, while the Democratic platform mentioned neither one. It was the most effective argument the Republicans could have offered.

The slavery issue, on the other hand, received hardly any attention in this particular section of the country. Campaign speakers alluded to it, hoping to strike a reminiscent chord in the hearts of those who once had fought for their own liberty in the Fatherland. But slavery could hardly be pictured as a threat to the farmer or laborer of the Northwest. If the Republicans had pledged themselves to nothing but its abolition, they could hardly have counted on many German votes. Only in so far as the interests of the "slaveocracy" could be identified with at-

59. Horace Greeley, ed., *Proceedings of the First Three Republican National Conventions of 1856, 1860 and 1864* (Minneapolis, 1893), pp. 138 ff.

60. Koerner, *Memoirs,* 2: 90.

tempts to prevent the distribution of the public domain could the Germans be induced to oppose a Democratic victory. "The vast majority cared little more for the fine moralities of the abolitionists than for the profound conceits of the slave-holders."[61]

Well aware of this fact, Douglas was eager to assure the settlers of the Northwest of his interest in the speedy passage of a homestead act. In a speech at Dubuque, Iowa, he said:

> I originated the idea of a Homestead Bill when a member of the House of Representatives sixteen or seventeen years ago. I have urged in the Senate over and over again the indispensable necessity of confining the public lands to the actual settler, and allowing no speculator to get possession except for cultivation. My policy has always been to make every inhabitant of the new States and Territories a landholder, as far as it was possible to do so, by our legislation.[62]

Doubtless these assurances coupled with the doctrine of popular sovereignty that seemed to bar slavery from the northwestern territories were not without effect. Cincinnati, Indianapolis, and Chicago accorded him enthusiastic receptions when he visited them in the fall of 1860.[63] In fact, to many Douglas' election alone seemed to guarantee the preservation of the Union.

Yet the record of the Democrats on the homestead issue was against him. The fact that his first wife had owned 100 slaves made him likewise suspect. Many believed him, but more turned to Lincoln, and the latter won. However, it was a close victory. Lincoln's majority in the northwestern states amounted to no more than 6,600 votes over all other candidates. The change of only one vote in twenty would have given the Northwest to Douglas.[64]

61. Frederic Bancroft, *The Life of William H. Seward,* 2 vols. (New York, 1900), 1: 529–30.

62. Dubuque *Herald,* October 17, 1860, quoted in George M. Stephenson, *The Political History of the Public Lands from 1840 to 1862* (Boston, 1917), pp. 236–37.

63. George F. Milton, *The Eve of Conflict* (Boston, 1934), pp. 495–96.

64. William E. Dodd, "The Fight for the Northwest, 1860," *American Historical Review* 16 (July 1911): 788.

It is generally recognized today that Lincoln could never have carried the Northwest in 1860, and with it the country, without German support.[65] Yet if the Republicans had hoped to win the support of the entire German element in the Northwest they were disappointed. Carl Schurz had claimed to speak for 300,000 German voters in that section when he insisted on definite commitments on the naturalization and homestead issues, and Hassaurek had asserted that he represented more than 20,000 Germans in Ohio, who would cast their vote "in a solid phalanx." But while both men exercised some influence over their fellow countrymen, they were far from controlling their vote.

The influence of the so-called Forty-eighters on their German contemporaries in this country has often been overestimated. Probably no voter was harder to move than the German farmer. As one of them boasted:

> We Germans, west, east, and everywhere in the United States, need no orators to induce us to vote. . . . We don't care to hear a man who does not follow anything else than stump speaking like any other trade. We know such men; their talk is nonsense. What they say don't come from their hearts, but they learn it like any schoolboy the A. B. C., and when you hear them talk it always goes from the same string.[66]

As intellectuals Schurz and his associates were looked at still more suspiciously by the average German. "His head was too much in the clouds for him to fraternize with the local politicians even of his own nationality," one of Schurz' neighbors in Watertown, Wisconsin, recalled years later.[67] Nor did Schurz seek easy popularity. Rather, he expected the Germans to follow him unquestioningly on the way he thought they should go. In complete misjudgment of their attitude he saw them "run after me

65. Ibid., pp. 786 ff.; Donnal V. Smith, "The Influence of the Foreign-Born of the Northwest in the Election of 1860," see above, pp. 1–15; George M. Stephenson, *A History of American Immigration, 1820–1924* (Boston, 1926), pp. 131 ff.

66. Cincinnati *Daily Gazette*, February 2, 1860.

67. William F. Whyte, "Chronicles of Early Watertown," *Wisconsin Magazine of History* 4 (1921): 297.

like children."[68] Actually, they refused to follow him blindly, and often sided with his opponents.[69]

Not even with those who knew him more intimately was Schurz more popular. In Watertown, where he had taken up his residence, he was generally known as a "d——d Republican," "whose few friends could easily be seated in one bus."[70] And while Jefferson County, in which Watertown was located, gave Lincoln a majority of 283 votes or 10.2 per cent in 1860, Douglas defeated him in Watertown itself by 181 votes and carried it by a majority of 40 per cent.[71] In Schurz' own ward the vote was 100 to 33 in favor of Douglas.

Other election returns likewise indicated the difficulty of the task Schurz and his friends had undertaken in trying to shepherd the Germans of the Northwest into the Republican fold. Although the Democrats had hardly any German speaker who could successfully compete with Schurz, Koerner, Hassaurek, and other German Republican leaders, the latter apparently succeeded only in winning just enough German votes to assure Lincoln's election. A great number of their countrymen remained faithful to the Democratic party in spite of all Republican efforts to draw them away.[72] Of the ten counties in Indiana in which the Germans had mainly settled,[73] only three were carried by Lincoln. True, the Republicans scored considerable gains over the returns of 1856 in all ten counties, but those increases were not out of proportion to Republican gains in other counties

68. Joseph Schafer, ed., "Intimate Letters of Carl Schurz," Wisconsin State Historical Society *Collections* 30 (1928): 224.

69. Carl R. Fish, "Carl Schurz—The American," *Wisconsin Magazine of History* 12 (1929): 349. See also Chester V. Easum, *The Americanization of Carl Schurz* (Chicago, 1929), pp. 114 ff., 137 ff.

70. New York *Staats-Zeitung* (weekly ed.), May 23, 1863.

71. Easum, *Americanization of Schurz*, p. 305; *Tribune Almanac for 1861*, p. 58.

72. H. A. Rattermann, in an editorial in *Deutsch-Amerikanisches Magazin* (Cincinnati) 1 (1887): 28.

73. Knox, Clark, Jefferson, Spencer, Floyd, Posey, Dubois, Dearborn, Marion, and Warrick counties. See William A. Fritsch, *German Settlers and Settlements in Indiana* (Evansville, 1915), pp. 22–23. For the election returns see *Tribune Almanac for 1861*, pp. 62–63.

in which only a few or no Germans were living. Of the Wisconsin counties with the strongest German concentrations,[74] Lincoln carried five and Douglas four. Douglas, moreover, carried Milwaukee by a majority of 40 per cent. Again, Republican gains in these counties were by no means greater than in others in which only a few Germans had settled. As a matter of fact, Gustave Koerner, himself one of the leading German Republicans, estimated that the majority of the Wisconsin Germans remained Democrats in 1860.[75] As for the German-settled counties in Iowa,[76] Lincoln carried four and Douglas one (by a majority of almost 50 per cent), while in another both polled an equal number of votes. In Allamakee County, which Lincoln carried by 30 votes, the Republicans gained 555 votes over the returns of 1856, while the Democratic gains totaled 651.

In Ohio the situation was similar. In Cincinnati, with a German population of 43,931 out of 161,044, Lincoln polled 1,091 votes more than Douglas.[77] In Michigan the majority of the Germans remained in the Democratic camp. There the Germans and the Irish were ardent followers of the doctrine of popular sovereignty, and they gave their votes to Douglas. The latter carried two of the three Detroit wards in which most of the Germans and Irish resided, and in the third he lost by only 18 votes. Rural German settlements in Michigan likewise gave the majority of their votes to Douglas.[78]

74. Washington, Milwaukee, Dodge, Jefferson, Ozaukee, Sauk, Sheboygan, Fond du Lac, and Manitowoc counties (Wilhelm Hense-Jensen, *Wisconsin's Deutsch-Amerikaner,* 2 vols. [Milwaukee, 1900], 1: 34 ff.; J. H. A. Lacher, *The German Element in Wisconsin* [Milwaukee, 1925], pp. 10 ff.).

75. Körner, *Das deutsche Element,* pp. 287–88.

76. Allamakee, Jasper, Buena Vista, Dubuque, Muscatine, and Scott counties (Joseph Eiboeck, *Die Deutschen von Iowa and deren Errungenschaften* [Des Moines, 1900], p. 310).

77. *Eighth Census,* 1860, *Population,* p. 612; Cincinnati *Daily Gazette,* November 8, 1860. However, Republican gains were largest in the German wards (ibid., November 7, 1860).

78. Floyd B. Streeter, *Political Parties in Michigan: 1837–1860* (Lansing, 1918), pp. 163 ff.; Frank, *Pionierjahre,* pp. 407 ff., 517–18.

The following table affords a basis for determining the significance of the vote in the northwestern states.[79] All figures are in percentages.

STATE	GERMAN POPULATION	IRISH POPULATION	LINCOLN'S MAJORITY OVER DOUGLAS
Illinois	7.65	5.12	7
Indiana	4.94	1.81	20
Iowa	5.71	4.16	26
Michigan	5.18	4.01	36
Minnesota	10.59	7.37	85
Ohio	7.19	3.28	24
Wisconsin	15.97	6.44	32

In Wisconsin where there were approximately two and a half times as many Germans as Irish, Lincoln's majority over Douglas was only 32 per cent, while in Minnesota where the Germans and the Irish stood in the ratio of one and a half to one, his majority was 85 per cent. In Iowa the Germans outnumbered the Irish by 30 per cent, and Lincoln's majority over Douglas in that state was 26 per cent. Yet, in Michigan where there were only about 25 per cent more Germans than Irish, Lincoln's majority was 36 per cent.

A similar inconsistency appears in the figures for St. Louis and Cincinnati. In St. Louis the Germans comprised 22 per cent of the population, and the Irish 14 per cent, and Lincoln's majority over Douglas was almost 100 per cent. In Cincinnati, on the other hand, where the Germans again constituted 22 per cent of the population and the Irish element amounted to 12½ per cent of the total, Lincoln polled but a small majority.

These figures indicate that Lincoln's victory in the Northwest cannot be attributed to the support of a solid German vote. Nor can it be said that the German vote went to Lincoln but was offset by the Irish vote which went to the Democrats. The above figures show that a solid Irish-Democratic vote could hardly

79. For the population figures see *Eighth Census,* 1860, *Population,* p. xxxi. The election percentages are based on the figures in the *Tribune Almanac for 1861.*

have annulled the effect of the German vote if the latter had gone solidly to Lincoln.

Thus, while it is correct to say that Lincoln's victory in the Northwest would have been impossible without German support, it is wrong to conclude that his German vote was out of proportion to the size of the German element in the northwestern states. In reality the Germans did no more to assure Lincoln's victory than did their American-born neighbors. Nor did they do so in any other section or in the nation as a whole.

Reprinted from the *Mississippi Valley Historical Review* 29 (June 1942): 55–76.

A professor of geography at Macalaster College in Saint Paul, Minnesota, Hildegard Binder Johnson earned her Ph.D. at the University of Berlin in 1934. She has written a variety of articles on the history and demography of German-immigrant settlements in the United States. More sophisticated in her quantification than her predecessors, Mrs. Johnson examines Minnesota evidence to conclude that even though the majority of Germans supported Lincoln's election in 1860, they were divided politically along religious lines.

The Election of 1860 and the Germans in Minnesota

HILDEGARD BINDER JOHNSON

"Did the Germans vote for Lincoln?" This question, which had been answered in the affirmative by historians and which for some time seemed to be settled, has recently been revived.

Of all the Middle Western states, Minnesota had the most liberal law for the enfranchisement of immigrants—the foreign-born resident was allowed to vote four months after applying for citizenship. In 1858 the Republicans had been defeated by a slight margin and, in view of the growing dissatisfaction over such issues as the railroad policy and the homestead bill, with its attendant land sales, the Republican party had good reason to hope for a decisive victory in 1859. The campaign of 1860 was, therefore, much less lively than that of the previous year; a Republican victory in Minnesota was taken for granted.

The German population of the state, comprising both German-born persons and their children, amounted to 23,309, or 15.8 per cent of the total population.[1] In 1860 probably more than one Minnesotan in five—the proportion usually estimated—

1. Hildegard Binder Johnson, "The Distribution of the German Pioneer Population in Minnesota," *Rural Sociology* 6 (March 1941): 31.

was a voter, since the entire white population of that year numbered 169,395, and the aggregate of all male persons above the age of twenty was 38,183. Among the Germans the percentage of voters was certainly higher, for 5,610 family heads were counted among them in the Minnesota census of 1860; that is, about forty-two in a hundred Germans were voters. The figure does not include single male persons of more than twenty-one years, a group numerous enough to neutralize the possible inclusion of German family heads who had not yet reached voting age or who were not enfranchised. Thus 5,610 of 38,183 Minnesota voters—or every seventh potential voter—were German in 1860. Naturally, the Republicans of Minnesota—as of the other Middle Western states—were as anxious to secure this powerful vote as the Democrats were to hold it. German and Irish settlers were known to be faithful Democrats until the late 1850's.

Political issues in the two parties both repulsed and attracted foreign-born voters. Know-Nothingism, which was directed against the immigrant, kept Germans out of the Republican party, but the failure to enact a homestead bill antagonized them toward the Democratic administration in Washington. An amendment to the Massachusetts constitution, passed in 1859, requiring foreigners to remain in the state for two years after naturalization before they could vote, aroused sharp protest among the Germans of the entire country against Republicanism in New England.[2] Again, a letter written by Lewis Cass, secretary of state, denying protection to a naturalized American citizen traveling in Germany and subject to Prussian draft regulations in Danzig, made German politicians cry out against the denial of their rights as citizens. The threat of land sales in Minnesota made a homestead bill a special concern of the German farmers in the state. As the Germans began to recognize the value of their votes to both parties, their resentment of the nativistic policies became more outspoken, their demand for protection as naturalized citizens was accentuated, and their cry for German candidates became louder. Much concern for their wishes was exhibited

2. Kirk H. Porter, *A History of Suffrage in the United States* (Chicago, 1918), p. 118.

in non-German newspapers, speeches, and public letters. In view of their experience, many of the readers of the *Minnesota Staats-zeitung* must have agreed with its editor, Albert Wolff, who re-marked bitterly, in the issue for May 26, 1860, on the unusual politeness of the English-language press toward the Germans.

On the whole, Minnesota, due to both its youth and its geo-graphic situation, had not received as large a share of well-edu-cated German liberals, like the political exiles of 1830 and 1848, as other Middle Western states. In Ohio, Illinois, Missouri, and Iowa, there were many German writers, lecturers, publishers, journalists, and teachers who corresponded with and visited each other frequently. Among those of similar caliber in Minnesota were Samuel Ludvigh and Wolff, both of whom were connected with the *Staatszeitung*. Ludvigh, a radical freethinker, was an extravagant personality who became nationally known through his quarterly literary magazine, *Die Fackel*, which he established in New York and published later in Baltimore without interrup-tion for twenty years.[3] In 1857 he went to Minnesota in search of new subscribers for his aggressive magazine, engaged in a speaking tour through the towns with large German populations along the Minnesota River, and settled in St. Paul in 1858. He took over the *Minnesota Deutsche Zeitung,* changing its name to *Minnesota Staatszeitung,* in conscious imitation of other lead-ing German papers, such as the *New York Staatszeitung* and the *Illinois Staatszeitung*. During his residence in Minnesota *Die Fackel* was published and printed in St. Paul.

Ludvigh wrote in the *Minnesota Staatszeitung* on September 24, 1859: "We have done our full duty during the period of nineteen years, to the Democratic Party till its absolute degen-eration under Pierce, and we have worked conscientiously since that time for the Republican Party—pausing a while after the proscribing measures of Massachusetts and reassuring our politi-cal Stand as Editor since the Massachusetts crime has been ex-

3. Albert Post, *Popular Freethought in America, 1825–1850* (New York, 1943), p. 73; Alexander Schem, *Deutsch-Amerikanisches Conversationslexikon* (New York, 1872), 6: 656.

piated."[4] The Republicans recognized the significance of Ludvigh's newspaper, for when he announced, on July 23, 1859, that it would be discontinued after three months because of lack of money, they came to his aid, ordering pamphlets and translations for which he was paid $150.00. About the same time new subscriptions brought in $163.50. Ludvigh himself published these figures after Friedrich Orthwein, his Democratic rival of the *Minnesota National Demokrat* in St. Paul, accused the Republican candidate for state treasurer, Albert Scheffer, of having handed $500.00 to Ludvigh.[5] Although Ludvigh left on a tour of the East on October 12, 1859, immediately after the state election, the *Staatszeitung* bore his name as editor until December 1, 1860. Charles Reuther and Christian Exel appear as owners of the paper after February 11, 1860, and Albert Wolff's name as editor appears for the first time in the issue of February 25, 1860.[6]

Although Wolff was not as radical as Ludvigh, like the latter he took pride in announcing that he was "free of any party yoke or party pay."[7] He recommended both Republican and Democratic candidates in the St. Paul city election of 1860; with one exception they were Germans. He worded his recommendation: "Show the Knownothings of both parties what the damned Dutchman can do."[8] In the issue of his paper for May 26, Wolff described the national Republican platform as "national and just," recommending at the same time a direct disavowal of the Massachusetts amendment, the revision of the Fugitive Slave Act, and a liberal homestead law. While he waited until after the second Democratic convention in Baltimore before he would openly

4. *Minnesota Staatszeitung,* September 24, 1859. The article appeared in English under the title "The Republicans of New Ulm and Their Resolutions."

5. *Staatszeitung,* September 24, 1859; *Minnesota National Demokrat,* September 11, 1859.

6. Wolff settled in Minnesota in 1853. He was associated with several German newspapers in the state before he became editor of the *St. Paul Volkszeitung* in 1877. See files of the *Staatszeitung* for 1860; Wolff's obituary in the *St. Paul Pioneer Press,* November 26, 1893; and Lynwood G. Downs, "The Writings of Albert Wolff," ante, 27: 327.

7. *Staatszeitung,* February 25, 1860. Translated from an article titled: "Die freie deutsche Presse von Minnesota an das gesamte Deutschtum."

8. *Staatszeitung,* March 31, 1860.

come out as a Republican, he favored the Republican party from the time of its Chicago convention because thirteen German delegates participated in it; he had found that Germans were entirely absent from the first Democratic convention in Charleston. Wolff did not follow the usual practice of the English-language papers, which for months preceding an election published in each issue the ticket of the party they supported. The Republican ticket was not printed in the *Minnesota Staatszeitung* until October 27, 1860.

A second German paper in Minnesota was the *New Ulm Pionier*. Its motto, "Free soil, free men, free labor, free press," designated it as Republican in 1859 and 1860, but its enthusiastic support of Seward made it reluctant to endorse Lincoln. It recommended Lincoln and Hamlin "only under protest," a stand that drew Wolff's criticism.[9]

A third newspaper, the *Minnesota National Demokrat,* was owned and edited by Orthwein, who earlier had published the *Minnesota Thalbote* in Carver and the *Minnesota Deutsche Zeitung* in St. Paul. His political leanings were apt to change with the support he obtained from either party; his unreliability appears to be established.[10] On the whole the situation with respect to the German press in the state favored the Republican party.

The English-language press varied in its attention to the German-born voter. Easily available files of county newspapers are not complete for the period in question; thus it is difficult to form a general opinion. In general, however, Republican newspapers showed greater solicitude for the Germans than the Democratic newspapers. The *Daily Minnesotian* and the *St. Paul Daily Times* were among those carrying frequent notes or articles of interest to German readers. They published notices of speeches by Carl Schurz, and expressed satisfaction over Germans leaving the Democratic party in other states or in certain districts of Minnesota. The *Times* voiced its admiration for the

9. *New Ulm Pionier,* June 2, 1860; *Staatszeitung,* June 16, 1860.
10. Daniel S. B. Johnston, "Minnesota Journalism in the Territorial Period," *Minnesota Historical Collections* 10: 286–88, 317.

thriftiness of German women in the fields, advising American women to "learn a lesson of the hard working German women of the fatherland." German festivals had often been obnoxious to American Puritan tastes, but a festival in St. Paul in August, 1860, drew the approval of the editor of the *Times,* who "saw no drunkenness and no disposition to disturb the pleasure of others." The *Minnesotian* ran a series of long articles by Ignatius Donnelly entitled "Letters to the Foreign-Born Citizens of Minnesota"; one of its headlines read "Naturalized Citizens Placed on Par with Runaway Slaves"; and it made much of William Windom's answer to a letter signed by thirty-five German citizens of Winona.[11]

The letter, dated September 14, 1859, illustrates the main grievances of the politically minded German voter—grievances that were no less acute in neighboring states.[12] The signers submitted four questions to Windom, the Republican candidate for Congress from the Winona district. Was he in favor of naturalization laws as they stood, and particularly against every extention of probation? Was he against every discrimination between native-born and naturalized citizens as to the right of suffrage? Did he specifically condemn the Massachusetts amendment which withheld the franchise for two years after naturalization? Was he in favor of a liberal homestead law? All questions were answered in the affirmative by Windom, who furthermore opposed the unjust discrimination against citizens of foreign birth attempted by the Democratic administration. This was a special addition to the answer required by the second question, and it showed how well Windom understood the German cause.[13]

Democratic papers were eager to assure foreign-born citizens that they actually were protected by American consuls in Europe,

11. *St. Paul Times,* June 26, July 3, August 3, 14, October 3, 6, 19, 1860; *Daily Minnesotian,* July 19, August 4, 1859; July 26, 1860.

12. Similar letters are enumerated by George M. Stephenson in his *Political History of the Public Lands* (Boston, 1917), p. 228. See also Frank I. Herriott, "The Germans in Iowa and the 'Two Year' Amendment of Massachusetts," *Deutsch-Amerikanische Geschichtsblätter* (Chicago, 1913), 13: 202–308.

13. The letter and Windom's answer may be found in the *Winona Republican,* September 28, 1859, and in the *Minnesotian,* October 1, 1859.

and they cited the cases of a former Hanoverian and a former Dane who were released in the countries of their birth after the intervention of American consuls. Notices appearing under such headings as "What the Germans Think," "Read This, Germans," "What Democracy Thinks of the Germans," and "To the Germans, Norwegians, and Swedes of Carver County" illustrate varying attitudes of Democratic papers.[14]

Slavery and abolition were not neglected. William Seward's great speech of September 22 in St. Paul—perhaps the most important event of the campaign of 1860 in Minnesota—dwelt on these issues. Morton S. Wilkinson, the Republican nominee for senator, dedicated a long speech in Mankato on August 27 exclusively to the discussion of slavery and the Dred Scott decision. But whenever the English-language press put the slavery issue before the foreign-born voter for his decision, the competition between white and Negro slave labor was emphasized, as it was by Donnelly in one of his letters to foreign-born citizens.[15] Appeals to the Germans to decide the question on the basis of principles, of freedom, of right and wrong were made by Germans like Ludvigh, Wolff, and Schurz.

There is evidence that pamphlet literature supplemented the newspapers during the campaign. The *National Demokrat* published a sheet called *Demokratisches Heer-Banner,* and the same paper complained that the Republicans distributed thousands of German and Swedish pamphlets in which the Massachusetts amendment was falsely represented. C. C. Andrews reprinted excerpts from articles against Know-Nothingism which he had published in Eastern papers in 1855 and distributed them with German translations in Stearns County.[16]

14. *Henderson Weekly Democrat,* September 28, 1859; *Scott County Democrat,* July 30, 1859; *Pioneer and Democrat* (St. Paul), August 12, 1859; *Central Republican* (Faribault), October 11, 1859; *Scott County Democrat,* October 27, 1859; *St. Paul Times,* July 3, 1860; *St. Cloud Democrat,* September 15, 1859; *Carver County Democrat,* August 1, 1859.

15. *Minnesotian,* July 19, 1859.

16. One copy of the *Demokratische Heer-Banner* is bound with the *Minnesota National Demokrat* of May 3, 1859, in the Minnesota Historical Society's file. See also C. C. Andrews, *Extracts from Letters and Articles against "Knownothingism"* (St. Paul, 1859).

The party platforms tried to appeal to the Germans. A resolution in the Republican state platform of August 27, 1859, declared that "we proscribe no man on account of his religion or place of nativity; we oppose any abridgement whatever of the right of naturalization now secured by law to emigrants, and all discrimination between native and naturalized citizens, whether by amendment of a state constitution, as in Massachusetts, or by Legislative or Congressional action; and we resist with indignation, as our fathers did in 1812, the monstrous doctrine of impressment of American citizens by foreign despotisms as recently proclaimed by the present Administration."[17]

The Democratic platform of August 19, 1859, declared that "American citizenship embraces persons of all creeds and nationalities, who under the laws, acknowledge and render allegiance to the American government, and that the Democratic party recognizes no distinctions between such citizens, whether native-born or naturalized, but guarantees to all, alike, the same political rights at home, and the same governmental protection abroad. And we further declare that the amendments to the Constitution of Massachusetts placing additional restrictions upon the admission of the foreign-born adopted citizens to the right of suffrage, is an act of the Republican party, and that we hold them responsible for it, as an open avowal of principles which are secretly and covertly held by that party in Minnesota, and wherever that sectional organization exists, which is manifested by the fact that they have placed in nomination for the suffrages of the native and adopted citizens of Minnesota, James H. Baker, for Secretary of State, Gordon E. Cole, for Attorney General, and William Windom, for Representative in Congress, three open and avowed Know Nothings." It was further declared in the platform that homestead principles were of Democratic origin, that land sales in Minnesota were contrary to the desire of the Democrats, and that the president should be urged to postpone the sales.[18] The Republican platform, on the other hand, held the Democratic administration responsible for the defeat of the

17. *Minnesotian,* September 5, 1859.
18. *Pioneer and Democrat,* August 20, 1859.

homestead law. For a German in the backwoods who had little knowledge of the political history of the issues involved, both platforms might have had equal appeal.

There was, however, a widespread distrust of both parties among the Germans, many of whom thought both corrupt and given to nativistic tendencies. Thus the bid for the German vote expressed itself in the nomination of many a German candidate on state and local tickets. In Minnesota each party had a German candidate on the state ticket in 1859. Francis Baasen of New Ulm had been elected secretary of state on a Democratic ticket in 1857. In 1859 he was renominated, and the Republicans named another German, Scheffer of St. Paul, as candidate for state treasurer.

It is significant that neither party derided the German candidate of its opponent for being a foreigner. There was little said against Baasen, who was in office at the time. The twenty-three-year-old Scheffer, a freethinking liberal who recently had moved to Minnesota from Wisconsin, was reproached for his youth and for being an infidel. His name is printed in different forms in the contemporary press, and a Democratic paper said that he was so unknown that nobody knew how to spell his name.[19] In 1860 each party named a German as one of the four presidential electors on its ticket—William Pfaender of New Ulm on the Republican, Joseph Weinmann of Benton on the Democratic.

The German candidates contributed speeches in their native tongue to the campaigns of 1859 and 1860. In 1860 A. H. Wagner of New Ulm, who had been one of the German delegates to the Chicago convention of 1860, joined Pfaender frequently on his speaking tours.[20] Their speeches were rarely printed. The Germans lacked reporters and newspapers, and though the Eng-

19. *Henderson Democrat,* October 12, 1859.
20. Speeches are reported for Baasen in the *Scott County Democrat,* August 27, October 1, 1859; for Scheffer, in the *St. Cloud Democrat,* September 22, 1859, and under the *Minnesotian,* November 3, 1860. Pfaender's and Wagner's schedule included Mankato, Henderson, Carver, Shakopee, St. Paul, and St. Peter between October 20 and 30, 1860. See the *Independent* (Mankato, October 25, 1860.

lish-language papers often mention the speeches, they do not give the contents. That public discussions provided a favorite entertainment for the Germans is indicated by the relieved "At last" with which Wolff announced a long-awaited debate between Pfaender and Weinmann in St. Anthony and St. Paul in October, 1860. It was reported in the Republican *Staatszeitung* of November 3. Weinmann's grammar, logic, and knowledge of statistics and history were found faulty, and he was said to have "made a laughing stock of himself, his party and Germanity" by his appearance, which was described as "a cruelty to animals." Praise of a speaker by a paper representing his own party or derision by the opposition press indicates little. The scales of public German oratory in Minnesota, however, tipped in favor of the Republicans without the weight of Carl Schurz.

Schurz has been called "the most ubiquitous as well as the ablest speaker in the German language if not the ablest Republican campaigner" of his time. He was glorified in German-American history and praised by Minnesota papers as the "illustrious German patriot and exile," as "one of the really great minds and men of the country," and as "a man of talent and education." Occasionally he was attacked, for instance in Hastings, where he was described as a "refugee who made his own land too hot to hold him." Quickly the *Faribault Republican* grasped the chance to ask "German citizens how they liked such specimens of democratic toleration and regard for foreigners."[21] It was evidently not advisable for either side to attack Schurz.

Schurz arrived in St. Paul on September 19, 1859, and he spoke in Shakopee, Chaska, Lexington, Henderson, Stillwater, St. Anthony, St. Paul, and St. Cloud, and perhaps in other communities. On October 1, when the German reading club of St. Paul opened the Athenaeum, Schurz was conducted to the clubhouse in a torchlight procession. There he delivered a German speech of ninety minutes, followed by another in English. The

---

21. Joseph Schafer, "Who Elected Lincoln?" see above, pp. 46–61; *Falls Evening News* (St. Anthony), September 24, 1859; *Minnesotian*, October 3, 1859; *Stillwater Democrat*, September 24, 1859; *Faribault Republican*, November 21, 1859.

contents were not printed; the *Staatszeitung* found the German
speech good and the English one a work of art. Short notices
appeared in the English-language papers, the reporters noting
the "good impression" that Schurz made on the German audi-
ence.[22]

The highlight of Schurz's appearance in Minnesota was his
debate with Emil Rothe of Wisconsin in St. Anthony and St.
Paul. The fact that the Democratic party sent its best German
orator from Wisconsin to Minnesota when Schurz was campaigning in the latter state illustrates the importance credited to him.
In Germany, Schurz and Rothe had been comrades in a student
fight for freedom; in America they became residents of the same
town in Wisconsin; now they opposed each other publicly in
Minnesota. Their debate in Stansfield Hall in St. Anthony was
a success for Schurz, according to the Republican papers and the
Pioneer. The latter newspaper declared that Rothe was at a dis-
advantage because Schurz was the first and the last to speak
and also because he could speak English, a language in which
Rothe could not reply. Schurz exposed the differences between
slave and free labor, and when Rothe defended slavery as traditional, Schurz asked poignantly if a historical wrong ever
could become a historical right. Rothe remarked that the
homestead bill was unjust to those who did not need or want
land—an unfortunate statement in a young agricultural state
like Minnesota. He reproached Schurz for adhering to the
Republican party after it failed to nominate him for governor
of Wisconsin, giving Schurz a chance to declare his faith in
essential convictions which "the Democrats obviously could
not understand." It was characteristic of Schurz to extoll principles rather than views on the issues of the day, leading his
opponents to think "that his acquirements appear to be more
of a philosophic cast than those of a statesman trained to grapple
with the realities of life." This tendency accounts for the only
praise the *Pioneer* could give its fellow partisan Rothe, who is

22. *Intimate Letters of Carl Schurz* (Madison, 1928), pp. 192–208; *St. Paul
Times*, September 23, 1859; *Minnesota State News* (Minneapolis), September
17, 1859; *Staatszeitung*, October 8, 1859.

described as a "practical talker, not a visionary essayist such as Schurz."[23]

English-speaking Republicans often found great merit in Schurz's political stand. The *Winona Republican* devoted three columns in each of two issues to a full report of his speech in St. Louis on August 1, 1860, because of its "profound political analysis of American politics." The speech was recommended to the "candid and careful perusal of every reader . . . whether of European or American origin." Further reports of speeches by Schurz appear in the *St. Peter Tribune* and in the weekly *New Ulm Pionier,* which needed five issues to give a full account of a speech in Massachusetts on January 4, 1860.[24]

A circumstance that favored the Republican cause in Minnesota in the eyes of the Germans was the friendly attitude toward them exhibited by the new Republican governor, Alexander Ramsey, and Lieutenant Governor Donnelly. As early as 1857 Ramsey was mentioned as a friend of the German-speaking people after he attended a lecture given by Ludvigh in St. Paul.[25] When Donnelly founded Nininger he wanted to attract Germans from the East, and his *Immigrant Aid Journal* issued to advertise the townsite contained two pages of English and two of German material in each number. On one occasion, Donnelly addressed the Germans of Minnesota in a letter to the *Staatszeitung:* "Germans, who have left your fatherland because you did not want to have your rights trampled on . . . if you desire to act as free citizens and to prove yourself worthy of the character which the Germans of Europe acquired as philosophers and thinkers, then you have to ask for an explanation and reason for your faith and you must not obey orders from small demagogues." He referred to the loyalty that the Germans—and the Irish as well—had shown for the Democratic party, for "Democracy."[26] The uprooting of

23. *Staatszeitung,* October 1, 1859; *Stillwater Democrat,* October 1, 1859; *Pioneer and Democrat,* October 6, 1859.

24. *Winona Republican,* August 15, 1860; *St. Peter Tribune,* February 29, March 28, May 23, 31, 1860; *New Ulm Pionier,* July 28, August 4, 11, 18, 25, 1860.

25. *Minnesota Deutsche Zeitung,* September 19, 1857.

26. Translated from an article entitled "An die Deutschen von Minnesota," in the *Staatszeitung,* October 9, 1858.

the traditional partisanship of the German voters represents one of the most interesting aspects of the election of 1860 in the Northwest.

The foregoing description of the attitude of the Minnesota press, the situation with respect to German-language papers, the political issues, and the campaign gives a background for German participation in the election of 1860 in Minnesota. It remains to ascertain, as far as possible, how the German-born immigrants voted.

The present study is concerned with the ten counties where the density of the German population was greatest, either throughout the country or in certain townships. They are Blue Earth, Brown, Carver, Hennepin, Le Sueur, Nicollet, Ramsey, Scott, Sibley, and Stearns. With the exception of Hennepin, all had heavy Democratic majorities in 1857. Carver, Le Sueur, Nicollet, Ramsey, Scott, Sibley, and Stearns showed Democratic majorities in 1859. In 1860 only Scott and Stearns retained them. Sibley could have had a Democratic majority if the vote had not been split over the two Democratic candidates for the presidency.[27]

In 1860 the votes returned throughout Minnesota amounted to 20.5 per cent of the total population. This would mean that every potential voter went to the polls, for every fifth person in the population is supposedly a voter. Obviously, this was not the case in Minnesota in 1860 or in 1859, when an even larger percentage voted despite frequent contemporary complaints that many voters did not go to the polls. Certainly all Minnesota's eligible voters did not participate in the election. A computation of the number of male persons above the age of twenty, in comparison with the number of votes returned in each county, results in the following percentages for participation: 78 for Blue Earth, 68 for Brown, 58 for Carver, 68 for Hennepin, 77 for Le Sueur, 68 for Nicollet, 70 for Ramsey, 81 for Scott, 79 for Sibley, 69 for Stearns, and 72 for the whole state. In reality, these percentages

27. Sibley County returned 397 votes for Lincoln, 384 for Douglas, and 18 for Breckinridge. Election returns for counties have been obtained from the *Tribune Almanac* (New York, 1868), p. 60.

were probably larger, since it cannot be assumed that every male person above the age of twenty had the right to vote.

The figures show deviations that are hard to explain. Was the numerous foreign-born element in Carver County responsible for the low proportion? If so, why should Stearns with a German population of approximately 60 per cent show a participation close to the average state? In Otter Tail County on the frontier the participation was as low as 15 per cent. But Brown County, also directly on the frontier, shows a participation of 68 per cent. The participation of 76 per cent in Fillmore County, where only 2 per cent of the people were Germans, might be attributed to the presence of a large native American element and a politically eager Norwegian group. Olmsted County, however, with very few Germans and an even larger native element, showed a participation of only 71 per cent; and Scott County, with a German population of 34.4 per cent and Sibley County with one of 35 per cent, participated in the voting to the extent of 81 and 79 per cent. For the counties no general tendency in the participation can be established with respect to national composition, urban or rural districts, Democratic or Republican majorities, or location.

Perhaps the township figures would be more revealing. The only sources for data on township returns, however, are local newspapers, since no detailed results for 1860 are preserved in the office of the secretary of state. For the present purpose, it is particularly unfortunate that no township results are available for Carver County.[28] Data for the composition of the population in townships can be derived only from the manuscript census. Such a count was undertaken, but the manuscript census of 1860 enumerates the population of Stearns County according to post offices, not townships. Thus no detailed comparison of the German population and election results is possible for that county.

By enumerating German-born persons and their children for each township and estimating the percentage of the German stock

28. No local newspaper was published in Carver County late in 1860, and no paper in the neighboring counties published detailed results for Carver County.

in the total population of the ten counties under consideration, the writer was able to list townships or city wards where German stock amounted to more than thirty per cent of the population.[29] Only six townships in other Minnesota counties had German populations of more than thirty per cent in 1860: Hampton in Dakota County, Wheeling in Rice, Hay Creek in Goodhue, and Jefferson, Mount Vernon, and Wilson in Winona.

Detailed data were not available for Carver, but scattered references were found to respective majorities in different townships.[30] The return of 504 votes for Lincoln and 324 for Douglas can leave no doubt that a substantial number of Germans must have voted for Lincoln, since more than half the population was German and there is no reason to suspect that the Germans were more indifferent than others toward the election. Chaska Township—the only one for which the number of votes was found—with a German proportion of 78.8, showed a considerably larger participation than the average for the county. A Republican newspaper commented with justifiable joy that "Carver County was redeemed" in 1860. In 1859, it had returned 473 votes for Ramsey to 524 for George L. Becker, the Democratic nominee for governor.[31]

The data for Scott County are misleading. The percentage for participation is exceptionally high—81 per cent on the basis of the male population above twenty years of age, and 26.2 per cent on the basis of the total population. There probably were some irregularities in the election, for the participation on the latter basis was 88 per cent in Helena Township and 45 per cent in Cedar Lake Township. Even if every potential voter went to the polls, it is imposssible to believe that 88 out of 100 residents of Helena had the right to vote. The startling percentages increase the average figure for participation in Scott County to

29. The writer has tabulated statistical information upon which she based the conclusions presented in the pages that follow. The Minnesota Historical Society has a copy of her table showing "Voting Participation and Election Results" in certain Minnesota townships in 1860.

30. *State News*, November 10, 1860; *Falls Evening News*, November 10, 1860; *Staatszeitung*, November 10, 1860.

31. *Falls Evening News*, November 10, 1860.

such an extent that most townships lag behind the average for the whole county.

. While Stearns County returned a Democratic majority, the Republicans gained there considerably. There were 255 Republican and 552 Democratic votes returned for the county in 1857; 375 Republican and 660 Democratic votes in 1859; and 438 Republican and 494 Democratic votes in 1860. The Democratic majority, which had amounted to 297 three years earlier, was reduced to 44 in 1860. It can hardly be assumed that the vote of 482 for Douglas and 12 for Breckinridge was exclusively a German vote, which it would have had to be if the 438 votes for Lincoln were attributed to the non-German population in a county where 59 per cent of the population was German. The population of Stearns County was largely Catholic, and it included a considerable number of Irish who voted as usual for the Democratic party in 1860.[32]

Certain conclusions can be reached, although the incompleteness of the data for Stearns and Carver counties must be kept in mind. Of the 29 townships or wards where a comparison with participation in the county is possible, 12 showed a participation above and 17 a participation below the average. Of the latter, 4 in Scott County are doubtful. In 10 out of 29 townships with a German population of more than 50 per cent, 6 had a participation above and 4 a participation below the average for the county. Of the 10 counties studied, only Hennepin and Carver lagged noticeably behind the participation in the state; Ramsey with 20.2 per cent was almost identical with the state's 20.5 per cent, and all others showed a higher participation. It may thus be concluded that the participation of the Minnesota Germans as voters in the election of Lincoln was at least as lively as that of the state's total population—a good indication of German interest in the issues of the election of 1860.

It would be impossible to determine exactly the number of Germans who voted for or against Lincoln unless the electoral units were made up of Germans only. A comparative study, how-

32. This can be checked in other townships, such as Cedar Lake and Credit River in Scott County, or Erin and Shieldsville in Rice County.

ever, of the majorities in the townships is revealing. Of townships where Germans amounted to more than half the population, 12 returned a Republican and 2 a Democratic majority. Even if it were possible to check the results in Stearns County with the German percentage in the various townships, the balance would remain in favor of the Republican vote, because of 12 townships in Stearns which reported in 1860, there were 7 with Republican and 5 with Democratic majorities. Of the townships where the German population amounted to 30 and 50 per cent, it is known that 10 returned Republican and 8 Democratic majorities.

How large were these majorities? In the first group of townships, 8 Republican majorities amounted to more than double the number of votes for Douglas. For 5 townships in Carver falling into this group, the check could not be made. There were 2 townships with Democratic majorities in the group where Germans amounted to more than half the population; only one returned more than double the number of votes for Lincoln. In the group of townships with a German population of between 30 and 50 per cent, 6 out of 10 Republican majorities amounted to more than twice the combined Democratic vote, and 4 were large enough to defeat a combined Democratic vote. Only 2 of the Democratic majorities in this group of townships amounted to double the number of votes for Lincoln. A summation of the number of votes returned in townships with more than 50 per cent of Germans results in 808 votes for Lincoln and 345 for Douglas. If the votes for Carver and Stearns counties are added, the vote for Lincoln is 1,673 and that for Douglas 1,096.

It is impossible to dissect the vote where it would seem to be most significant, that is, where the returns were highest in absolute numbers, such as all St. Paul, the fourth ward of Winona, with 40.8 per cent Germans in a population of 1,200, or in the most densely populated counties. Either the German percentage was not high enough to warrant definite conclusions or the data are unobtainable.[33] It has been necessary to restrict the present investigation to the districts where German settlers were

33. No results are reported for the city wards of Winona in which the German proportion varied from 7 to 40.8 per cent.

most numerous. Democratic majorities were found where Catholics prevailed, as in Belle Plaine and Louisville in Scott County, in and about Mankato, and in Stearns County. In centers of Lutheran settlement, where the Germans were mainly from Prussia and Hanover, Republican majorities were returned. Among such settlements were Arlington and Dryden townships in Sibley County, Courtland Township in Nicollet County, and Hamburg in Carver County. New Ulm offers proof of the frequently mentioned support for Lincoln by German freethinkers and liberals. There, according to a check of the manuscript census, every man who had a right to vote must have done so, with the result that 155 votes were returned for Lincoln and 31 for Douglas, the latter probably by the group that supported Baasen. Wherever Turners and freethinkers were active, as in Henderson, Carver, and Shakopee, testimony of their Republican partisanship can be found in newspaper notices, and election results support the traditional impression.

It cannot be claimed that the Germans in Minnesota contributed a very significant absolute number of votes for Lincoln. Minnesota returned 4 electoral votes for Lincoln, as did Iowa. Wisconsin returned 5. Minnesota's electoral vote represented 22,069 single votes for Lincoln and 11,920 for Douglas. In regions where a test was possible, and where the Germans amounted to more than half the population, 808 votes were returned for Lincoln and 345 for Douglas—proof that the Germans contributed their share to the Republican victory of 1860.

Reprinted from *Minnesota History* 28 (March 1947): 20–36. One footnote omitted.

George H. Daniels (b. 1935) received his Ph.D. from the University of Iowa in 1963. Presently on the faculty of Northwestern University, he is primarily interested in American intellectual history and in the history of science. This article, written while its author was still a graduate student, is an early effort to employ analytical concepts and systematic methods in the study of ethnic political history. By tabulating data for other nativity groups in addition to the Germans, Daniels made meaningful comparisons possible. Unlike Charles Wilson Emery, he concludes that the Iowa Germans tended to prefer Stephen A. Douglas for president.

Immigrant Vote in the 1860 Election: The Case of Iowa

GEORGE H. DANIELS

The influence of the immigrant vote in the presidential election of 1860 has been a subject of continuing controversy since the date of the election. The disagreement, though, is not usually in terms of how a given immigrant group voted; it is in terms of how much influence its vote exerted on the outcome of the election. There is a consensus of opinion among historians about the partisan leanings of every major immigrant group. The starting point of this paper was the recognition that there is still some question on the more fundamental level; before it is reasonable to dispute about the influence of a group's vote, the most elementary considerations require that one first determine how the group voted. No adequate evidence has yet been offered on this basic question. This paper is an effort to determine as exactly as possible, on the basis of a study of township voting returns, how the major immigrant groups in Iowa voted in the election of 1860.

When historians try to analyze political trends, there are a number of courses open to them; they may reach a judgment on the basis of an impressionistic survey of the data; they may—in the manner of the modern pollster—accept the judgment of contemporary opinion; or they may use statistical analysis of the votes on the question at issue. Although the third of these alternatives seems to have much to commend it, statistical analysis has not, until recently, been widely used.

Lee Benson has suggested that a closer analysis of voting on the precinct level might reveal the unsoundness of many of our commonly accepted impressionistic judgments about past political behavior. By simply using state voting statistics, he was able, for instance, to disprove the generalizations of Allan Nevins about the Cleveland victory of 1884 and that of Arthur M. Schlesinger, Jr., concerning the Jackson victory of 1824. But he was not able, using the figures available to him, to do more than show that the generalizations of German influence in the election of 1860 were not proved.[1]

The German vote is usually credited with being a major factor in Lincoln's victory in 1860, and on the surface at least, there is a great deal of evidence for this viewpoint. The seven states then known as the Northwest are generally regarded as a crucial area in that election. The area was just emerging from the frontier stage, its population was rapidly increasing, and it represented more than enough electoral votes to determine the outcome of the election. The total vote in Illinois, Indiana, Iowa, Michigan, Minnesota, Ohio, and Wisconsin increased by 440,223 in the quadrennium in 1856–60. In the same period, 976,678 immigrants arrived, many of whom went to the Northwest and most of whom were Germans.[2] Since Lincoln captured the 66 electoral votes in these states, winning them all by narrow margins over Douglas, a large bloc of united voters in this area could very easily have carried the election to Douglas. Lincoln's plurality in the Northwest was only 149,807—far less than the most

1. Lee Benson, "Research Problems in American Political Historiography," in *Common Frontiers in the Social Sciences,* ed. Mirra Komarovsky (Glencoe, Ill., 1957), pp. 113–83.

2. Frederick F. Schrader, *The Germans in the Making of America* (Boston, 1924), p. 195.

conservative estimate of the number of German voters in the area.

Addressing the Chicago Republican Convention in 1860, the German-American politician Carl Schurz promised the party 300,000 German votes in the Northwest. Since that time, it has been traditional to assert that the immigrants in general, and in particular the Germans, were largely responsible for Republican success in 1860. Both panegyrists who wished to laud the immigrants for their peculiar humanitarian concern for liberty, and apologists who wished to blame "foreigners" for Democratic losses in the Midwest and for the purely American chaos which followed the election of Lincoln in 1860, have advanced the claim continuously. The *Des Moines Valley Whig* of Lee County remarked in October, 1859: "Verily, Germany is a power in Lee County."[3] The editorial observed that there were no Germans campaigning for the Democrats and estimated that over three-fourths of Lee County Germans had gone over to the Republican party. On the unfriendly side, the *Sioux City Register* predicted that if the Republicans "refuse to accede to the demands of their German allies they will be defeated in every state west and north of the Ohio."[4]

Historians have generally fallen in line with the thinking of contemporary observers. When they have not maintained that the Germans were responsible for the victory in 1860, they have, at least, listed them as an important factor. The most extreme claim was that of Schrader, who, basing his estimate on German immigration into the Northwest between 1856 and 1860, estimated the German Republican vote in those states in 1860 to be nearly 450,000.[5] Faust, in his two-volume study of German immigrants, maintained that a large majority of German immigrants joined the Republican party in an "unselfish effort to advance the interests of humanity, i.e., to banish slavery from the country."[6] Faust based his conclusion on a study of the spokes-

3. *Des Moines Valley Whig,* October 17, 1859.
4. *Sioux City Register,* June 16, 1859.
5. Schrader, *The Germans in the Making of America,* p. 195.
6. Albert B. Faust, *The German Element in the United States* (Boston, 1909), 2: 130–31.

men of the German community, who undoubtedly did, both in Iowa and the Midwest generally, campaign vigorously for the Republican party. The same type of evidence led Herriott to conclude that the Germans voted heavily Republican in the Iowa gubernatorial election of 1854,[7] and, more recently, two historians to conclude that Midwestern Germans poured into the Republican party en masse during the decade in a "spontaneous overflow of powerful emotions."[8]

Among all of these studies, only Herriott actually made an effort to determine how the German masses voted, but since his analysis was on the county level, he had to confess that the returns were "somewhat perplexing."[9] Dissent from the majority opinion first came in 1942 when Dorpalen tentatively concluded that the Germans were generally conformists, tending to vote as their neighbors did.[10]

Following the suggestion in Benson's essay, this study was specifically designed as a test of the thesis that Germans were overwhelmingly Republican in 1860. For reasons that will appear later in the essay, this could not effectively be done without at the same time considering the other population groups. I selected Iowa purely as a matter of convenience on the grounds that it would serve quite as well as any of the others. The situation in Iowa at that time was similar to that in the other midwestern states. It had been solidly Democratic in 1850 and subsequent elections began showing a marked Democratic decline. Whig strength increased, the Free Soil party registered small percentages in 1852 in several counties, and the first opposition success came in 1854 with the election of James W. Grimes as governor on a combined Whig and Free Soil platform. The Grimes supporters were later active in forming the Republican

7. Frank I. Herriott, "A Neglected Factor in the Anti-Slavery Triumph in Iowa in 1854," *Deutsch-Americanische Geschichtsblätter; Jahrbuch der Deutsch-Amerikanischen Historischen Gesellschaft von Illinois,* 18–19 (1918, 1919), pp. 174–335.
8. Lawrence S. Thompson and Frank X. Braun, "The Forty-eighters in Politics," in *The Forty-eighters,* ed. Adolf E. Zucker (New York, 1950), p. 120.
9. Herriott, "A Neglected Factor," p. 342.
10. Andreas Dorpalen, "The German Element and the Issues of the Civil War," see above, pp. 68–91.

party, which carried every election in Iowa from 1856 until long after the Civil War. The period of Republican rise coincided with the period of greatest increase in Iowa's population, and also with a definite shift in the focus of immigration from the southern states and the southern part of the Ohio Valley, to the northern Ohio Valley, the Middle Atlantic states, and Europe. In 1850, the population stood at 192,214, and by 1856 had reached 517,875. Thereafter, immigration from all quarters greatly decreased, and by 1860 only another 150,000 was added to the population. Native Germans in 1860 formed 5.79% of the entire state population of 674,913.[11]

In order to apply systematic data in the analysis of a political problem, it is first necessary to translate the question of what happened into a question of who (what voting groups) caused it to happen. In this case, we have a state which over a period of ten years changed its political allegiance from one party to a rival party. The German-Americans allegedly were a casual factor in the change. If this be the case, one would hypothesize that in a national election at the end of the transition period, a relationship would be found between the Republican vote and the presence of large numbers of German-Americans in a given area. The hypothesis can be tested by listing the various nativity groups, or at least the larger ones, found in Iowa at the time and comparing the vote in areas of their dominance. If place of origin does, indeed, play a determining role in the way one votes, a clear pattern should emerge when a large number of areas are compared.

Still, there is one other difficulty which could interfere with the validity of the results. If a historian selects a group and then studies only those areas where it is numerically strong, he will be in danger of neglecting other groups in other areas, equally or more important as casual agents for the trend. For this reason, the author has not considered population as a factor in selecting the areas of study. The only criterion was intensity of partisanship. In making this kind of selection, the only necessary assump-

11. *Population of the United States in 1860; Compiled from the Original Returns of the Eighth Census* (Washington, 1864).

tion is that if a group be notably partisan, it will be almost certain to emerge in a tabulation of extremes.

Two methodological conclusions emerged quite early in this study: first, that the township was the largest political unit that could yield the desired answers, and second, that total population figures were untrustworthy as guides to political strength. On the county level, population groups are so evenly divided and so many changes are occurring at once that no pattern can readily emerge. If, for example, the vote is fairly well split on the county level, as it was in Lee County in the presidential election of 1860 when 51.5% of the vote went to the combined Democratic parties, and if no one group of voters is clearly dominant, as was also the case in Lee County, there is little that the historian can properly deduce about the election. But the Democratic vote in the townships of Lee County ranged from 14% to 74%, and since groups originating from the same locality did tend to settle close together, a clearly dominant group can be distinguished in most of the townships.

The only disadvantages in this approach are in the labor involved and in the difficulty of locating returns by townships. In most cases, the counties themselves did not retain the returns for any great length of time, and one must resort to newspapers for their report. Where no newspaper existed, or where the newspaper did not choose to print such returns, the historians must usually admit failure and try another county. Although this lack of complete evidence does make it impossible to utilize any normal scientific sampling methods, it does not make it necessary to leave the existing material unstudied. The historian must, rather, make the best use he can of the materials he can find. This has been the procedure followed in this study. Township returns for twenty-six counties were located for the presidential election of 1860, and eleven more for the gubernatorial election of 1859. In addition to these, there were twenty-two counties so sparsely populated that for election purposes they were regarded as comprising one township each, and they can be so regarded by the investigator. The fifty-nine counties (from a total of ninety-nine) are distributed throughout the state, and they contained in 1860 over 70% of the total population of Iowa. Considering the present state of scientific sampling techniques, it can be seriously argued that covering this large a percentage of the total population is at least as conducive to accuracy as any sample could be.

While the desirability of pursuing one's study in terms of townships is hardly a controversial issue, there is a deficiency of the census that has not been so often remarked. A look below the surface of the county returns drives one to the conclusion that census figures showing the total population do not necessarily reflect the distribution of voting power. In studies of group voting behavior, historians have characteristically assumed that there is a real relationship between total and voting population, but the results of this study show not only that it is not necessarily so, but also that in a frontier community, it is highly unlikely to be so.

A comparison of the two kinds of population statistics for any of Iowa's counties will demonstrate that the formal ethnic divisions of the census do not reflect voting power. Comparative figures for Clay County, a particularly revealing example, are shown below:

TABLE I

Voting Strength in Clay County

	Percent of Total Population	Percent of Potential Voters
Middle Atlantic	28.0	20.0
Ohio Valley	20.0	13.3
Germany	22.0	46.7

In other words, the census showed that the Middle Atlantic natives were the largest group and the Ohio Valley group followed closely behind the Germans, while in terms of the voting population, the Germans greatly outnumbered the two combined. In all of the other cases, the greatest discrepancies occurred along the normal migration lines of the most numerous group outside the Ohio Valley, and discrepancies increased in direct relation to proximity to Iowa. Missouri and Illinois were consistently overrated by the census and the immigrant groups consistently underrated in terms of their actual voting power. In cases where, for example, New England was listed as the birthplace for a large percentage of adult males, the Middle Atlantic states without exception received disproportionate representation in the census.[12]

The meaning of all this, so far as this particular study is concerned, is clear. Although we have no way of determining who actually did vote, it is apparent that in order to determine the relative strength of those who could possibly have voted, it will be necessary to count only adult males. This has been done in all the townships used.

The analysis in the remainder of this paper is largely based upon the group of counties for which township returns are available for the election of 1860. The other categories are used as a check upon the conclusions and will only be mentioned when necessary for clarification. While the desirability of including materials for an earlier period is unquestionable, returns before 1859 are so extremely fragmentary that they could add very little to the study.

In order to have a large number of townships for comparison, all those voting over 65% Democratic and all those voting less than 25% Democratic were tabulated along with the most Democratic and the most Republican townships in each county. The only significance which is attached to these percentages is that they undoubtedly deviate a great deal from the state averages and that they yield an equal number of Democratic and Republican townships (40 each). These, then, are the extremes and their

12. The three frontier counties of Boone, Decatur, and Marshall, which in 1850 had 2,051 residents, were used to determine whether this kind of distribution was peculiar to the later period in Iowa, or whether it could be applied more generally to frontier communities. Four hundred seventeen, or about one-fifth, of the total residents were adult males and could possibly have voted in the gubernatorial election of that year. The same pattern is found as in 1860. At one extreme is the foreign group, which had 33 potential voters from a total foreign population of 55, and at the other extreme are the neighboring states of Missouri, Indiana, and Illinois, which together furnished only 42 voters out of a total of 802 immigrants from those states.

populations are compared in Table II. According to the table, the Middle Atlantic states of New York, Pennsylvania, and New

TABLE II

LARGEST NATIVITY GROUPS IN MOST DEMOCRATIC AND
MOST REPUBLICAN TOWNSHIPS
PRESIDENTIAL ELECTION OF 1860

Nativities	Most Democratic Townships	Most Republican Townships
New England	0	1
Middle Atlantic	3	21
Upper Ohio Valley	21	16
South	4	0
Germany	7	0
Great Britain	1	0
Ireland	4	0
Scandinavia	0	1
Holland	0	1

TABLE III

LARGEST NATIVITY GROUPS IN MOST DEMOCRATIC AND
MOST REPUBLICAN TOWNSHIPS
GUBERNATORIAL ELECTION OF 1859

Nativities	Most Democratic Townships	Most Republican Townships
New England	0	1
Middle Atlantic	2	4
South	0	0
Upper Ohio Valley	7	5
Germany	1	1
Ireland	2	0

Jersey supplied the most consistent Republicans.[13] The Ohio Valley states were split, while Germans, Irish, and Southerners

13. Although New Jersey is included as a Middle Atlantic state, only an insignificant number from this state ever came to Iowa. New Yorkers and Pennsylvanians are about equally represented. No differences were noted when the Ohio Valley states were considered separately.

were clearly Democratic. There are no other groups which appear often enough in a dominant position for one to judge.

These results were taken a step further in Table IV, which shows that in every case, an increase in the dominance of a nativ-

TABLE IV

MEDIAN DEMOCRATIC VOTE OF TOWNSHIPS ACCORDING TO THE
PERCENTAGE DISTRIBUTION OF SELECTED NATIVITY GROUPS
PRESIDENTIAL ELECTION OF 1860

Nativity	+20% of Voting Population Median Vote		+40% of Voting Population Median Vote	
Ireland	86.7	83.0	89.2	86.7
Germany	70.0		81.1	
South	67.1	66.3	75.1	
Upper Ohio Valley	56.4	56.0	68.4	67.7
Middle Atlantic	22.2		22.2	17.8

ity group increased the trend of the township vote. The first entry in the table shows the median Democratic vote of all the townships studied which contain more than 20% of a given nativity group; the second entry shows the median vote of townships containing more than 40% of the group. In townships where the Germans, for example, supplied over 20% of the voting population, the median Democratic vote was 70%. But if one considers only those townships where Germans numbered more than 40% of the population, the median Democratic vote rose to 81.1%. This is a clear indication that Germans in these townships did contribute to the Democratic vote.

Every item on the chart, except that pertaining to the Germans, is in accord with the standard interpretation and will require little further comment. It does seem worthwhile to remark that if the known Republicanism of immigrants from the Middle Atlantic states and their known influx into the Midwest during the decade 1850–60 be considered in connection with the migration pattern alluded to in this study, historians will in all probability find that their migration into the Midwest was the sole cause for the political shift. Although the percentage of population from the Ohio Valley was also increasing phenomenally at the same time, these immigrants were, as it seems, mostly women and children who could have had no immediate political influence. The fact that townships dominated by Ohio Valley immigrants were evenly divided reflects the divided sympathies of their background. There only remains the problem of reconciling the conflict between the statistics on German voting and other types of evidence.

Even though all of the German townships located in this study were Democratic in 1860, the theory of Dorpalen, which was endorsed by Benson, is suggestive when it is applied to the Germans in Iowa's large cities. In all of the German townships studied, there was really no chance for the Germans to conform to anything; conformity requires frequent contact in order for the political attitude to be transferred. The situation in all seven of the townships precluded such contact and transfer, for the Germans all lived and worked in purely German communities. Iowa's two largest cities, Davenport and Dubuque, were also the cities which contained the largest number of Germans in an urban environment, where contact and presumably outside political influence would be almost a daily occurrence. And, the Germans in both cities seemed to adopt the prevailing political attitudes. Dubuque voted Republican only once in the thirteen statewide elections between 1850 and 1860, and Davenport voted Democratic only twice during the same period. The Germans entering between 1852–54 seemed to do no more than increase the already prevailing trend in each case. According to a census taken in 1858, there were approximately 496 Germans who could have voted in Davenport in that year, and the Republican majority of that year was 438 out of the total 1,864 votes cast for representative in Congress.[14] While similar population figures for Dubuque (Julian Township, Dubuque County) do not exist, contemporary reports indicate that the German population must have been about the same as in Davenport. Here the Democratic majority in 1858 was 503 out of 2,339. It would require a great

14. The census returns can be found in Franc B. Wilkie, *Davenport Past and Present* (Davenport, 1858), p. 325.

stretch of the imagination to believe that either city would have voted differently had there been no Germans in them.

Although the situation in Dubuque and Davenport may be explained in terms of conformity, as Dorpalen and Benson would have it, outside of these two areas, the great majority of Germans in Iowa were not diffused throughout the population. Instead, they normally formed communities of their own and enjoyed relative political isolation. In these cases, they did not conform to the political attitudes of the counties in which they lived; in every instance this study shows that they were a great deal more Democratic than their neighbors in 1860. The seven Democratic townships in which Germans formed the largest group were in six different counties, four of which were Republican in 1860, and one of which was only slightly Democratic. In this connection, it is significant to note that while 21% of Scott County's population in 1860 was German, Germans did not appear as a large group in any of the highly Republican townships in that county. On the other hand, in Dubuque County, which contained only 15.6% Germans, they were the largest group in the two townships which voted more than 80% Democratic. The one German township voting Republican in the election of 1859 (Amana, Iowa County) is easily explained on the grounds that being a pietistic religious colony, it would have little ideological affiliation with other German groups in the state.

Any way the problem is approached, except by taking the word of interested politicians, German intellectuals and newspapers, it seems that Iowa Germans were definitely inimical to Republican aspirations in the election of 1860, and the indications are that a study would show that the same was true in 1856.[15]

Actually, there were two very potent reasons why German-Americans should have been attracted to the Democratic party during that particular decade. Republicanism was linked, at least in the popular mind, with Know-Nothingism, and in Iowa

15. At least five of the seven German townships found in the election of 1860 were also highly Democratic in 1856. Records do not exist for the other two.

it was also linked to prohibition. Democrats, on the other hand, tended to favor free liquor, and in their convention of 1856, had roundly denounced native Americanism and read the Know-Nothing element out of the party. Events outside the Midwest also reflected a basic difference between the two parties in their treatment of immigrants, and the Iowa Democratic press seized every opportunity to play up Know-Nothingism in the Republican ranks. When the "two year" amendment was passed by the heavily Republican Massachusetts legislature in March, 1859, every Democratic paper in Iowa featured it in their editorials. Obviously aimed at eliminating immigrant influence at the polls, the Massachusetts amendment provided that naturalized citizens must have resided in the state for two years before being eligible to vote. Iowa papers claimed that the Massachusetts action demonstrated that Republican love for humanity extended only so far as the African, while the Democratic party "places the adopted citizen . . . on a basis of perfect and entire equality with the native."[16] The *Weekly Independence Civilian* prophesied that if the Republicans of Iowa "were strong enough to do without foreign votes, they would soon be walking in the steps of Massachusetts."[17]

In answer to the Republican defense that the nativist attitude was purely local, not reflecting any national Republican attitudes, the Democrats pointed out that the New York and the Connecticut Republican party were sponsoring a similar proscriptive amendment. Democrats also claimed that the union of the American and the Republican parties in Hamilton, Ohio, proved that Know-Nothingism was not a local element in the Republican party.[18]

There is abundant evidence that German-Americans in Iowa were aroused by the nativist tendencies in the Republican party. One German immigrant, a resident of Burlington, Iowa, wrote a lengthy public letter to the press, urging Germans not to vote

16. *Iowa Weekly Democrat* (Sigourney), March 25, 1859.
17. *Weekly Independence Civilian*, May 12, 1859.
18. *Sioux City Register,* June 30, 1859; *Page County Herald* (Clarinda, Iowa), July 29, 1859.

for the party of nativism and prohibition. Denunciatory resolutions were drawn up by an association of Germans in Scott County, and a group of German political leaders submitted a questionnaire to the Congressional delegation from Iowa asking them, in effect, if they condemned the Massachusetts legislation.[19]

All historians who considered the subject have noted these less attractive—at least from the German viewpoint—features of the Republican party, but have insisted that because of their love of liberty, the Germans overlooked these minor points. Speaking of the German intellectuals, this seems to be perfectly true; and the masses were also lovers of liberty. But like masses everywhere, the rank and file Germans who did the bulk of the voting considered their own liberty to be of paramount importance. Apparently ignoring the advice of their leaders, they cast their ballots for the party which consistently promised them liberty from prohibition and native-American legislation.

At least one German-American businessman expressed the same opinion just before the election of 1860. Samuel Stern of Boston, in an open letter to Carl Schurz, claimed that he had been in the Revolution of 1848, and had learned enough of "radicalism and idealism to learn to be conservative and look after my own interests." Although he offered no statistics to prove his contention, Mr. Stern's experience had convinced him that the bulk of the Germans who had become adopted citizens and could vote were largely Democratic. Only the newly arrived masses, he said, were fooled by Schurz and the other politicians who were really thinking of their own advancement.[20] Although Stern could hardly be called a disinterested observer, his analysis is suggestive, and would seem to be largely borne out by the results of this study. An editorial in the *New York Demokrat* which was widely reprinted in midwestern newspapers, although it did not speak so frankly of conservatism and self-interest, came to roughly the same conclusions. The editor described German-Americans who were still voting Republican after all the kicks

19. *Weekly Independence Civilian*, June 16, 1859; *Iowa Weekly Democrat* (Sigourney), May 13, 1859; *Weekly Maquoketa Excelsior*, May 17, 1859.
20. *Mississippi Valley Register* (Guttenberg, Iowa), November 1, 1860.

they had received as "stupid."[21] Whatever the merits of the arguments of Stern and the *New York Demokrat,* it is evident that large numbers of German voters, at least in Iowa, must have taken them seriously.

Although the prohibition issue was undoubtedly a factor, it was probably not as important as Republican native-Americanism. Had a split occurred over prohibition, one would expect a religious pattern to emerge. But an inspection of the *Census of 1860, Social Statistics* and the appropriate county histories indicates that the German Democrats ranged from Roman Catholic in Dubuque and Johnson counties to Methodist-Episcopal and Mennonite in Lee, and Baptist in Des Moines. Any religious issues were apparently subordinated to the general German hatred of native-Americanism.

Even though it be granted that Iowa Germans were largely Democratic in 1860, it does not automatically follow that Germans throughout the Midwest were Democratic. Conclusions drawn from a study of one state cannot be automatically applied elsewhere, for it is possible that there were conditions peculiar to Iowa which caused the split between the German spokesmen and the German masses, but this conclusion is important for another reason. In a sense, this paper has been a case study in the relationship between the pronouncements of group spokesmen and the actions of group members. And, since no significant relationship existed in this case, it does call into question all generalizations about group voting based upon the opinions of leaders. Historians, accepting the statements of contemporary observers as true, had found reasonable grounds for assigning a large majority of the German vote to Frémont and Lincoln. That they were wrong in at least one case has been demonstrated in this study, for well over half the Germans in Iowa lived in the six counties where the most Democratic townships were dominated by Germans. It is important to recognize that in every case conclusions of German Republicanism have been made on the same ground —acceptance of contemporary opinion. The broadest generalizations that can be made from this study are that the masses do

21. Ibid., October 6, 1859.

not necessarily vote the way their spokesmen are campaigning, and that contemporary opinion, including that of newspapers, is a poor guide. If the historian would discover how any group actually voted, he must turn to an analysis of voting returns in terms of the smallest possible units. Only in a unit the size of a township can groups be isolated with enough precision for the historian to be sure that his conclusion is correct. If this study has any applicability outside of the immediate area considered, it is only in adding evidence to Benson's claim that historians must utilize systematic data in political studies if their statements are to bear scrutiny.

Reprinted from *Mid-America* 44 (July 1962): 146–62. Several footnotes have been modified.

APPENDIX A

THE DEMOCRATIC VOTE BY TOWNSHIPS ACCORDING TO NATIVITY GROUPS
PRESIDENTIAL ELECTION OF 1860

MIDDLE ATLANTIC TOWNSHIPS

Township	County	Democratic Vote (%)
Putnam	Fayette	9.4
Fremont	Buchanan	13.6
Jefferson	Butler	17.3
Boardman	Clayton	18.6
Scott	Johnson	16.4
Wayne	Jones	17.8
Cue	Benton	20.0
St. Claire	Benton	21.2
Taylor	Dubuque	35.4
Liberty	Scott	25.7
Union	Boone	31.4
Amity	Page	2.2
Douglas	Page	22.2
Fulton	Muscatine	22.7
Mitchell	Mitchell	9.9
Albion	Butler	17.5
Fremont	Butler	25.0
Sumer	Buchanan	18.8
Ohio	Webster	24.1
Washington	Webster	22.0
Harlan	Fayette	25.0
Clear Creek	Johnson	66.3
Auburn	Fayette	56.4
Rockingham	Scott	57.9

UPPER OHIO VALLEY TOWNSHIPS

Township	County	Democratic Vote (%)
Wayne	Henry	0.8
Gower	Cedar	11.3
Yellow Springs	Des Moines	16.9
Brown	Linn	20.7
Bruce	Benton	7.3
Harrison	Benton	23.6
Cedar	Lee	24.8
Valley	Page	11.4
Indiana	Marion	32.5
Milford	Story	30.0
Center	Pottawattamie	20.8
Crawford	Washington	15.2
Clay	Washington	14.7
Richmond	Wayne	27.6
Drakeville	Davis	43.5
Springdale	Cedar	17.2
Jefferson	Lee	73.9
Roscoe	Davis	71.6
Dodge	Boone	67.1
March	Boone	78.7

APPENDIX A (Continued)

UPPER OHIO VALLEY TOWNSHIPS (Cont.)

Township	County	Democratic Vote (%)
Buffalo	Linn	63.3
Jackson	Jones	60.0
Augusta	Des Moines	73.1
Massilon	Cedar	57.2
Jackson	Butler	71.4
Baltimore	Henry	70.9
Buchanan	Page	70.8
Pierce	Page	68.4
Polk	Marion	79.2
Jefferson	Mahaska	70.7
Collins	Story	56.0
Rocky Ford	Pottawattamie	67.3
Pleasant Grove	Des Moines	67.7
Salt Creek	Davis	81.9
Lick Creek	Davis	73.0
Marion	Davis	74.5

SOUTHERN TOWNSHIPS

Township	County	Democratic Vote (%)
Fabius	Davis	88.7
Clay	Wayne	66.1
Fox River	Davis	75.1
Yell	Webster	63.2

NEW ENGLAND TOWNSHIPS

Township	County	Democratic Vote (%)
Denmark	Lee	13.7

GERMAN TOWNSHIPS

Township	County	Democratic Vote (%)
West Point	Lee	70.0
Liberty	Dubuque	86.6
Mossalem	Dubuque	81.1
Liberty	Johnson	83.2
Clayton	Clayton	56.6
Benton	Des Moines	66.7
Moscow	Muscatine	55.8

IRISH TOWNSHIPS

Township	County	Democratic Vote (%)
Prairie Creek	Dubuque	83.0
Iowa	Dubuque	89.2
Union	Benton	86.7
Washington	Jones	93.4

SCANDINAVIAN TOWNSHIPS

Township	County	Democratic Vote (%)
Cedar	Mitchell	1.4

DUTCH TOWNSHIPS

Township	County	Democratic Vote (%)
Black Oak	Mahaska	31.7

APPENDIX B

The Democratic Vote and Dominant Nativity Groups by Townships
Gubernatorial Election of 1859

Township	County	Democratic Vote (%)	Dominant Nativity Group
Butler	Jackson	100.0	Irish
Washington	Clinton	88.9	Irish
Warren	Keokuk	84.6	Ohio Valley
Sioux City	Woodbury	69.5	Middle Atlantic
Clear Creek	Jasper	69.4	Ohio Valley
Walnut	Jefferson	63.7	German
Iowa	Iowa	60.2	Ohio Valley
Columbia	Tama	59.0	Ohio Valley
Sugar Creek	Poweshiek	57.4	Ohio Valley
Green	Wapello	77.8	Ohio Valley
Union	Black Hawk	70.0	Ohio Valley
Amana	Iowa	3.2	German
Buckingham	Tama	8.1	Middle Atlantic
Richland	Jasper	8.6	Ohio Valley
Grinnell	Poweshiek	13.9	New England
Berlin	Clinton	19.9	Ohio Valley
Prairie	Keokuk	21.9	Ohio Valley
Richland	Wapello	23.4	Ohio Valley
Correctionville	Woodbury	25.0	Middle Atlantic
Monmouth	Jackson	25.7	Middle Atlantic
Liberty	Jefferson	33.5	Ohio Valley
Black Hawk	Black Hawk	15.4	Middle Atlantic

APPENDIX C

Democratic Vote and Dominant Nativity Groups
of Counties Not Organized into Townships
Presidential Election of 1860

County	Democratic Vote (%)	Dominant Nativity Group
Audubon	55.1	Upper Ohio
Sac	72.7	Upper Ohio
Clay	61.9	German
Ida	60.0	Middle Atlantic
Palo Alto	87.9	Irish
Kossuth	23.8	Middle Atlantic
Grundy	11.9	Middle Atlantic
Hancock	12.1	Middle Atlantic
Dickinson	13.2	Middle Atlantic
Humbolt	24.7	Middle Atlantic
Emmet	0.0	Middle Atlantic
Crawford	39.7	Middle Atlantic
Cherokee	23.1	New England
Shelby	39.0	Upper Ohio
Plymouth	15.8	Upper Ohio
Pocahontas	32.3	Irish

A professor at Kent State University in Ohio, Robert P. Swierenga (b. 1935) is the third historian in this volume to examine Iowa sources. In this study of a Dutch colony and its leader, he specifically attacks the traditional assumption that the partisan preferences of an immigrant group can be inferred from the behavior of its elite. By stressing the tenacity with which voters hold to established voting habits, Swierenga suggests that historians have traditionally exaggerated the importance of issues.

The Ethnic Voter and the First Lincoln Election

ROBERT P. SWIERENGA

Scholars, particularly those interested in the impact of ethnic groups on key national elections, have long been intrigued by Abraham Lincoln's victory in 1860. Ever since Professor William E. Dodd's classic article it has been axiomatic in the works of historians that the foreign-born of the Old Northwest, voting in solid blocs according to the dictates of their leaders, cast the decisive ballots. Lincoln could not have won the presidency, Dodd suggested, "but for the loyal support of the Germans and other foreign citizens led by Carl Schurz, Gustav Koerner, and the editors of the *Staatszeitung* of Chicago."[1]

A decade later, taking his cue from Dodd, Donnal V. Smith scrutinized the immigrant vote in 1860 and confidently declared that "without the vote of the foreign-born, Lincoln could not have carried the Northwest, and without the Northwest . . . he would have been defeated." Smith's statistics also confirmed the premise that the social solidarity characteristic of ethnic groups

1. "The Fight for the Northwest, 1860," *American Historical Review* 16 July 1911): 774–88. The idea was quickly accepted. See, for example, Arthur C. Cole, *The Era of the Civil War* (Springfield, 1919), pp. 341–42.

invariably translated itself into political solidarity, and that because of the language barrier the immigrants needed leaders to
formulate the political issues for them. "The leaders who were
so trusted," Smith maintained, "were in a splendid position to
control the political strength of the foreign-born." And in the
election of 1860, he continued, even to the "casual observer"
the ethnic leaders in the Middle West were solidly Republican.[2]
Therefore, except for isolated, insignificant minorities, the foreign-born of the Old Northwest voted Republican.

Most midwestern ethnic leaders, it is true, were predominantly
in the Republican camp in 1860. Foreign-language newspapers
generally carried the Lincoln-Hamlin banner on their mastheads;
prominent immigrants campaigned actively for Old Abe and
played key roles at the Chicago convention.[3] It is also widely
conceded that the anti-slavery movement, the free homestead
idea, and the Pacific railroad issue were key factors attracting
ethnic leaders to the Republicans.[4]

The really crucial question however, concerns not the foreign-
born leaders but the masses that they supposedly represented.
Did the naturalized immigrants vote as their spokesmen desired?
Except for Dr. Joseph Schafer's deathbed protest in 1941 that
the Wisconsin Germans did not fit the pattern,[5] the Dodd-Smith
thesis has stood unchallenged.[6] But a recent analysis of the 1860

2. "The Influence of the Foreign-Born of the Northwest in the Election
of 1860," see above, pp. 1–15. See also Frank I. Herriott, "Iowa and the First
Nomination of Lincoln," *Annals of Iowa*, 3d ser. 8 (1907): 196.

3. Besides Schurz of Wisconsin and Koerner of Illinois, prominent foreign-
born campaigners included Frederick Hassaurek of Ohio, Theodore Hielscher
of Indiana, and Henry P. Scholte and Nicholas Rusch of Iowa. See M. Halstead, *Caucuses of 1860: A History of the National Political Conventions*
(Columbus, 1860), pp. 123, 127; Reinhard H. Luthin, *The First Lincoln
Campaign* (Cambridge, 1944), pp. 185–87; Charles W. Emery, "The Iowa
Germans in the Election of 1860," see above, pp. 16–45.

4. Luthin, *First Lincoln Campaign,* p. 187; Paul W. Gates, *Fifty Million
Acres: Conflicts over Kansas Land Policy, 1854–1890* (Ithaca, 1954), pp. 104–5.

5. "Who Elected Lincoln?" see above, pp. 46–61.

6. For textbook examples see Carl N. Degler, *Out of Our Past: The
Forces That Shaped Modern America* (New York, 1959), p. 287; Ray Allen
Billington, *Westward Expansion: A History of the American Frontier,* 2d ed.
(New York, 1960), p. 611.

election statistics for Iowa suggests that the foreign-born, and particularly the Germans, may not have supported Lincoln as strongly as historians have long assumed to be the case.[7]

A possibly critical factor thus far ignored in studies of the ethnic impact on the first Lincoln election is the time gap between the date of immigrant settlement and the year 1860. That ethnic leaders initially influenced the ballots of their countrymen is highly probable. Yet it seems reasonable to assume that a leader's power would steadily wane as the rank-and-file newcomers attained a measure of economic security and cultural acclimatization. If true, the student of ethnic voting must be careful when relying on what spokesmen said as an indication of how the foreign-born voted, particularly if ten or fifteen years had elapsed since the trans-Atlantic migration. The collective experience of the Netherlanders who migrated to central Iowa in the mid-nineteenth century, in illustrating this danger, is a case study of the complex influences actually molding immigrant political patterns in the years immediately preceding the Civil War.

In 1847 the Hollanders—some eight hundred strong—established their colony, with the new town of Pella at its center, in Lake Prairie Township, Marion County. To insure complete control of the area, the colony's leaders had earlier bought up the claims and improvements of almost all pioneer squatters in the township. Along with the purchase of vacant government land the Netherlanders were thus able to engross some eighteen thousand choice acres between the Des Moines and Skunk rivers. Through the antebellum years the settlement grew rapidly under a continuing Dutch immigration, augmented by a growing minority of native Americans. In the decade of the fifties potential voters in the township increased by 340 European-born and 152 native-born men. With a maximum voting majority of 85 per

7. George H. Daniels, "Immigrant Vote in the 1860 Election: The Case of Iowa," see above, pp. 110–128.

cent in 1850 and 72 per cent in 1860, therefore, the Dutch clearly dominated local politics.[8]

The Reverend Mr. Henry Peter Scholte (pronounced Skol'-tuh), founder of the Pella colony, was one of the ethnic leaders cited by Donnal Smith as typical of those who led the foreign-born into Lincoln's camp.[9] The basis of Scholte's political influence, dating from the Old Country, was his position as president of the Netherlandish Association for Emigration to the United States, formed at Utrecht in 1846 and consisting mainly of members of his religious congregation. Having seceded from the state-supported Dutch Reformed Church because of its alleged lack of spirituality, Scholte and his flock suffered a mild persecution from government officials. This, coupled with economic distress, prompted the Dutch minister to lead his followers to America.

Until his death in 1868, the "Dominie," as his followers affectionately addressed him, played an important part in the intellectual, economic, and political life of Pella, Marion County, and the state of Iowa. His versatility was truly remarkable. He served as minister, as editor of the English-language Pella *Gazette,* as lawyer, real estate developer, justice of the peace, school inspector, and mayor ex officio. Scholte was also an energetic capitalist. Besides owning almost one-third of the land in and around the town of Pella, his investments in local industry were substantial. He owned a brick kiln, steam flour mill, and limestone quarry, founded the Pella National Bank, and was a benefactor and trustee of the local college. Although he failed in his bid for nomination as state senator in 1852, he served as delegate-at-large and vice-president of the 1860 Republican national convention at Chicago. In 1864 President Lincoln appointed him United

8. Voting population figures were compiled from manuscript censuses on microfilm at the State Historical Society of Iowa, Iowa City. Lake Prairie Township was the only township in Iowa in this period (1850–60) in which the Dutch were a clear majority over native American voters.

9. "Influence of the Foreign-Born," see above, pp. 3, 6.

States minister to Austria, although the Senate refused to confirm nomination because he was not a native American.[10]

The early political views of the Pella leader were decidedly Whig. Idolizing Henry Clay while still in the Netherlands, Scholte espoused the Whig cause upon his arrival in Iowa. Like Clay, he possessed a typical Whig attitude toward slavery and the important economic questions of the day. While no admirer of the Peculiar Institution, he condemned abolitionism more than slavery since it embodied the greater threat to the survival of the Union.[11] The American economy, he divined from his study of recent history, "always flourished" under Whig administrations and slumped during Democratic misrule. Moreover, the Whigs were "more respectable and more intellectual," while the Democrats were "poorer and slower-witted citizens." The only explanation for the Democrats' ascendancy in Iowa since the state's birth in 1846, he convinced himself, was the constant influx of "poor folks from other states and from abroad. . . . All the poverty-stricken Irish and Germans that arrive are immediately incorporated by the Democrats who inform them that the Whigs are the wealthy aristocrats and blood-suckers of the common man."[12]

10. Biographical data in Scholte Collection, Central College Archives, Pella, Iowa. A full-length biography—Lubbertus Oostendorp, *H. P. Scholte: Leader of the Secession of 1834 and Founder of Pella* (Franeker, Netherlands, 1964)—is mainly concerned with Scholte's theological ideas and his religious career. But see also Jacob Van Der Zee, *The Hollanders of Iowa* (Iowa City, 1912); Henry S. Lucas, *The Netherlanders in America: Dutch Immigration to the United States and Canada, 1789–1950* (Ann Arbor, 1955); Lenora Scholte, "A Stranger in a Strange Land: Romance in Pella History," *Iowa Journal of History and Politics* 37 (1939): 115–203.

11. Unpublished autobiographical sketch, Scholte Collection. The best expression of Scholte's views on slavery is in his pamphlet, *American Slavery in Reference to the Present Agitation of the United States* (Pella, 1856), p. 5. George M. Stephenson, *A History of American Immigration, 1820–1924* (Boston, 1926), errs in maintaining that Scholte affiliated with the Democrats "shortly after his arrival in this country" (p. 130).

12. A. E. Dudok Bousquet to John Bousquet, January 1, 1851, in "Letters of Abraham Everardus Dudok Bousquet to His Brother, John, 1849–1853," trans. Elizabeth Kempkes, Scholte Collection. For a similar expression of sentiment see Komer Van Stigt, *Geschiedenis van Pella, Iowa, en Omgeving* (Pella, 1897), 2: 81.

Political observers assumed that the Pella Dutch would follow the usual pattern and line up with the other immigrants behind the Democratic standard.[13] But they failed to contend with the Dutch leader and his Whig sympathies. The presidential election of 1852, the first in which the newcomers were eligible to vote,[14] clearly demonstrated the Dominie's power over his immigrant band. Contrary to all expectations, over 80 per cent of the new voters cast Whig ballots, as the table of election statistics indi-

ELECTION STATISTICS,
LAKE PRAIRIE TOWNSHIP, 1851–60

ELECTIONS	WHIG/REPUBLICAN		DEMOCRATIC		KNOW-NOTHING	
	No.	%	No.	%	No.	%
1851 State	9	18.0	41	82.0		
1852 National	89	60.1	59	39.9		
1854 State	52	34.9	97	65.1		
	(FOR)		(AGAINST)			
1855 Prohibition	31	11.1	250	88.9		
1856 State	98	24.7	299	75.3		
1856 National	136	27.7	345	70.3	10	2.0
1857 County						
(spring)	55	20.4	214	79.6		
1857 County (fall)	58	17.1	282	82.9		
1857 State	56	16.3	287	83.7		
1858 County	102[a]	27.8	265	72.2		
1859 State	146	28.6	364	71.4		
1860 National	199	33.9	388	66.1		

SOURCE: Marion Co. newspapers and published county histories.
[a] Includes 66 (18 per cent) Independent votes.

13. "Marion County will shortly become an important part of the Democracy of the State, for, besides being thoroughly democratic ever since her organization, she is about to receive an acquisition of a thousand Hollanders" (Davenport *Gazette,* October 17, 1847).
14. Iowa law prescribed a five-year naturalization period, except with respect to voting in township elections *(Iowa Revised Code,* 1851, pp. 562–63).

cates.[15] The thumping Whig majority can largely be explained in terms of Scholte's influence. The language barrier isolated the Hollanders from their neighbors and rendered unintelligible the newspaper editorials of the day. Therefore, they were completely dependent on the few bilingual leaders like Scholte.[16]

Dutch ethnic antagonism toward native Americans in the immediate locale apparently aided Scholte's effort to indoctrinate his followers with Whig dogmas. Such cultural conflict was by no means unique to Marion County. New York state, originally settled by the Dutch, had long witnessed bitter antagonism between "Yankees" and "Yorkers," as Professors Dixon Ryan Fox and Lee Benson have shown. Fox traced nineteenth-century Yankee-Dutch antagonisms back to the seventeenth century and Benson demonstrated that in the Jacksonian period the Dutch "ranged themselves politically against the Yankees and Negroes— and voted accordingly."[17] The Pella settlers soon fell into this pattern. A bitter county seat contest, for example, evoked native American–Dutch ill-will.[18] Even such seemingly minor concerns as different conceptions of proper farming techniques and ani-

15. In the August, 1851, election, when only native American settlers in Lake Prairie Township participated, the Democrats captured forty-one out of fifty ballots (or 82 per cent), demonstrating a solid Democratic predilection for this group. In the presidential contest of 1852, with ninety-eight additional votes cast, the Democrats gained eighteen and the Whigs eighty. There is no evidence that the native Americans switched parties; and since the Dutch monopolized the land of the township (refusing as a matter of policy to sell to incoming Americans) it is safe to assume that almost all the new voters of 1852 were Hollanders.

16. Historians of the Pella colony were later unable to comprehend the magnitude of Scholte's early power. Failing to consult the township vote, they assumed that the native Americans led their Dutch neighbors into the Democratic fold immediately upon their arrival. See Van Stigt, *Geschiedenis van Pella,* 2: 81–82; Cyrenus Cole, "Pella—A Bit of Holland in America," *Annals of Iowa,* 3d ser. 3 (1898): 257–58; Van Der Zee, *Hollanders of Iowa,* p. 231; Lucas, *Netherlanders in America,* p. 542.

17. Dixon Ryan Fox, *Yankees and Yorkers* (New York, 1940), passim; Lee Benson, *The Concept of Jacksonian Democracy: New York as a Test Case* (Princeton, 1961), p. 301.

18. A. E. Dudok Bousquet to John Bousquet, July 14, 1852, "Letters," Scholte Collection.

mal husbandry, and proper dress and domestic habits of women, proved irritating.[19]

Between the national elections of 1852 and 1856 the political patterns in the state, as well as in Lake Prairie Township, changed radically. In the so-called revolution of 1854 the Iowa Whigs finally overturned the Democratic ascendancy in the state. Among the Dutch, however, the trend was in the opposite direction as Scholte and more than 80 per cent of the Lake Prairie voters now switched to the Democratic party.[20]

Why did most of the Iowa Hollanders defect to the Democrats? Scholte's newspaper editorials perhaps provide the answer. The final plank in the 1854 platform of the Iowa Whigs pledged the party to enact a state liquor prohibition law. Scholte and his people bitterly opposed prohibition, which they viewed as an unwarranted intrusion into their traditional way of life.[21] Comparable to the liquor issue in generating anger and anxiety was the nativist movement then gaining ground in the United States —a crusade against Roman Catholicism in particular but all recent immigrants in general. By 1856 almost one in every ten voters in Marion County supported ex-President Millard Fillmore, candidate of the American (or "Know-Nothing") party, which had pledged itself to limit the political rights of naturalized citizens.[22] The Iowa Democrats, on the other hand, promised in their platform to resist "every attempt to abridge the

19. One Dutchman reported to friends in the Netherlands that American farmers had no regard for their animals and that their women "are terribly lazy." Moreover, he said, American consumption of whiskey was "scandalous" (quoted in Sjoerd Aukes Sipma, *Belangrijke Berigten uit Pella* [Dockum, Netherlands, 1849], pp. 14–15).

20. There were 343 more votes cast in 1856 than in 1852. Of this increase, 286 (or 83.6 per cent) were new Democratic votes and fifty-seven (16.4 per cent) were new Republican votes.

21. Scholte, in one of his early promotional broadsides, asserted that Pella needed a brewery. He added, however, that "I would not encourage a distillery, since I think that an increase in strong beverages would be harmful for the colony" (*Tweede Stem uit Pella* [Bosch, Netherlands, 1848], p. 32).

22. Fillmore collected 225 out of 2,616 votes cast, or 8.6 per cent (*Census of Iowa,* 1869, p. 261).

privilege of becoming citizens," a plank that obviously appealed to the Dutch.[23]

Following their 1854 election victory, the new Whig majority in the Iowa legislature immediately pushed through a proposed constitutional amendment "for the suppresion of intemperance," and in early 1855 submitted it to the electorate for approval.[24] The Dominie campaigned heatedly against the measure. From February through April, 1855, every issue of the Pella *Gazette* devoted itself almost exclusively to this subject. On February 15, editor Scholte printed the bill in its entirety and promised to "disect the corpse" in subsequent editorials. He emphasized that "no man in the State of Iowa" was more strongly opposed to intemperance and the "debasing practice of drunkedness" than he. The "Whig law," however, was "an abomination" which would "subvert . . . the principle of common justice. . . . We [must not] try to effect by law," he reasoned, "what can only be effected by the Gospel."[25]

A counterattack by the prohibition forces was immediate. Levi Leland, popular agent of the Iowa Temperance Society, lectured in Pella on two successive evenings. Besides issuing other inflammatory statements, he charged Scholte with advocating "intemperance and drunkedness" and remarked that judging from the faces he had seen about town the Dutch used too much alcohol.[26] Native Americans throughout central Iowa joined the anti-liquor clamor, specifically attacking Scholte.[27] The Dutch

23. Herbert S. Fairall, ed., *The Iowa City Republican Manual of Iowa Politics* (Iowa City, 1881), p. 36.

24. Dan E. Clark, "History of Liquor Legislation in Iowa, 1846–1861," *Iowa Journal of History and Politics* 6 (1908): 55–87.

25. Pella *Gazette,* March 1, 1855. The only extant file of this newspaper is in the Scholte Collection.

26. Ibid., March 8, 1855.

27. The Eddyville *Free Press,* March 8, 1855, published a bitter three-column editorial, and a Knoxville resident, Charles Burnham, sent Scholte a lenghty letter-to-the-editor which leveled a variety of charges. See Pella *Gazette,* March 8, 1855. Native Americans, of course, harbored similar opinions of their Dutch neighbors. Recalled one pioneer Marion County resident: "The writer will never forget the Hollanders coming into Pella—strange people, at least strange at that time, in their appearance, their strange ways, their forms of dress and language" (Pella *Chronicle,* July 18, 1912).

leader, possibly anticipating real trouble, advised his "Christian soldiers" to "put your trust in God and keep your powder dry."[28]

On March 10, a group of native Americans at Pella, led by Francis A. Barker, warden of the state penitentiary, met and drew up resolutions charging Scholte with "retarding the progress of the temperance cause." Unless the Dutchman capitulated on the issue, they threatened to urge readers to cancel their subscriptions to the *Gazette*. Scholte disdainfully replied that to him "pecuniary profit is a secondary thing."[29]

Politicians from Knoxville, the local county seat, staged the next rally in Pella. William M. Stone, a future Republican governor of Iowa, was the main speaker. He not only charged the Dominie with injuring the anti-liquor movement, but he ridiculed "Father Scholte's" foreign birth and asserted that the Dutch leader was scheming to open a "saloon or doggery" in Pella for the sale of imported liquors. Stone's attack on Scholte was the beginning of a bitter personal vendetta. The feud took the form of a newspaper war, since Stone edited and published the Knoxville *Journal*. More important, Stone's blatant prejudice against foreign-born citizens demonstrated to the Dutch in a most personal way that the emerging Republican party was no place for them, thoroughly permeated as it was with nativism.

The next issue of the *Gazette* contained a four-column letter charging that Scholte merely wanted a law that was harsh on the drinker but lenient on the seller—the former being mostly native Americans and the latter German and Dutch. In reply Scholte labeled this charge "Know-Nothingism" and declared that "it would perhaps be difficult to find ten beer shops kept by Dutchmen; they are commonly Germans. In the cause of temperance," he continued, "it is perfectly wrong to set the Hollanders or Dutchmen on the side of favoring drunken[n]ess, it is just the

28. Pella *Gazette*, March 8, 1855.
29. Ibid., March 29, 1855.

contrary." He ended by demanding that native Americans never lay upon the Netherlanders "what they will never bear."[30]

Scholte's bitterness was now open. He considered all antagonists to be Know-Nothing types and grew overly sensitive to references to his European birth. In one sarcastic editorial he wrote that

> Some men have sneeringly alluded to the foreign birthplace of one of the editors of our Paper. Men tainted with, or immersed in Know-Nothingism have in their native presumption supposed that they had only to open their native babbling instrument, and bellow out their native wind-pipe, and the foreign-born citizen would tremble upon his feet, his hearer would shudder for fear of the native ignoramouses. . . . They are mistaken.[31]

Election day proved Scholte a correct judge of the local temper. Lake Prairie Township rejected the prohibition law by an overwhelming 89 per cent, although state-wide the voters approved the law by a small majority. Nearby Knoxville Township, consisting mainly of native Americans, also rejected prohibition—but only 51.5 to 48.5 per cent. Significantly, on the liquor issue as on the county seat question, Pella and Knoxville were sharply divided.

An important county election that occurred shortly afterwards further increased the Democratic sympathies of the Dutch and prompted Scholte openly to endorse a Democratic slate. The contest pitted the Democratic machine which controlled the courthouse at Knoxville against a slate of ex-Whigs who styled themselves "Independents" but who were in fact incipient Republicans.

A secret midnight political caucus of the Independents at Pella on a July evening in 1855 became a crucial event. Several Dutch Democrats learned of the meeting and immediately declared it to be a Know-Nothing conclave. They strengthened their charge by swearing an affidavit before a Pella justice of the peace. "In our Government," Scholte observed,

30. Ibid., May 17, 1855. The letter was written by S. N. Lindley of Monroe, Jasper County.
31. Ibid., March 29, 1855.

it is unfair, unmanly, and unchristian to so work in the dark, and to shun an open contest with political opponents. . . . Is it a wonder that the people begin to have strange thoughts about men, who . . . resort to such secret policy? No! It is no wonder, true and genuine Democrats must detest such an organization.

The Dutch leader demanded that the Independent candidates pledge under oath that the charge of the affidavit was not true. The aspirants promptly refused, claiming Scholte was merely "the tool of certain party managers, who exult in their power of wielding at their pleasure the votes of our Holland fellow-citizens. . . . We most emphatically deny the right of any man, or set of men in the town of Pella or elsewhere to establish a censorship over the minds of our people." At the same time, the men denied that they were members of the Know-Nothing party. In reply Scholte argued that the candidates, if innocent, should have taken the oath because "the voters have a right to know. . . . To ask citizens of foreign birth to vote for men who are bound to exclude such citizens from office is more than an insult, it is to ask them to commit political suicide."[32]

The Dominie's editorial remarks soon bore fruit. The Dutch remained convinced that the Pella "midnight meeting" provided a clear indication of the linkage of Know-Nothingism and Republicanism. Anyone who claimed otherwise, said Scholte, committed an "open, bare-faced falsehood." From now on, he concluded, the Pella Dutch had a clear-cut choice between the nativist and Democratic parties and the decision would "not be difficult" to make.[33] On election day the colonists flocked to the polls and delivered "a heavy majority" against the Republican ticket.[34]

Following the two emotion-charged elections of 1855, the Dutch and their leader clearly and consistently espoused the Democratic cause. In the local election of April, 1856, the Democrats carried the county by two hundred votes, the largest majority ever. A few days before the election a Knoxville citizen had predicted that Pella did not have enough wooden shoes to gain

32. Ibid., August 2, 1855.
33. Ibid., November 29, 1855.
34. Ibid., August 9, 1855.

the victory. Afterward Scholte reported prophetically: "The men with wooden shoes . . . kicked the Know-Nothing Republicans badly now, and they will do it [again] next August."[35]

As the citizens prepared for the important state election of August 4, 1856, just three months prior to the presidential contest, Scholte worked hard to gain another Democratic victory. He delivered a series of lectures in Pella in the final week of the campaign in both the English and Dutch languages. So forceful were these speeches that an anonymous nativist charged him with driving the citizens of Lake Prairie to the polls "like cattle to the slaughter."[36] Despite the complaint, the great bulk of the Dutch inhabitants applauded Scholte's zeal. On election day, Lake Prairie went Democratic by 75.3 per cent, enough to put the entire county in the Democratic column.

To swell this majority for the Democratic presidential nominee, Scholte inserted three political columns in the weekly *Gazette* in the Dutch language for the duration of the national campaign. Since Republican politicians considered victory in Lake Prairie a prerequisite for gaining Marion County, they countered by importing their most prestigious personality, Governor James W. Grimes. The governor's rhetoric proved of little help. After the Pella rally Scholte observed that Grimes had gained very few converts and that "the demonstration was a total failure." This prediction proved correct. In one of the largest turnouts in the decade Lake Prairie gave Democrat James Buchanan 70.3 per cent of their ballots. Republican John C. Frémont attracted 27.7 per cent and Millard Fillmore of the nativist American party 2 per cent. The increased total vote reflected Scholte's heated editorials in the Dutch language, and his efforts to have all eligible aliens naturalized so as to cast ballots. In response to his urging some fifty Hollanders had appeared at the August session of the district court.[37]

Politically, the years 1857–58 saw little change in Lake Prairie. Citizens balloted five times, with the Democrats consistently

35. Ibid., April 17, 1856.
36. Ibid., August 21, 1856.
37. Ibid., August 21, September 4, 1856.

garnering 70 to 80 per cent of the vote. These impressive majorities placed Marion County well within the Democratic fold, whereas neighboring counties returned strong Republican votes in all these elections.[38] Scholte, however, was beginning to have second thoughts about the Democracy. He blamed President Buchanan for the sectional violence in Kansas and expressed dissatisfaction with the increasingly proslavery complexion of the party.[39]

Disillusionment with the Buchanan administration in no way aided local Republicans, however, for in the spring of 1858 the Republican-controlled legislature proposed an election law which discriminated against naturalized citizens whose ballots were challenged at the polls.[40] Scholte declared the bill an "outrageous affront" which clearly illuminated the nativist bias of the new party. "We did not dream," he wrote,

> that the stupidity and recklessness of our Iowa Nativists would go so far. . . . Native puppyism was never better illustrated. . . . It is a narrow mind indeed that cannot devise a law to preserve the purity of elections without exposing naturalized citizens to repeated insults. The proposed outrage will sink deep into the minds of Hollanders, and they will take care to resent it. . . . The Hollanders were nursed and craddled under the enjoyment of Republican liberties for centuries and . . . will not, without a remonstrance submit to the ignomy of begging for a vote . . . at the pleasure of any Know-Nothing demagogue that may choose to challenge them! . . . But we know also that the day of reckoning is coming. . . . Whenever there is an opportunity . . . the despised wooden shoe nation will be at hand to kick would-be despots and exclusivists into the abyss of political oblivion.[41]

The statistics of the 1858 election, in which Lake Prairie voters gave almost three-fourths of their ballots to the Democrats, prove that Scholte's desire to "kick would-be Republican despots" was

38. Knoxville *Journal,* October 27, 1857, February 2, 1858.
39. Pella *Gazette,* December 3, 24, 1857, January 7, 14, February 11, March 11, 1858.
40. Naturalized citizens would have to swear under oath they were indeed naturalized, then prove it by presenting their papers, and then swear to the veracity of the papers (Iowa *House Journal,* 7th G.A. [1858], p. 233).
41. Pella *Gazette,* February 18, 1858.

shared by most Pella Dutchmen. This was the fourth straight year that the community returned solid Democratic majorities, but their convictions would soon be put to a severe test.

In 1859 the over-confident Democratic party of Marion County was rocked by two jarring blows which all observers predicted would change the political complexion of the county. In April a longtime Democrat, Sebra U. Hammond, editor of the *Democratic Standard* of Knoxville, bolted his party with an editorial blast in which he labeled the local Democratic leadership a "selfish and unprincipled clique."[42] The second jolt came with the defection of the man who was believed to control the crucial Dutch votes of Lake Prairie Township—Henry Scholte. The Dominie had planned his move carefully to obtain maximum newspaper coverage and squeeze out the last ounce of propaganda value. On June 18, the county Democratic convention named the Pella leader as one of its thirteen delegates to the state convention at Des Moines on June 23.[43] To the astonishment of all, however, on June 22 Scholte appeared at the Republican convention (also meeting in the capital city) at the head of the Marion County delegation. Eager to publicize this coup, the state's Republicans honored Scholte with the convention vice-presidency.

Almost every prominent newspaper in Iowa commented on this "Incident at the Convention." The Republican press reported that Scholte had fallen in with a number of Republican delegates on the steamer en route for Des Moines. These partisans supposedly had convinced him of the error of his way. On the morning of the convention, the story went, the Marion County Republicans elected him as a delegate since he had "privately declared himself a Republican, and wanted to have done with modern Democracy forever."[44] The Democratic journals lamely asserted that Scholte had "wandered into the Republican

42. Knoxville *Democratic Standard,* April 5, 14, 1859.

43. Ibid., April 14, 1859; Pella *Gazette,* July 22, 1859.

44. Muscatine *Weekly Journal,* July 1, 1859; *Iowa Citizen* (Des Moines), June 29, July 13, 1859; *Des Moines Valley Whig* (Keokuk), July 4, 1859; Dubuque *Daily Times,* June 30, 1859.

Convention by mistake."[45] Scholte himself ambiguously explained that "the foolish and unreasonable action of the democrats of nominating me as a delegate to their State Convention, against my will and without my knowledge, has accelerated my decision to take an active part in the Republican Convention, where I did belong in reality."[46]

That the Dominie belonged in the Republican fold is obvious from his editorials. Whig even before coming to America, he had adhered to that dying party until convinced that abolitionists and Know-Nothings had captured it. Thereafter, along with many former Whigs, he supported the Buchanan administration "for the purpose of saving the Union."[47] But the President's support of the fraudulent proslavery Kansas constitution and the eruption of violence in the Sunflower State dissillusioned him. Scholte, in short, had joined the Democrats only as a last resort and soon grew disenchanted.

The most important question is not why Scholte changed his party allegiance, however, but whether the Pella Dutch would follow his lead. Opinions of contemporaries varied widely, depending on political viewpoint. Typical of Republican editors was a flat statement that "the accession of Mr. Scholte and those he represents will give us Marion County, with a gain of two Representatives and one Senator."[48] The Knoxville *Journal* editor assured his readers that Scholte's defection was "likely to work a complete revolution in the political character of Marion County. The feeling and conviction that led Scholte to abandon the black democracy, has also induced most of his countrymen to take the same step."[49] Democratic newspapers, on the other hand, predicted that "Mr. Scholte will take with him into the Republican party exactly four men, himself one of the number. And a number of Hollanders, whose dislike to Scholte has placed

45. Dubuque *Express and Herald,* cited in Burlington *Hawk-Eye,* July 30, 1859.

46. Pella *Gazette,* July 22, 1859.

47. Scholte, *American Slavery,* p. 78.

48. Burlington *Hawk-Eye,* June 28, 1859. See also Iowa City *Republican,* July 6, 1859.

49. Cited in Des Moines *Citizen,* July 6, 1859.

them with the Republicans, will now come over to the Democracy."[50] The Oskaloosa editor labeled Scholte "another Benedict Arnold," whose "unprincipled course" would result in a larger majority for the Democracy of Lake Prairie "than they ever yet had."[51] A Netherlander from Muscatine, professing some acquaintance with the Pella colony, also judged that Dutchmen "possess a mind of their own," and could not be "turned by the voice of a traitor. . . . Hollanders are not such a set of fools as to change their political principles at the bidding of a man in whom they have no confidence."[52]

Republican politicians, particularly ex-Governor Grimes and the gubernatorial nominee, Samuel J. Kirkwood, were unwilling to accept this verdict. On July 29, Grimes encouraged Kirkwood to discount rumors that the Republicans were losing strength in Iowa, as just the reverse was true. "I just saw an intelligent man from Marion County," Grimes wrote. "He says the Hollanders are nearly all going with Scholte and that we shall carry the county by as large a maj[ority] as the democrats have usually done it, viz. 200."[53]

Because of the wide publicity given to Scholte's defection, winning the Dutch vote became a matter of prestige for both parties. A Knoxville editor spoke for many when he noted the election was "one of unusual importance because all eyes are turned on Marion."[54] Maintaining the support of the Hollanders was a must for the Democrats. Should the Dutch defect, other Iowa immigrant groups, particularly the Germans, might be influenced to follow suit.

The politicians worked diligently as the gubernatorial election of 1859 approached. Scholte sponsored several Republican caucuses in Lake Prairie, thereby effecting the first permanent

50. Des Moines *State Journal,* reprinted in *Daily Iowa State Democrat* (Davenport), July 3, 1859.

51. Oskaloosa *Times,* July 28, 1859.

52. Davenport *Democrat,* July 6, 1859.

53. "Correspondence of James W. Grimes," *Annals of Iowa,* 3d ser. 22 (1941): 556.

54. Knoxville *Standard,* August 12, 1859.

Republican organization in the township.[55] As in previous contests, the key issues seemed to be ones affecting the Dutch as an ethnic group. Instead of squatter sovereignty, free land, and a transcontinental railroad, local attention centered on the nativist Massachusetts naturalization law and the protection of naturalized Americans abroad.[56] The Massachusetts Act, an expression of eastern Republicanism which other states were being urged to emulate, banned foreign-born citizens from the polls of that state for a minimum of two years after gaining citizenship. Iowa Democrats, citing this issue, argued that for the Dutch to vote Republican was tantamount to "putting the rope around their own necks."[57] Republicans, however, countered by stressing the refusal of Buchanan's Secretary of State, Lewis Cass, to protect naturalized citizens from induction into foreign military service while temporarily visiting their old homelands.[58]

The balloting took place on October 10, 1859. Despite Scholte's strongest urgings, Lake Prairie citizens again cast Democratic votes in undiminished numbers. Over 71 per cent of the total went to the Democrats whereas in 1856, with Scholte campaigning ardently for the Democracy, the party had captured but 70.3 per cent. The turnout in both contests varied little—491 in 1856 to 510 in 1859. Instead of wholesale desertions to the Republicans, therefore, the Democrats actually showed a slight net gain. The Knoxville *Standard* editor was obviously correct when he concluded that "H. P. Scholte does not control the Hollanders."[59]

Scholte's loss of power highlights a significant fact—that the initial power of the ethnic leader to control the ballots of the

55. Pella *Gazette,* August 17, September 14, October 5, 1859.
56. Ibid., September 14, 21, 28, 1859.
57. Ibid., August 17, September 14, October 5, 1859; Knoxville *Standard,* June 14, 1859.
58. Pella *Gazette,* July 22, 1859; Oskaloosa *Times,* July 28, August 4, 1859.
59. Knoxville *Standard,* October 22, 1859. Scholars, entirely ignoring the township vote, have assumed that Scholte's defection had a tremendous influence on his countrymen. See Stephenson, *History of American Immigration,* p. 130; Frank I. Herriott, "Republican Presidential Preliminaries in Iowa, 1859–1860," *Annals of Iowa,* 3d ser. 9 (1910): 253.

immigrant could be short-lived. It is difficult, however, to pin-point when the Dominie's political influence began to decline. A few disgruntled colonists had criticized him and dissentions already had erupted within his church in the early years, and by 1855 a group of "young Turks" had pushed through the municipal incorporation of Pella and taken office against Scholte's wishes.[60] Undoubtedly he had made enemies. Yet this probably had little impact on the outcome of the 1859 election. The voting pattern had been set and, regardless of attitudes toward Scholte, the people continued to think in terms of prohibition and nativism, as the Dominie subsequently complained.[61] No doubt the bitterness of these issues, both associated with Republicanism, still smarted within the rank-and-file. The sophisticated Scholte, his political contacts transcending the local scene, apparently proved to his own satisfaction that the Republican party had purged itself of nativism and that prohibition had become a relatively minor issue. But the mind of the average Dutchman, still largely isolated by the language barrier, could not easily be changed. "I don't bother much about politics," remarked a Dutch carpenter. "I put a Democratic ticket in the box and leave the rest to God."[62]

Seemingly not discouraged, Scholte labored for the Republicans throughout 1860. Returning full of enthusiasm from the national convention in Chicago, he penned splendid tributes to Lincoln and castigated Democratic leaders.[63] He also publicized

60. Sipma, *Belangrijke Berigten*, pp. 27–30; Pella *Gazette*, August 9, 16, 23, 1855; Oostendorp, *H. P. Scholte*, pp. 168–73; "The Garden Square Controversy, April 1835," Scholte Collection.

61. "The Democratic leaders," wrote Scholte, "are continually trying to influence foreign-born citizens . . . [to think] that the Republican party is under the control of the party generally known as the Know-Nothing or Native Americans." This was "slander," he concluded (Pella *Gazette*, January 25, 1860).

62. Quoted in John Scholte Nollen, *Grinnell College* (Iowa City, 1953), p. 249.

63. The Pella *Gazette* succumbed to financial difficulties in February, 1860, and thereafter Scholte published his views in the Burlington *Hawk-Eye* and the Sheboygan (Wis.) *Nieuwsbode*, a Dutch-language paper read by many Pella Hollanders.

the Republican platform planks on the supposedly key issues—no extension of slavery into free territory, a homestead bill, a transcontinental railroad.[64]

The homestead principle, in particular, should have appealed to the Dutch of Marion County. By 1860 most of the vacant land within twenty miles of Pella had been taken up and the community considered itself overcrowded.[65] Colonists were discussing the feasibility of a mass migration to northwest Iowa where government land was still available. The idea of free—or at least cheap—land should have been decisive. Yet Hollanders rejected both the Republican platform and the party's rough-hewn candidate.[66] In November, 1860, Lake Prairie Township awarded Lincoln only 33.9 per cent of its ballots.[67]

Scholte's post-election editorials gave no indication that the Pella colony had repudiated his political leadership; other politicians and editors continued to treat him as an important ethnic leader. Only the township statistics now contradict the assumption by historians that the Dominie continued to deliver the

64. Burlington *Hawk-Eye,* November 3, 1860.

65. Lucas, *Netherlanders in America,* p. 333.

66. There is other evidence in addition to this negative Dutch vote that Buchanan land policy and the homestead issue may have been overemphasized by historians such as Paul W. Gates ("The Homestead Law in Iowa," *Agricultural History* 38 [1964]: 73). Many northwest Iowa newspapers welcomed Buchanan's land sales of 1858–60 and ignored his homestead bill vetoes, while Stephen A. Douglas ran far ahead of his ticket in the same area.

67. Although this was a net Republican gain of 5.3 per cent over the gubernatorial contest of 1859, the Republican increase was likely due to the influx of native Americans attracted to Pella by Central Iowa University, which opened its doors in 1857. A comparison of the 1850 and 1860 population censuses in Lake Prairie Township shows that nearly two-thirds of the non-Dutch newcomers of the fifties were from the New England, Middle Atlantic, and Upper Ohio Valley states. Daniels, "Immigrant Vote," table II, demonstrates that most migrants to Iowa from these areas voted Republican in 1860.

Dutch vote.[68] Scholars might well be cautious of other immigrant spokesmen who professed political leadership of their people.

But there is a larger lesson to be learned from the case of the Pella Dutch. In recent years some students of the ethno-cultural approach to voting—in stressing nativism and prohibition as hidden issues—have implied that immigrants "rationally" defended their Old Country ways of life at the ballot box. The case of the Pella colony, however, suggests that after the first few years sheer political inertia governed—as Scholte himself discovered. Influenced by personal attacks on himself and his followers (attacks that he translated to the rank-and-file), the Dominie created such a staunch tradition of Democratic voting that he was unable to alter it. Hence, while Scholte in 1860 fulminated against Democrats as slave-mongers, as opponents of the Pacific railroad and homestead bills, and as destroyers of the Constitution, the Dutch citizens blithely ignored him and the national issues he propounded and voted against nativism and prohibition—the issues of 1854–56.

One suspects that if Scholte had initially championed slavery abolition and had refrained from emphasizing the Know-Nothing and anti-liquor movements, he might have created a Whig-Republican tradition. Indeed, in failing to gravitate to Lincoln's support in 1860 the Pella Hollanders apparently ran counter to what occurred in Dutch settlements in Michigan, Illinois, and

68. See Stephenson, *History of American Immigration*, p. 131; Van Stigt, *Geschiedenis van Pella*, 3: 44; Van Der Zee, *Hollanders of Iowa*, pp. 229, 408 n. Lucas alone concluded the reverse. "In Pella," he wrote, "the majority still stubbornly adhered to the Democratic position and were suspicious of the abolitionist elements in the new party" *(Netherlanders in America,* p. 562). The "official abstract" of the Marion County vote was printed in the Knoxville *Republican,* November 20, 1860. The only issue of the newspaper for that year known to be extant, it now reposes in the State Historical Society of Iowa.

Wisconsin.[69] Lake Prairie Township, in fact, has been in the Democratic column in *every* national election since 1860 except for the Eisenhower and Kennedy contests.[70] For those who would understand this longtime rejection of the party of Lincoln the peculiar historical circumstances within which the tradition began provide the decisive insight.

Reprinted from *Civil War History* 11 (March 1965): 27–43. One footnote shortened.

69. Lucas, *Netherlanders in America*, pp. 529 ff. Daniels, "Immigrant Vote," table II and appendix A, lists the Iowa Dutch as strong Lincoln supporters. This conclusion resulted from an examination of the Hollanders of Black Oak Township, Mahaska County. Although the largest ethnic group in that township, these Dutch were outnumbered by native American voters by a more than two-to-one margin. It is likely, therefore, that the native Americans, rather than the Dutch, accounted for the heavy Republican vote there. The Black Oak Netherlanders represented a contiguous segment of the Pella colony.

70. In gubernatorial races the township has voted Democratic in every election except in 1930. The Pella city wards, separated from the rural precinct since the turn of the century, remained consistently Democratic until 1928. Since then a two-party trend has emerged. All votes are in the yearly editions of the *Iowa Official Register*.

Paul J. Kleppner received his Ph.D. from the University of Pittsburgh in 1967 and now teaches at Northern Illinois University at De Kalb. By utilizing coefficients of correlation in association with ethnic, religious, and electoral data, he shows that in Pittsburgh German-born voters divided along religious lines as they identified the Republican party with anti-Catholicism. Kleppner thus makes a major contribution to both the methodology and the conceptualization of ethnic political history as he asserts that religious belief rather than ethnicity itself was the prime determinant of electoral choices among the Germans in 1860.

Lincoln and the Immigrant Vote:
A Case of Religious Polarization

PAUL J. KLEPPNER

The role played by German-American voters in the election of Abraham Lincoln to the presidency in 1860 has been a matter of continuing concern to analysts of political history. Impressed with the extent to which leaders of the German-American community espoused the cause of Republicanism, these analysts have attempted to assess the importance of the German vote to the Republican victory. Rarely, however, have they troubled themselves with the more basic problem of determining to what extent German-Americans voted for the Republican candidate. Even more rarely have they made explicit the possibility of polarization within the German-American community along lines other than ethnic.

The present study was designed to test systematically the hypothesis that German-Americans supported the Republican party in 1860. The reasoning implicit in that hypothesis is that the members of the German-American ethnic group were more likely than non-members to possess characteristics making them responsive to the Republican appeal. Therefore, verification of the hypothesis requires a demonstration that German-Americans grouped within the geographic area in question, the city of Pittsburgh, made similar voting decisions.[1]

The systematic testing of this hypothesis will involve three separate lines of argument. First, it will be demonstrated that the Republicans attempted to capture the German-American vote by injecting into the campaign a specific causal factor to which they expected the German-Americans to respond favorably. Second, the hypotheis will be systematically compared with the election and demographic data to determine whether it is empirically verifiable. Third, the generalizations deduced from the empirical data will be explained either in terms of the original hypothesis, or a revision thereof.

I

The Republicans sought to win the vote of the German-Americans. At both the national and local levels they developed appeals specifically designed to attract the support of German-American voters.

At the national level three specific aspects of Republican political action were shaped to this end. In response to the demands of German-Americans at the Republican National Convention, the final platform contained a resolution declaring the party's opposition to any restrictive changes in federal or state naturalization laws.[2] Second, the selection of Lincoln as the

1. Lee Benson, "Research Problems in American Political Historiography," in Mirra Komarovsky, ed., *Common Frontiers of the Social Sciences* (Glencoe, Ill., 1957), pp. 172–75.
2. The resolution in question is the fourteenth one in the Republican platform, in Horace Greeley and John F. Cleveland, eds., *Political Textbook for 1860* (New York, 1860), p. 27. For the debate in the Republican Convention and the reflection of sentiment on the issue see *Proceedings of the First Three Republican Conventions of 1856, 1860 and 1864* (Minneapolis, 1893), pp. 137 ff. For the reactions of the two German-Americans who served on the Committee on Resolutions see Wayne Andrews, ed., *The Autobiography of Carl Schurz* (New York: 1961), p. 158; and Thomas J. McCormack, ed., *Memoirs of Gustave Koerner* (Cedar Rapids, 1909), 2: 74–75 and 87. The resolution which was adopted originated in a pre-convention meeting of the German-American delegates to the convention. See F. I. Herriott, "The Conference in the Deutsches Haus, Chicago, May 14–15, 1860," *Transactions of the Illinois State Historical Society* (1908), pp. 101–94.

presidential nominee was the result of a compromise of divergent interests in which those of the German-American were consciously taken into consideration. While not the first choice of the German-American delegates, Lincoln's availability for the nomination was enhanced by his known antipathy to the antiforeign current which permeated some quarters of the party and by his earlier overt courting of German-American support.[3] Lastly, in the course of the campaign itself, the Republicans enlisted the aid of Carl Schurz, one of the more vocal, if not influential, members of the German-American community. The objective here was to mobilize systematically the German-American vote by employing a German-speaking leader who was assumed to be influential among the non-leadership strata of the German community.[4]

At the grass-roots level, in Pittsburgh, the Republicans took similar steps to attract immigrant voters, and particularly those of German origin. The Republican Executive Committee of Allegheny County established a Naturalization Committee which was "happy to aid in seeking prompt naturalization of Republican voters of foreign birth."[5] The leading Republican newspaper undertook a comprehensive attack designed to project an image of the Democratic party as a nativist organization. Beginning on August 20, 1860, with the blanket accusation that

3. Lincoln's anti-nativist views were clearly expressed in his letter of August 24, 1858, to Joshua F. Speed, in Roy P. Basler, ed., *The Collected Works of Abraham Lincoln* (New Brunswick, N.J., 1955), 2: 320–23. His speech in Belleville, Illinois, in the 1856 campaign in which he lauded the Germans for their enthusiastic support of the cause of freedom was duly noted by leading German-Americans; see McCormack, ed., *Memoirs of Koerner*, 2: 32–33. For Lincoln's pre-convention courting of the German-American vote, which included his purchase of the *Illinois Staatzeitung* as a means of enhancing his political ambitions, see Reinhard H. Luthin, *The First Lincoln Campaign* (Cambridge, Mass., 1944), pp. 83–84; and Carl Wittke, *Refugees of Revolution* (Philadelphia, 1952), p. 214.

4. Andrews, ed., *Schurz Autobiography*, p. 164; Carl Schurz to Abraham Lincoln, May 22, 1860, in Frederic Bancroft, ed., *Speeches, Correspondence and Political Papers of Carl Schurz* (New York, 1913), 1: 116–18; A. Lincoln to Carl Schurz, June 18, 1860, in Basler, ed., *Works of Lincoln*, 4: 78.

5. *Pittsburgh Gazette*, September 18, 21, and 22, 1860. The Democracy in the county had a similar organization; see *Pittsburgh Post*, October 2, 1860.

the Know-Nothings supported Douglas, the *Gazette* proceeded, in chronological sequence, to claim that the anti-foreign orientation of the Democracy was manifest in its attacks on men such as Schurz; that the Democrats in Pennsylvania would emulate Michigan and impose a property qualification on alien voting; and that the Democratic gubernatorial candidate, Henry Foster, had voted in Congress in 1847 against appropriating money for the relief of the starving people of Ireland.[6]

The importance of such a line of attack as a potential means of attracting the immigrant vote can be adduced from the manner in which the opposition responded. The major Democratic organ repeatedly denied the allegations against Foster and pointed out that he had taken the lead in promoting private relief to Ireland.[7] Moreover, borrowing from the opposition's set of tactics, the Democrats countercharged that it was a Republican legislature in Massachusetts which in 1859 had extended the residence period required for naturalization, and that the Republican gubernatorial candidate, Andrew Curtin, was a Know-Nothing.[8] Thus, each party in its appeal to the immigrant vote not only emphasized its own pro-alien feeling, but attempted to apply a nativist image to its opponent.

In addition to this general appeal for the immigrant vote, the Republican party conducted a campaign specifically designed to attract German-American voters. Since Carl Schurz was believed to be influential with the German-American community, he alone among the national figures of the party was paid to conduct a speaking tour of Pennsylvania.[9] To enlist the German-Americans of Pittsburgh into the Republican ranks, Schurz twice spoke in that area. Both on the 10th and 27th of September he appealed to his fellow countrymen to support the

6. *Pittsburgh Gazette,* August 20, September 19 and 27, October 1, 8, and 9, 1860. The *Pittsburgh Daily Dispatch,* another, although less vociferous, Republican organ, added its weight to the charge on October 8, 1860, and to the allegation that the Democrats were anti-foreign because of their attacks against Schurz on September 24–26, 1860.

7. *Pittsburgh Post,* October 2, 8, and 9, 1860.

8. Ibid., October 6, 8, 9, 13, 16, and 27, 1860.

9. Alexander K. McClure, *Old Time Notes of Pennsylvania* (Philadelphia, 1905), 1: 418. McClure managed the state Republican campaign.

Republican party and its candidates, and he assured them that the party was free of Know-Nothing influence.[10] Whether with reason or not, it was felt that Schurz's activities rendered an "inestimable service" to the local Republican cause.[11]

The second aspect of the local Republican attempt to capture the German-American vote was conducted by the German-language newspapers of the city. On varied bases these Republican organs appealed to their German-reading public to support the Lincoln candidacy. Claiming that the Democrats and Stephen Douglas preached one slavery doctrine in the North and another in the South, German-Americans were admonished to remember that only the Republican party favored free soil, free labor, and free homesteads.[12] The *Pittsburger Volksblatt,* lamenting the corruption of the incumbent Democratic administration and the disunity which made it incapable of governing effectively, urged German Democrats to vote for Lincoln and against the administration.[13] In addition to this type of frontal attack, and possibly with the intention of creating a type of band-wagon psychology in the minds of their readers, both German-language organs repeatedly claimed that German-Americans by the hundreds and thousands were deserting the Democratic ranks and enlisting in the cause of Lincoln and the Republican party.[14]

The value of looking at the specific means chosen by a political party to mobilize support in a particular election, and the

10. Unfortunately, no complete text of the Schurz speech remains. At best, only this one line of argument is noted by the following fragmentary accounts: *True Press* (Pittsburgh), *Pittsburgh Evening Chronicle,* and *Pittsburger Volksblatt,* September 11, 1860; and *Pittsburgh Gazette,* September 28, 1860, and *Pittsburger Volksblatt,* October 5, 1860.

11. McClure, *Notes,* 1: 418. With typical modesty Schurz would have heartily agreed with such an evaluation. See his letters to Mrs. Schurz of September 24 and 28, 1860, in Bancroft, ed., *Papers of Schurz,* 1: 160–62.

12. *Freiheits Freund und Pittsburger Courier,* October 2. 5, 8, 12 and 22, and November 6 and 7, 1860.

13. *Pittsburger Volksblatt,* October 16 and 19, 1860.

14. *Freiheits Freund und Pittsburger Beobachter,* August 24, 1860; *Pittsburger Volksblatt,* October 19, 1860; and *Freiheits Freund und Pittsburger Courier,* October 22, 1860. Despite the three separate names, there were but two German-language papers in the city. The *Freiheits Freund und Pittsburger Volksblatt,* October 19, 1860; and *Freiheits Freund und Pittsburger* and thereafter was known as *Freiheits Freund und Pittsburger Courier.*

countermeasures employed by its opposition, lies in the fact that it enables the analyst to determine the viewpoint of practical politicians concerning contemporary voting behavior. In the case of the election of 1860 in Pittsburgh certain inferences emerge quite clearly. In the first place, the very fact that political action was shaped in such a way as to appeal to ethnic groups indicates that contemporary opinion must have held that these groups, or some portions thereof, tended to have common voting attitudes which could be mobilized for particular political parties. The specific nature of political action in Pittsburgh, the fact that the Republicans were anxious to deny the charge of a nativist orientation and to label their opposition as anti-foreign, and the fact that the Democrats sought to pin a similar label on their Republican opponents, indicates that Know-Nothingism was an important causal factor in this locality. One final significant inference can be drawn from the fact that the German-language newspapers claimed that the German-Americans were deserting the Democratic party in favor of Lincoln. Such a claim implies that some portion of the German-Americans had previously voted with the Democratic party. To whichever subdivision of the German-American population in Pittsburgh this inference applied, it seems that they had judged the Know-Nothing issue in favor of the Democratic party.

If these inferences are correct, a precise description of the Know-Nothing or nativist movement in Pittsburgh should also provide a clue to the nature of the prevailing pattern of voting behavior. Whatever the earlier nature of that behavior, a matter which will be dealt with in some detail in the last section of this study, the fact remains that in 1860, at both the national and the grass-roots levels of political action, the Republicans sought to appeal to German-Americans. They injected into the campaign a specific causal factor to which they expected the German-American voters would respond. Whether that hope was stillborn or not can be adequately determined only through a quantitative analysis of the patterns of voting behavior which prevailed in the city of Pittsburgh in the presidential election of 1860.

II

The dramatic shifts in comparative voting strength of the contesting parties and the relatively homogeneous political subdivisions which have been employed by other analysts of the 1860 election as the basis for camparisons and, hence, indicators of voting behavior, were not found in Pittsburgh. Indeed, Pittsburgh voters had but rarely since 1848 given a plurality, and even less frequently a majority, to a Democratic candidate in local, state, or national elections.[15] Ethnocultural heterogeneity was the pattern characteristic of most of the political subdivisions of the city. This factor makes it necessary to take into account the voting behavior of groups other than the one in focus.

The data in Table I provide the basis for the initial steps in attempting to identify those voter groups which supported each of the contesting major parties.

TABLE I

PERCENTAGE DISTRIBUTION OF ELECTORIAL AND
DEMOGRAPHIC DATA: PITTSBURGH, 1860[16]

Ward	Percent Democratic	Percent Republican	Percent German	Percent Irish
1	24.9	69.0	19	25
2	25.4	70.4	11	24

(Continued Next Page)

15. Including the elections of 1860, the Democrats had captured the city only three times in thirty-one elections since 1848. See *Pittsburgh Gazette, Daily Dispatch,* and *Evening Chronicle,* 1848–60.
16. The percentage strength was computed from the official election returns which were published in the *Pittsburgh Gazette,* November 10, 1860. In computing the Democratic percentage strength, the number of votes which Douglas received on the "Fusion" ticket and the "Straight" ticket was totaled. That an addition of the percentages for the two major parties in each of the wards does not total 100% is due to the vote for the Constitutional Union party. The percentage distribution of each of the ethnic groups was derived from the 1860 Census MSS, microfilm. The percentages here deal only with those persons who by reason of age, sex, and race could have qualified to vote. In short, they reflect only the adult white males. For a justification of this approach to the quantification in question see George A. Boeck, "A Historical Note on the Uses of the Census Returns," *Mid-America* 44 (January 1962): 46–50.

TABLE I (Continued)

Ward	Percent Democratic	Percent Republican	Percent German	Percent Irish
3	42.3	55.6	23	41
4	26.9	70.8	14	26
5	37.8	61.5	47	26
6	27.1	70.3	16	36
7	27.2	71.6	26	30
8	24.7	73.5	30	27
9	26.0	69.9	18	24

While the Democrats did not succeed in capturing a single ward, their greatest percentage strength was registered in the third and fifth wards, in that order. The Republican party found its greatest percentage strength in the eighth and seventh wards, wards which ranked second and third, respectively, in the percentage of German-Americans of the total of the potentially eligible voters who resided there. On the other hand, the fifth ward, which was second in Democratic percentage strength and eighth in Republican percentage strength, was the most heavily German ward. The data provide still another suggestive fact: The most heavily Irish ward, the third, was also the most heavily Democratic ward, although the second-ranking Irish ward, the sixth, was the third-ranking Republican ward.

The distribution of both the vote and the demographic characteristics is such that this "eye-inspection" is inadequate to isolate the prevailing patterns. Some summary device is needed to enable the analyst to make a generalization concerning the relationship between the vote and the characteristics in point. For this purpose the Pearsonian coefficient of correlation has been used. The relationships between the vote and the demographic characteristics are presented in Table II.

Taken in isolation, the correlations indicate a negative relationship between high values of the Republican vote and high

TABLE II
CORRELATIONS BETWEEN PARTY PERCENTAGE STRENGTH AND PERCENTAGE DISTRIBUTION OF ETHNOCULTURAL GROUPS[17]

	Percent Republican	Percent Democratic
Percent German	−.346	+.511
Percent Irish	−.547	+.602

values of German and Irish concentration.[18] Yet two facts are significant. First, the magnitude of the correlations is not such as to account for a major proportion of the variability of the vote. Second, in particular cases the Republicans fared quite well in voting units with high concentrations of Germans and Irish.

In light of these observations it is entirely conceivable that the relatively high negative correlations between the Republican vote and the demographic characteristics reflect a spurious rather than an explanative relationship. To test this possibility an additional variable was introduced, *viz.*, religious orientation.

The demography of religious groups poses unique problems for the historical political analyst. Frequently either the necessary data are not available, or they are not reported in terms of political divisions. For the analyst the problem is to use what data are available to estimate the *relative* strength of religious groups within the political divisions being studied. In the hope that the

17. For the computation and interpretation of the Pearsonian correlation coefficient see Hubert M. Blalock, Jr., *Social Statistics* (New York, 1960), pp. 273–325 ;and Mordecai Ezekiel and Karl A. Fox, *Methods of Correlation and Regression Analysis: Linear and Curvilinear,* 3d ed. (New York, 1959), pp. 434–77. It is important that historians recognize the ways in which statistics can be useful, but it is equally important that they be aware of what statistics *cannot* do. In the case in point, a correlation coefficient, as a statistical procedure, can never tell anything about causality.

18. For the problems which inhere in correlational analysis of this type see W. S. Robinson, "Ecological Correlations and the Behavior of Individuals," *American Sociological Review* 15 (1950): 351–57; and especially see Paul F. Lazarsfeld and Herbert Menzel, "On the Relation between Individual and Collective Properties," in Amitai Etzioni, ed., *Complex Organizations: A Sociological Reader* (New York, 1961), pp. 422–40.

method devised for the present study can be utilized by other analysts, it will be explained in some detail.

In its bare outlines the task was one of locating each church, determining the number of potentially eligible voters who attended, and locating their residences. The initial portion of the task, locating each church, posed no particular problem. Using a city directory which gave the address of each church in the city, and a street map of the city on which the ward boundaries were marked, it was a simple task to locate each church in terms of the political division in which it was located.[19]

The next step was to determine the size of each church's congregation. For this purpose Catholic church membership was used as a point of reference since the records for that church were more complete than those for the other large denominations. In addition, while there were only five Catholic churches, the membership of each was far greater than that of the membership of any single Protestant church. Unfortunately, the Catholic parish membership figures did not cover the year 1860. The first year for which precise parish membership figures were available was 1877.[20] These figures were used as the basis for an interpolation through which the 1860 membership could be estimated. Using the membership for a single Catholic church in 1877, it was compared to the total population of the diocese for that year.[21] In this way the percentage of Catholics of the diocese who were members of a single given church could be derived. Assuming a certain degree of stability in the proportion, this percentage was applied to the total number of Catholics who lived in the diocese in 1860. Thus a fairly reasonable approximation could

19. The church addresses were found in George T. Thurston, comp., *Directory of Pittsburgh and Vicinity for 1859–60* (Pittsburgh, 1859).

20. The membership figures were obtained from the Parochial Reports for the Year 1877, MSS in the Archives of the Diocese of Pittsburgh.

21. The total number of Catholics in the diocese in 1877 is reported in the *Catholic Almanac and Directory* (Baltimore, 1877).

be made of the membership of each Catholic church in the diocese in 1860.[22]

The fact that an individual attended a church in one particular ward does not indicate, especially in a compact geographic area, that the person lived and voted in the same ward. Therefore, the next step was to determine the ward distribution of the membership of each of the Catholic churches involved. For this purpose lists were compiled of the names of Catholic laymen who could be identified by parish affiliation.[23] These names were checked against a city directory, and the addresses obtained plotted on a street-ward map.[24] Assuming that the names involved represented a reasonably random cross-section of that parish's membership, whatever percentage of the known names was found to reside in a given ward was predicated for the total membership of the parish. Thus, since 12% of the known members of St. Paul's Cathedral lived in the first ward, it was assumed that 12% of the total church membership lived in that ward. Following the same pattern for each of the churches, it was possible to reconstruct the religious composition of each of the wards in terms of the number of Catholics who resided there.

The number of Catholics in each ward then had to be expressed in terms of potentially eligible voters. The ratio between the number of potentially eligible voters and the total population of each ward was predicated for the Catholic population of that ward to derive this estimate. In turn, the number of potentially eligible Catholic voters in each ward was then classified according to ethnic group membership. This classification was facilitated

22. That the proportion was reasonably constant is a judgment made following an examination of a wide range of qualitative sources. In addition the validity of the method was confirmed by comparing the derived figures with the actual 1860 membership figures for two of the five churches. For the latter figures see Fr. Bernhard Beck, *Goldenes Jubiläum des Wirkens der Redemptoristenväter an der St. Philomena Kirche in Pittsburg und Umgegend* (Maryland, 1889), and *Brochure Commemorating the Diamond Jubilee of Holy Trinity Church* (N.p., 1932).

23. The names were obtained from the diocesan newspaper, the *Catholic* (Pittsburgh), 1859 and 1860.

24. George H. Thurston, comp., *Directory of Pittsburgh and Allegheny Cities and the Adjoining Boroughs . . . for 1860–61* (Pittsburgh, 1860).

by the fact that four of the five were nationality parishes.[25] By using this procedure, the Catholic population of each ward, as well as the number of German and Irish Catholics in each ward, could be estimated with a reasonable degree of accuracy.

For purposes of this analysis it was adequate to categorize the population as Catholic or Protestant, with the latter term connoting a frame of mind rather than a specific denominational affiliation. By using the figures for the Catholic population a similar quantification of the remainder of the voting population could easily be made.[26]

The product of this procedure, the quantification of ethnic groups in terms of their religious attitudes, is presented in Table III.

TABLE III

Distribution of Ethnic Groups
by Religious Attitudes

Ward	German Population		Irish Population		Total Population	
	% Cath.	% Prot.	% Cath.	% Prot.	% Cath.	% Prot.
1	10	90	55	45	20	80
2	15	85	65	35	20	80
3	35	65	75	25	40	60
4	75	25	70	30	30	70
5	75	25	30	70	45	55
6	30	70	55	45	25	75
7	5	95	35	65	15	85
8	5	95	15	85	10	90
9	5	95	45	55	15	85

25. The fifth, St. Paul's Cathedral, while not a nationality parish, was almost exclusively Irish.

26. As a check against the accuracy of the procedure, the measurements and impressions thus derived were verified against as broad a range of useful sources as was available. Data for Baptist, Presbyterian, Methodist, and Lutheran churches were obtained. In some cases precise data were available; in other instances membership figures could be reconstructed or estimated from congregational and denominational histories, records, minutes, and anniversary pamphlets and brochures.

The data indicate that some 75% of the German-American voters in the fifth ward, the second most heavily Democratic ward, were Catholics; whereas in the most heavily Republican wards, the seventh and eighth, the German-American voters were only 5% Catholic. If the religious orientation of the total population is considered, it can be seen that wards three and five, which registered the heaviest Democratic percentage strength, were the most strongly Catholic; and the strongest Republican wards were among the most heavily non-Catholic wards in the city.

The correlations between the vote and the religious variable, presented in Table IV, established the same type of pattern.[27]

TABLE IV

CORRELATIONS BETWEEN PARTY PERCENTAGE STRENGTH
AND PERCENTAGE DISTRIBUTION OF RELIGIOUS GROUPS

	Percent Republican	Percent Democratic
Percent German Catholic	−.454	+.496
Percent German Protestant	+.454	−.496
Percent Irish Catholic	−.225	+.141
Percent Irish Protestant	+.225	−.141
Percent Total Catholic	−.854	+.855
Percent Total Protestant	+.854	−.855

The original hypothesis being tested was that German-Americans supported the Republican party in 1860. To verify the hypothesis required a demonstration that German-Americans made similar voting decisions. The data suggest that German-American voters in Pittsburgh did *not* make similar voting decisions. Rather they suggest that the voting behavior of the German immigrant group, as well as that of the Irish, tended to conform to religious rather than purely ethnic lines.

27. For the ethnic group in focus, the German-Americans, the coefficient of partial correlation makes the point even clearer. The coefficient of partial correlation between the Republican vote and percent German, holding percent Protestant constant, is −.445.

The empirical data suggest an alternative hypothesis to describe the central tendency of group voting behavior in Pittsburgh in 1860: German-American and Irish-American Protestants were more likely to vote for Lincoln than were their fellow countrymen of the Roman Catholic faith. Similar voting decisions seem to have been made not by each of the ethnic groups collectively, but by specific subdivisions within each. The polarization of the vote cannot be explained in terms of ethnic responses, but in terms of differences in religious attitudes within each group. The analytical task at this point is to explain how religious attitudes were able to serve as an effective counterpressure to ethnic factors.

III

The earlier examination of the nature of political action by each of the contesting parties in Pittsburgh in 1860 permitted the deduction of a series of inferences which, taken collectively, were suggestive of the voting behavior of ethnic groups. Briefly, these inferences indicated that practicing politicians believed that ethnic groups, or some particular subdivisions thereof, responded collectively to specific causal factors. The Know-Nothing movement seemed to be one of these factors. It also appeared that prior to 1860 some portion of the German-American ethnic group had voted with the Democratic party. This implied that at least some of the Germans had judged the Democratic party to be less nativist than its opposition.

From the foregoing argument it appears that an examination of Know-Nothingism in Pittsburgh might provide an important clue to the voting behavior of the specific subgroups of the ethnic communities. If the patterns revealed here correspond to those derived from the quantified statistical analysis of the election results, the role of religious attitudes as determinants of voting behavior will become clearer.

The impetus behind the Know-Nothing movement in Pittsburgh was not so much a generally anti-immigrant sentiment as it was an anti-Catholic attitude. Feeling that their traditional values were being threatened by what they conceived to be the sinister machinations of Romanism, Protestants mobilized to resist the encroachments of the Papists. In Pittsburgh, the support of societies such as the Protestant Association, composed largely of Irish and native Protestants, and the Muscovies, predominantly German Protestants, gave an additional anti-Catholic flavor to Know-Nothingism.[28] In reaction, the Catholics who were thus under attack came to oppose the Know-Nothing movement. This social and religious conflict assumed political salience because of the identity of the Know-Nothings with a major portion of the Whig party. With Know-Nothings and numerous Whigs in tacit alliance, the anti-Know-Nothings, particularly Catholics, supported the opposition party, the Democrats.[29]

A further indication that the Know-Nothings drew the bulk of their support from the ranks of the Whigs can be adduced from the election statistics for the period 1848 to 1854. While the percentage strength of the Democratic party in the city

28. Ray Allen Billington, *The Protestant Crusade, 1800–1860* (New York, 1952), p. 129, and "Maria Monk and Her Influence," *Catholic Historical Review* 22 (October 1936): 283–96; and Carl Wittke, *The Irish in America* (Baton Rouge, 1956), pp. 117–18. For the activities of the Protestant Association in Pittsburgh see Billington, *Protestant Crusade*, pp. 167 and 184; *Pittsburgh Daily Dispatch*, January 4 and December 14, 1855; and *Pittsburgh Gazette*, September 12, 1854, and September 26, 1855. For the role of the Muscovies see *Pittsburgh Daily Dispatch*, January 4, 9, and 11, 1855; *Pittsburgh Gazette*, September 26, 1855; and *Pittsburgh Post*, September 27, 1855.

29. This statement is not meant to imply that Catholic support for the Democrats originated in response to Know-Nothingism. The view that Catholics had earlier supported the Democratic party and that, therefore, the anti-Catholics were led to another political party in order to express their opposition to Romanism is not in issue at this point. Whatever the temporal order of the causative sequence, the fact remains that Catholics, in Pittsburgh, to the extent that they were anti-Know-Nothings, supported the Democratic party. For a general discussion of this Catholic reaction see Helen Dorothy English, "Political Background and Republicanization of Allegheny County, 1854–56" Master's diss., University of Pittsburgh, 1936), p. 79; Warren F. Hewitt, "The Know-Nothing Party in Pennsylvania," *Pennsylvania History* 2 (April, 1935): 75–76. For specific indications of Catholic support of the Democracy in opposition to the Whig–Know-Nothing faction in particular elections, see *Dispatch*, January 4, 9, and 11, 1855; *Gazette*, October 9, 1852, September 12 and 25, 1854, October 3, 4, and 6, 1854, January 4 and 9, 1855, September 26, 1855, October 11, 1855; *Post*, October 3 and 5, 1848, November 6, 1848, September 23 and 28, 1852, October 2, 1852, September 8, 12, 15, and 21, 1854, October 2, 7, 10, 1854, September 27, 1855, and January 4, 1856.

showed a marked degree of relative stability, that of the Whigs varied in an inverse proportion to the strength of the Know-Nothings. For example, while the correlation between the Democratic mayoralty vote in 1849 and 1850 is +.717, the Whig vote in the same two contests correlates at only +.159. But the gains made by the nativist candidate in the 1850 contest correlate at +.846 with the Whig losses, and at −.959 with changes in the Democratic vote.[30] Moreover, it was commonly accepted by contemporary observers, of all shades of partisanship, that such a relationship existed between the Whig and Know-Nothing organizations.[31]

This tendency of Catholics to gravitate toward the Democratic party can be further explained in terms of the presence within the Whig–Know-Nothing entente of three distinct strains of thought which were anathema to the average Papist. The fusion of temperance agitation, Sabbatarianism, and abolitionism with the overt anti-Romanism of the Whig–Know-Nothing attitude intensified the antipathy of Catholics and thereby reinforced their proclivity to support the Democratic party.[32]

From its inception the temperance movement in Pittsburgh had very strong support from religious groups. The preponderance of this support emanated from the Protestant portions of

30. This is not an isolated instance but describes the central tendency derived from a correlational analysis of party strength at every successive pair of elections over the period 1848 to 1854. For the elections in point see *Pittsburgh Gazette* and *Pittsburgh Daily Dispatch,* 1848–54.

31. *Pittsburgh Daily Dispatch,* January 4, 9, 11, 1855; *Pittsburgh Gazette,* September 12 and 25, 1854, October 4 and 6, 1854, January 9, 1855, September 26, 1855, and October 11, 1855; *Pittsburgh Post,* October 3 and 5, 1848, September 12, 15, and 21, 1854, October 2, 7, 10, 1854, September 27, 1855, and January 4, 1856.

32. Whether the anti-Romanism of the Whig–Know-Nothing faction was an overt and quantifiable manifestation of the divergence of Protestant and Catholic attitudes on these three issues, or was the product of a fear of Papal encroachments existing independently, but reinforced by the conflicts over these problems, remains a question whose resolution does not materially affect the substance of this analysis. It suffices here to accept the consensus that there was a Protestant fear of Catholicism and that there was a divergence of attitudes between the two groups over the three aforementioned issues.

the population, and particularly from among the Presbyterians.[33] While the spiritual leader of the Roman Catholic Diocese of Pittsburgh, Bishop Michael O'Connor, had supported the temperance movement prior to his resignation, his endorsement did not exert a sufficient degree of counter-pressure against the ethnocultural characteristics of his German and Irish Catholic flock to engender any wide-spread support for the movement among the Catholic laity.[34] As a consequence, the temperance issue remained a divisive one between Catholics and those portions of the Protestant population of the city which supported it. The projection of this issue into the realm of political action, its advocacy by the Whigs and then the Know-Nothings, and the failure of the Democratic party to advance the temperance cause further reinforced Catholic support of the Democracy.[35]

33. John N. Boucher, ed., *A Century and a Half of Pittsburgh and Her People* (N.p., 1908), 1: 526; Hare, "The Presbyterian Church in Pittsburgh," pp. 104–5; William W. McKinney, *Early Pittsburgh Presbyterianism* (Pittsburgh, 1938), p. 449; and Lloyd L. Spohnholtz, "Pittsburgh and Temperance, 1830–1854," *Western Pennsylvania Historical Magazine* 46 (October 1963), p. 378. For an indication of the attitude of one of the major temperance movement leaders see Jane Grey Swisshelm, *Half a Century*, 2d ed. (Chicago, 1880), pp. 148–49.

34. Colman J. Barry, *The Catholic Church and German Americans* (Milwaukee, 1953), p. 17; and the letter of Bishop Michael O'Connor to Dr. Cullen, January 10, 1842, quoted in Paul E. Campbell, "The First Bishop of Pittsburgh," in *Catholic Pittsburgh's One Hundred Years* (Chicago, 1943), p. 35. The view that the temperance movement never gained a considerable degree of support among the Catholic laity of the area is derived from a knowledge of the ethnocultural characteristics of the groups in question, from the continued Protestant opposition to Catholics on the issue, and from the fact that those geographic areas in Pittsburgh which were most heavily Catholic also contained the largest number of retail liquor outlets and taverns whose annual volume of business in 1860 was, on the average, far greater than that of such establishments in any other area of the city; see *Pittsburgh Daily Dispatch*, November 16, 1860.

35. The Catholic-Protestant dichotomy which underlay the temperance issue and the political effect of same was admitted by contemporary observers. See *Pittsburgh Daily Dispatch*, November 7, 1849, January 9, September 15, and October 9, 1855; *Pittsburgh Gazette*, October 15, 1852, September 18, 1854, January 4 and 9, October 11 and 15, 1855; and *Pittsburgh Post*, September 8, 1854.

The issues of Sabbatarianism and abolitionism had a somewhat similarly divisive impact in both religion and politics. The evangelical Protestant attitude toward Sabbath observance, replete with its puritanical implications, was seen by German and Irish Catholics as modern Phariseeism.[36] Even more markedly did the abolition issue produce a dichotomy along religious lines within the German and Irish ethnic groups. Despite the fact that their precise attitudes on the problem of effective remedial action reflected a relatively wide range of opinions, Protestant Germans and Irish could agree that slavery was an intrinsic evil whose presence was a blight upon the social order.[37] The Catholic consensus that slavery was not necessarily evil, that it was not intrinsically opposed to divine or natural law, led to the view among anti-slavery forces that Catholics were in alliance with the Southern Slave Power. That this generalization was both logically and empirically fallacious does not alter the fact that it was the attitude generally advanced by the anti-slavery groups in Pittsburgh. The maintenance of such an attitude by these groups, and the responsive attitude of Catholics that abolitionists were enemies of religion, served to exacerbate the tensions be-

36. The *Catholic* (Pittsburgh), October 22, 1859. The attitude of Irish Protestants on this issue led to frequent charges by the *Catholic* of a growing fanaticism and hysteria among the ranks of that group; see the editorials of October 15, 1859, September 15, 22, and 29, 1860. The *Pittsburgh Gazette*, a virulently anti-Catholic paper, identified Know-Nothingism with Sabbatarianism, January 9, 1855.

37. Boucher, ed., *Pittsburgh and Her People*, 1: 542; Ernest Bruncken, "German Political Refugees in the United States during the Period from 1815–1860," *Deutsch-Amerikanische Geschichtsblätter* 4 (January 1904), p. 45; Hare, "Pittsburgh Presbyterianism," pp. 140, 154–55, and 269; George F. Swetnam, "The Growing Edge of Conscience," in William W. McKinney, ed., *The Presbyterian Valley* (Pittsburgh, 1958), pp. 285–86; Carl August Voss, *Gedenkschrift zur Einhundertfünfundzwanzigjährigen Jubel-Feier der Deutschen Ev. Prot. Gemeinde zu Pittsburgh, Pennsylvania* (Pittsburgh, 1907), pp. 98–99.

tween the groups and to intensify the religious polarization of political allegiances.[38]

Viewed in perspective, it is obvious that not all of those who supported the Whig–Know-Nothing entente did so for the same reasons. Nor did all Protestant religious groups share precisely the same attitudes on the issues of temperance, Sabbatarianism, and abolitionism. The consensus of the Protestant Irish seemed to have been in favor of temperance and Sabbatarianism and to have been opposed to slavery. However, with the exception of the New Light and Cumberland Presbyterians, they were not rabid abolitionists. The Protestant Germans, while not sharing the pro-temperance and Sabbatarian ideas of their Irish counterparts, were abolitionist in their orientation. The significant fact which emerges is that Irish and German Catholics favored neither temperance, nor Sabbatarianism, nor any shade of abolitionism.

Taken independently these issues might not seem to be able to explain the polarization of the Irish and German ethnic groups along religious lines. The fact is, however, that the issues were not taken independently by contemporaries, but were viewed collectively and within the broad context of an anti-Catholic sentiment which permeated the Protestant mentality. The fact that the Know-Nothing movements can be seen from the present perspective as an agglomeration of disparate and even contradictory interests in no way affects the fact that it was seen in the decade of the 1850's, both by its adherents and its opponents, as a vehicle for the expression of an anti-Catholic sentiment. While

38. John Tracy Ellis, *American Catholicism* (Chicago, 1956), p. 87; Madeleine Hooke Rice, *American Catholic Opinion in the Slavery Controversy* (New York, 1944), pp. 109, 153–55, and 157; C. Maxwell Myers, "The Rise of the Republican Party in Pennsylvania: 1854–1860" (Ph.D. diss., University of Pittsburgh, 1940), pp. 3 30–1. For a specific indication of a Pittsburgh abolitionist's reaction to the Catholic attitude, see Swisshelm, *Half a Century*, pp. 150–51. The identification of the anti-slavery groups with the anti-Catholic forces was made by the *Pittsburgh Gazette*, October 10, 1848, and January 9, 1854. For some indication of the nature of anti-slavery sentiment in this area, see B. E. Browne to John Covode, May 12, 1858, and J. J. Coffey to Covode, August 23, 1854, in Covode MSS, Library of the Historical Society of Western Pennsylvania.

on a given issue the Know-Nothing appeal might otherwise have been able to elicit an ethnic group response, the fact that the issues could not be so sharply delineated, that they were fused into a type of primitivistic ideology which was anti-Catholic in its essential orientation, resulted in the view of contemporaries that the movement was in substance an anti-Catholic one. Perceived in these terms, on no basis could the Know-Nothing movement elicit a favorable response from Catholics. Since the Democratic party favored neither temperance, Sabbatarianism, nor abolitionism, it was the logical vehicle of political expression for those who could on no basis find solace in the ranks of the Know-Nothings. Since the latter group was confined to Catholics, it follows that they formed a core of Democratic support which was augmented from time to time by other groups in response to the nature and intensity of the specific issue in any particular Democratic–Know-Nothing contest.

The emergence of a new political organization, the Republican party, in the later 1850's, might be expected to have produced a reorientation of voting behavior on the local scene. Closer scrutiny of the composition of that party explains why such was not the case.

The nascent Republican party of the 1850's should not be viewed as an organization which arose solely in response to the further westward expansion of slavery augured by the passage of the Kansas-Nebraska legislation. Rather it was born of an amalgamation of puritanical Protestantism with abolitionism. It is only in such terms that its continuity with the earlier expressions of the ideology of moral trusteeship can be perceived. The rise of the Republican party did not represent the advent of new forces of social protest, but the reorganization and consolidation of old ones.[39]

This reorganization of the old forces of social protest into a new vehicle of political expression was not confined to the national level. In Pittsburgh temperance supporters, Sabba-

39. Clifford S. Griffin, *Their Brothers' Keepers* (New Brunswick, N.J., 1960), passim.

tarians, and abolitionists united behind the new party.[40] Heir to the same bases of social support as those of the Know-Nothing movement, the Republican party in Pittsburgh could not have been expected to alter drastically the patterns of voting behavior which had already been well defined. If German and Irish Catholics had opposed Know-Nothingism, to the extent that the Republican party was identified with that movement they would oppose the new party as well. While the divisive issues of the previous decade were not dwelt upon in the local campaign, the antagonisms that had been aroused by them remained and continued to influence voting behavior. Catholics and Protestants continued to view each other as negative reference groups whose values, beliefs, and attitudes were in diametric opposition.[41] The most logical manner for Catholics, regardless of their ethnic group membership, to express their hostility to the Protestant mentality with which they found the Republican party imbued was to persist in their traditional patterns of voting behavior, i.e., to persist in their support of the Democracy.

Having identified the nature of the Know-Nothing movement, it is now possible to reexamine the local election of 1860 to determine what practical politicians felt were the causes of group voting behavior. The fact that both Democrats and Republicans vied with one another to pin the Know-Nothing label on their opposition suggests an awareness that Know-Nothingism did fluence voting behavior.[42] Since Know-Nothingism was essentially an anti-Catholic movement, the attempt here must have been to attract a Catholic vote. Similarly, the Democratic at-

40. Even its most ardent partisans admitted the nature of the party composition. See William H. Egle, *Andrew Gregg Curtin* (Philadelphia, 1895), p. 35; McClure, *Notes,* 1: 259, and *Lincoln and Men of War Times* (Philadelphia, 1962), p. 47; Swisshelm, *Half a Century,* pp. 158–62; and J. G. McQuaide to J. J. Covode, August 11, 1858, in Covode MSS.

41. For the negative reference group concept see Robert K. Merton, *Social Theory and Social Structure,* rev. ed. (Glencoe, Ill., 1963), pp. 225–386. For an illustration of the use of the concept in explaining voting behavior see Lee Benson, *The Concept of Jacksonian Democracy* (Princeton, 1961), pp. 162–63, 279–80, and 322–26.

42. *Pittsburgh Gazette,* October 8 and 9, 1860; *Pittsburgh Post,* October 6, 9, 16 and 27, 1860; and *Freiheits Freund und Pittsburger Courier,* October 6, 1860.

tacks against Carl Schurz, attacks in which he was labeled a "Red Republican infidel," an abolitionist, and a "German Jacobin," suggest that his personal and political views must have aroused a measure of opposition among some segment of the German-American voters.[43] The fact that the *Pittsburger Volksblatt*, a paper which otherwise supported the Republican party, refused to endorse the Republican gubernatorial candidate, Andrew Curtin, because of his past affiliations with the Know-Nothing movement would imply that some segment of the German-speaking population was still aroused by the Know-Nothing factor.[44] Since Know-Nothingism was manifestly an anti-Catholic phenomenon, it would appear that the German element so aroused was a Catholic-German element. Furthermore, the acrimonious public controversy between the official organ of the Catholic diocese and one of the leading Presbyterian ministers of the city, Dr. Melancthon W. Jacobus, leads to the inference that old religious antagonisms still persisted and that contemporaries were indeed aware that they did.[45]

The tactical approach of the leading Republican newspaper in the city, the *Gazette*, largely centered on the religious question. Initially the *Gazette* sought to identify the Democrats with Catholicism. It charged that a leading Catholic publication and the "American primate" were supporting Douglas. These facts it explained on the basis that Douglas's wife was a Catholic. One week later, on August 28, 1860, the *Gazette* explained the Catholic hierarchy's open support of Douglas on the grounds that he himself was a Catholic. At the same time it laid bare the allegation that Catholic priests in Pennsylvania were openly supporting the Democratic gubernatorial candidate. To allay the Democratic countercharges that Andrew Curtin was a Catho-

43. *Pittsburgh Post*, October 22, 24, 25, and 26, 1860.
44. *Pittsburger Volksblatt*, September 12 and 28, and October 5, 1860.
45. For Dr. Jacobus's anti-Catholic views see *Pittsburgh Daily Dispatch*, December 28, 1859, and January 10, 1860. The *Catholic* (Pittsburgh) pointedly took issue with Jacobus in its editorials of December 3 and 17, 1859, January 7, 14, and 28, 1860, February 4, 11, and 18, 1860, and June 9, 1860. Moreover, the *Catholic* pointed out, and Dr. Jacobus admitted, that he had used his pulpit to propagate his views.

lic, the *Gazette* assured its readers that "he comes of a good Presbyterian family."[46]

Viewing such an approach as a whole, it appears that the *Gazette,* and therefore the party for which it was the semi-official organ, recognized the fact that anti-Catholicism played a role in determining voting behavior. Its attempts to pin a Catholic identification on the Democrats, and to deny such for the Republicans, were aimed at reinforcing traditional party loyalties. At the same time, its denial of a Know-Nothing orientation and its charge that Democrats were supporters of that movement represented an effort to attract Catholic voters to the Republican banner. Whatever might be said of the internal consistency of this tactical approach, it implicitly admits the belief in a Catholic versus anti-Catholic voter response. The nature of the Democratic attacks against Schurz, coupled with the *Pittsburger Volksblatt*'s concern with the Know-Nothing issue, implies that the portion of the German population aroused by Know-Nothingism was roughly identical with that portion of it which the Democrats hoped would respond favorably to their lines of reasoning. In short, the Germans aroused by Know-Nothingism were Catholic Germans.

IV

This study was designed to test the hypothesis that the German-American voters in Pittsburgh supported the cause of the Republican party in 1860. The verification of the hypothesis required a demonstration that Germans voted in similar manner. But the data failed to verify the hypothesis. Instead they suggested the alternative proposition that both German and Irish-Americans voted in terms of religious distinctions within each group.

46. *Pittsburgh Gazette,* July 2, August 21 and 28, and October 3 and 4, 1860. The Catholic paper which was alleged to be a Douglas supporter was the *Boston Pilot,* while Archbishop John Hughes was identified as the American Primate. Confirmation that the charge that Curtin was a Catholic was upsetting to the Republicans can be found in McClure, *Notes,* 1: 421. For the reaction to the *Gazette*'s line of attack see the *Catholic,* September 1, 8, and 15, 1860.

The specific causal factor responsible for this polarization of voting behavior along religious, rather than ethnic, lines was found in the Know-Nothing movement. This latter phenomenon, supported by temperance agitators, Sabbatarians, and abolitionists, was imbued with an anti-Catholic orientation. Therefore, regardless of their ethnic group membership, Know-Nothingism elicited a negative response from Catholic voters. The reorganization of these Know-Nothing elements into a new political organization meant that the Republican party assumed a negative reference group characteristic *vis-à-vis* Catholic voters. The cumulative effect of the negative reference group reaction was to encourage a continuation of the polarization of German-American voting behavior into Catholic-Democratic and Protestant-Republican subdivisions.

Reprinted from *Mid-America* 48 (July 1966): 176–95. A few footnotes have been omitted or shortened.

Michigan politics is the subject of a social analysis by Ronald P.
Formisano (b. 1939), assistant professor at the University of Rochester.
As Joseph Schafer, Hildegard Binder Johnson, and Paul J. Kleppner
discovered earlier, Formisano also finds that religion was a funda-
mental conditioner of electoral behavior among German, Irish, Dutch,
and New British voters. Approaching ethnic political behavior from
the vantage point of the larger society, he warns against placing ex-
cessive importance on isolated variables subject to quantification.

Ethnicity and Party in Michigan, 1854-60

RONALD P. FORMISANO

The presidential election campaign of 1860 surpassed all contests of the previous two decades in extravagance of display.
Electoral armies trooped in endless parades with bands and singing groups sounding a cacophony of partisan enthusiasm. Uni-
formed in caps and capes and carrying torches, the quasi-military
Republican Wide Awake clubs drilled, watched polls, and
guarded Republican mobilization.[1] Republicans turned out in
force to cheer William H. Seward and Democrats whooped it
up for Stephen A. Douglas when he campaigned through Michigan. Yet the Democrats lacked the flair and especially the fervor
of the Republicans, whose crusading energy was reminiscent of
the Whigs' political revivalism in 1840.[2]

Almost 155,000 votes were cast for president. Lincoln captured the state with 88,480 votes, or 57.1 per cent, of the total,

1. *Michigan Christian Herald,* September 27, 1860. The Preamble and
Constitution of the "Zach Chandler Wide Awakes" is in the *Hillsdale Stand-
ard,* September 4, 1860; a description of one of their marches, ibid., Septem-
ber 18, 1860.
2. For evidence of political heat being generated early in 1860 see Detroit
Advertiser, April 4, 1860; Centreville *Western Chronicle,* April 12, 1860;
George S. May, "Politics in Ann Arbor During the Civil War," *Michigan
History* 37 (March 1953): 53.

while Douglas attracted 65,057 votes, or 42 per cent.[3] Although voter turnout slipped proportionately from 1856, there was an absolute increase of 23.2 per cent in the total number of votes cast. The 1860 election, like that of 1856, was one in which masses of men who did not normally vote went to the polls in a year of unusual political excitement.[4] This phenomenon favored the Republicans in 1860 as it had in 1856. In the exceptional showing of anti-Democratic voters, the party which had enjoyed almost unbroken political hegemony in the state until 1854 lost even its traditional stronghold of Detroit and Wayne County. This loss, though temporary, symbolized all the short-run influences working against the Democracy: anti-Southernism, anti-party feelings, social tensions, high voter turnout, and more.

The social bases of the election returns in 1860 were of course complex. Hundreds of variables might influence individual voting decisions, but usually only a few are subject to quantitative analysis. Even then, the historian, more than the political scientist working with recent elections, must be wary of the "law of available data" by which it is assumed that significant causes are those which can be measured. Saturation in traditional sources as well as a historian's sense of the relevant can keep quantitative analysis in perspective. And careful study of election and demographic data over time can help identify the relevant with at least some relative precision.

Enough data exist for Michigan's election of 1860 to generalize about several variables which traditionally have been deemed important influences on voter decisions that year. The Democrats won only in some northern Michigan counties straddling the Straits of Mackinac and lining upper Saginaw Bay. They were relatively undeveloped, thinly populated, and agriculturally poor areas where lumbering, mining, fishing, and a linger-

3. Breckinridge polled 805 votes, or .6 per cent, and Bell and the Constitutional Unionists attracted 400, or .3 per cent. The Constitutional Unionists nominated national but not state candidates (Detroit *Free Press*, October 6, 1860). See Detroit *Advertiser*, August 31, 1860, for names of electors. As the vote indicated, the minor parties received little attention.

4. See Angus Campbell, "Surge and Decline: A Study of Electoral Change," *Public Opinion Quarterly* 24 (Fall 1960): 397–418.

ing fur trade provided the chief occupations. The foreign-born—English, Irish, Germans, and French Canadians—were common in most of these counties, but the population was not strongly religious.[5] Though the Democratic strongholds in 1860 were back country, systematic investigation reveals no consistent differences in party preference between urban and rural voters in 1860 or in preceding elections.[6] In fact, neither social, economic, demographic, nor technological conditions seem to warrant classifying any areas "urban" in 1860, except perhaps Detroit.

Examination of socioeconomic variables yields mixed results. Comparison of the general economic condition of townships across the state shows that prosperous units tended to vote Republican; yet other evidence demonstrates that the very poor also contributed mightily to Republican strength. Among the undeveloped frontier counties the returns resembled those in the state as a whole. While voters in newly organized counties holding elections for the first time in 1856 or in 1860 were divided in party, more often than not they showed a Republican preference.

A study of Detroit and Wayne County's economic elite of 1860 can further define party preferences among social groups.[7] The elite generally tended to be Republican, but not because of any narrow economic or class interest. Landowners, for example, displayed a strong Democratic tendency, while capitalist, entrepreneurial, and unspecialized business elements, with the exception of bankers, tended to favor Republicanism. Religious and ethnic influences, however, seem to have been more closely tied

5. Angus Murdoch, *Boom Copper: The Story of the First U.S. Mining Boom* (New York, 1943), pp. 67, 68, 69, 199; Arthur Cecil Todd, *The Cornish Miner in America* (Glendale, Calif., 1967), pp. 114–50; Caroline M. McIlvaine, ed., *The Autobiography of Gurdon Saltonstall Hubbard* (Chicago, 1911), pp. 15–17, 20; George Robinson, *History of Cheboygan and Mackinac Counties* (Detroit, 1873), pp. 17–22; Ormond S. Danford, "The Social and Economic Effects of Lumbering on Michigan, 1835–1890," *Michigan History* 26 (Summer 1942): 355–57; Robert James Hybels, "The Lake Superior Copper Fever, 1841–47," *Michigan History* 34 (June 1950): 97–120.

6. This assertion rests on detailed investigation of all major villages and "cities" in Michigan in 1860.

7. Alexandra McCoy, "Political Affiliations of American Economic Elites: Wayne County, Michigan, 1844, 1860, As A Test Case" (Ph.D. diss., Wayne State University, 1965), pp. 115, 166–67, 175–77, passim.

to party choice among the elite than was economic role. Yankee Presbyterians disproportionately preferred the Republican party, while Episcopalians tended to align with the Democrats.

Similarly, among the masses of voters in Michigan in 1860 religion and ethnicity appear to have been predominant in shaping partisan loyalty, although this conclusion must be qualified. Generalizations about ethnic group voting, for example, are as hazardous as those regarding the voting patterns of any other type of social group. A detailed consideration of the major immigrant groups' party loyalties in Michigan in the later 1850s shows the difficulties inherent in generalizing about any one of these groups.

Of all the immigrant groups voting in 1860 the Germans have received the most attention. Ethnocentric German and patronizing native scholars both established a tradition that the German vote of the Northwest elected Lincoln. Recently such claims have been tested in controlled investigations of how Germans in particular areas voted and why some supported Lincoln while others did not. Taken together, old and new studies suggest a formidable number of variables influencing German political behavior: length of time in America, personal and family loyalties, class, economic role, education, urban or rural environment, degree of isolation, loyalties to associations such as labor unions, and religion. Data that permit the systematic testing of all these variables in Michigan are not available, but there is enough evidence at hand to determine certain central tendencies.

In the 1850s Michigan Germans were, in the words of a Free Soil editor in 1854, "in the transition state." He claimed that "a great majority were now awakening" and moving away from the Democrats. During the 1856 campaign Republicans called attention to German activities in their ranks as Whigs never had. In Detroit, Republican campaigners regularly exhorted voters in both the English and German languages; more German names appeared among lists of Republican ward officers than before; and German bands and "lager beer hall" keepers gained prominence in Republicanism. In townships across the state German Republican clubs appeared. Republicans labored to create an impression of German movement to their side and after the election made large claims about the extent of German defection to their ranks.[8] Indeed, a new German-language newspaper endorsed Frémont as had the previously Democratic *Volksblatt,* though the latter returned to the Democracy after 1856.[9]

Indications of German movement continued through the later 1850s. The Republican state administration encouraged it in 1859 by reviving the post of immigration commissioner and appointing successively as commissioners two Germans, Rudolph Diepenbeck of Detroit and George F. Vennfliet of Saginaw County.[10] One of the motives behind such an action was indirectly expressed by an Ann Arbor Republican who in 1859 recommended to the state treasurer "one of our German Republicans" for a job at the Sault Canal works. "The Republicans of Ann Arbor will be much obliged," he wrote; "we are so situated here that we need all the help we can get."[11] In 1860 the Wayne County Republicans, after a well-reported discussion of the matter, urged upon the Republican state convention "the propriety and justice of selecting a German delegate" for the national convention in Chicago. The state convention not only chose the Wayne County German candidate, John Pieterson, but added another "tribute to the German members" by sending a second national delegate of German origin, Dr. M. T. C. Plessner of Saginaw. And on the list of electors for Lincoln in 1860 stood

8. Detroit *Daily Democrat,* February 11, 1854; Detroit *Advertiser,* July 1–31, August 1, 13, September 1, 3, 20, 29, October 3, 4, 9, 14, 15, 25, 1856; Detroit *Advertiser,* August 26, September 8, 1856; Marshall *Statesman,* November 19, 1856; Lansing *Republican,* October 21, November 11, 1856. For similar claims in 1858, see Grand Rapids *Daily Eagle,* November 12, 1858. *Republican,* November 2, 1858.

9. Mark O. Kistler, "The German Language Press in Michigan: A Survey and Bibliography," *Michigan History* 44 (September 1960): 306; Detroit *Advertiser,* July 8, 1856.

10. William L. Jenks, "Michigan Immigration," *Michigan History* 28 (January–March 1944): 69–70, 78, 79–80; Grand Rapids *Daily Eagle,* March 4, 16, 1859; Jackson *American Citizen,* March 10, 1859.

11. James McMahon, Ann Arbor, to John McKinney, May 6, 1859, Department of Treasury Papers, Letters Sent and Received, 1857–82, Michigan Historical Commission, Lansing (MHCom).

the name of Eduard Dorsch of Monroe, scholar, politician, and German "Forty-eighter."[12]

What did all this activity add up to in votes? To a surprising extent, available quantitative data suggest that Germans remained far more loyal to the Democracy than has usually been supposed. Some Republican gains were made, primarily among German Protestants and a smaller group of anticlerical rationalists, but the evidence indicates that a majority of the Germans stayed with the Democracy in 1860. Lutherans were the most numerous religious group resident in the areas listed in Table I; yet the data do not show a uniform movement away from the Democracy for them, nor can it be presumed that they were responsible for all that did occur. In Saginaw County, for example, Germans probably participated in the aggregate shift away from the Democratic party, but the fact that the Democrats still handily carried the homogeneous German Lutheran town of Franken-

TABLE I

PERCENTAGE OF DEMOCRATIC VOTE, 1852 AND 1860,
IN AREAS WITH A CONCENTRATION OF GERMAN LUTHERANS

	1852	1860
Saginaw County	61	45
Waterloo, Jackson County	67	64
Riga, Lenawee County	77	58
Freedom, Washtenaw County	67	81
Warren, Macomb County	67	50
Harrison, Macomb County	74	58
New Buffalo, Berrien County	62	40
Bainbridge, Berrien County	68	51
Bridgewater, Washtenaw County	58	60

12. Detroit *Advertiser*, April 13, 1860; the secretary of the Wayne convention was a Detroit German. J. Elaine Thompson, "The Formative Period of the Republican Party in Michigan, 1854–1860" (Master's thesis, Wayne State University, 1949), pp. 103–5; Harold G. Carlson, "A Distinguished 48'er: Eduard Dorsch," *Michigan History* 19 (Autumn 1935): 429, 435; M. Evangeline Thomas, *Nativism in the Old Northwest, 1850–1860* (Washington, D.C., 1936), p. 240.

muth[13] shows that rural German Lutherans did not move en masse away from the Democrats.

Rural German Catholics also maintained their Democratic loyalty. Springwells and Hamtramck in Wayne County both had large enclaves of German Lutherans and Catholics—mostly the latter—in 1860. Both units fell only slightly in Democratic percentage in 1860. The isolated German Catholic community of Westphalia, a homogeneous ethnoreligious enclave, voted 94 per cent Democratic in 1860 as it had in 1852.[14]

In Detroit, the cleavage between Catholics and Protestants among the Germans bore a close relation to party differences. In 1859 the Republicans encouraged the drift away from the Democrats by nominating for mayor Christian H. Buhl, a wealthy Protestant whose parents had come from Saxony.[15] Buhl ran very well in wards of high German density, surpassing the previous Republican candidate for mayor as well as all Republican candidates for alderman on his own ticket. His showing also exceeded Lincoln's in those wards in 1860 (see Table II), but

TABLE II

PERCENTAGE OF VOTE FOR REPUBLICAN CANDIDATES, 1857 AND 1859, IN THE "GERMAN WARDS" OF DETROIT

	Mayor, 1857	Alderman, 1859	Buhl, 1859
Ward Seven (48)[a]	43	51	57
Ward Ten (44)	40	50	62
Ward Six (41)	46	58	60
Ward Four (40)	33	41	51

[a]Numbers in parentheses indicate the percentage of the potential electorate in 1860 that was German.

13. Floyd B. Streeter, *Political Parties in Michigan, 1837–1860* (Lansing, 1918), p. 226.

14. Nearby Dallas Township, which received some German Catholic and Lutheran settlers in the 1850s, went from 43 per cent Democratic in 1852 to 66 per cent in 1860 (*History of Shiawasee and Clinton Counties* [Philadelphia, 1880], pp. 416, 420–21).

15. Streeter, *Political Parties, 1837–1860*, p. 282. The *Advertiser* commended the "independent Democrats and especially the Germans of the Fourth, Sixth, Seventh, and Tenth wards" for supporting "justice and humanity" (November 9, 1859). Buhl was not only a Protestant but also a member of the Whig-Republican Yankee Presbyterian elite.

German Democrats were more likely to jump party lines in a local election, where party loyalties often count for less than in a state or national contest.

In Detroit's four "German wards" from 1852 to 1864 (Seven, Ten, Six, and Four), the Democrats generally did well: three were Democratic in 1858, and all four were Democratic in 1862. Sharp declines were registered in two wards, Four and Seven, in 1860. Yet even in that year the fourth ward remained loyal to the Democracy, and only in this ward, significantly, did Catholic Germans outnumber Protestant Germans. Thus with the exception of 1860, most urban Germans seem largely to have retained their Democratic loyalty. The Republican party enlarged somewhat its minority strength among Germans, but this limited phenomenon probably occurred chiefly among German Protestants.

TABLE III

PERCENTAGE OF DEMOCRATIC VOTE IN MAJOR ELECTIONS,
1852–64, IN THE "GERMAN WARDS" OF DETROIT

	1852	1854	1856	1858	1860	1862	1864
Ward Seven (48)a	55	57	56	59	48	58	65
Ward Ten (44)				48	46	57	58
Ward Six (41)	52	39	41	51	40	52	48
Ward Four (40)	64	70	64	68	53	67	65

aNumbers in parentheses indicate the percentage of the potential electorate in 1860 that was German.

Even modest gains of the Republicans among Michigan Germans are somewhat remarkable in view of the origins of Republicanism in Michigan. To begin with, the new party fell heir to the evangelical, moral reform tradition of Whiggery which had contained deep strains of nativism and anti-Popery. In 1836 the Whig party had made its first appearance in Michigan, in fact, over a fight with the Democracy about alien voting. Whig insistence on citizen voting, accompanied by nativist outbursts insulting to Irish and German immigrants, had been a key element shaping ethnic patterns in politics during the birth of the party system in Michigan.[16] Republicanism not only inherited many Whig traditions and attitudes, but was itself forged in the ethno-religious controversy of the mid-fifties. The Democracy had been beaten in 1854 by a party which not only opposed the Kansas-Nebraska bill, but which, much more importantly, included powerful anti-Catholic and nativist elements. The victors of 1854 were a coalition of anti-Democratic groups called at that time "Fusion" or "Independency" but only rarely "Republican." In short, nativist Know-Nothingism pervaded the new, emerging Republican party. Why, then, were Germans not wholly repelled by what some newspapers characterized "the know nothing republican candidates"?[17]

The answer lies in part in the exceptional treatment given to the Germans by the Republicans. Independency's anti-Popery need not have offended and probably appealed to many Protestant Germans. To a lesser extent perhaps, Germans also recognized that the Know-Nothings had infiltrated and influenced the Democratic party in many areas.[18] Republican platform pledges of support for the rights of naturalized citizens were aimed squarely at the Germans. "English and Scotch and Protestant German citizens"[19] occupied a very different place in Republican feelings than did Irish Catholics. Republicans deliberately played off Germans and Irish against one another, frequently using the German Protestants as examples of good immigrants who favored American interests while the Irish served always to define the bad foreigner. Republican rhetoric portrayed Germans as true to the principles of freedom for which they came, while the Irish obeyed the slavery of party.

Despite these favorable omens, most Germans who sold or drank alcoholic beverages opposed Republicanism because of its identification with prohibition. Germans who cherished their

16. Ronald P. Formisano, "A Case Study of Party Formation: Michigan, 1835," *Mid-America* 50 (April 1968): 83–107.
17. Niles *Republican*, November 8, 1856; Detroit *Free Press*, November 3, 1859.
18. The Saginaw *Enterprise* published a letter from a German claiming this was true in Saginaw, Detroit *Advertiser*, July 22, 1856.
19. The phrase is from the Detroit *Advertiser*, March 13, 1855.

traditional leisure pleasures were as repelled by the Republicans as they had been by the evangelical Whigs. Christian Buhl perhaps represented the Americanized, upper-status Protestant who could identify with moral reform, but Catholics, many Lutherans, and many unchurched Germans adhered to a different value system. One Saginaw Valley German said he saw little choice in politics in 1855, with "slavery on the one side, the temperance humbug on the other." Sectionalism and the slavery extension question added to the many pressures bearing on Germans in the 1850s but the relative weight of these issues is not clear. Certainly many Germans responded to the intense anti-Southernism of 1856 and 1860, but close examination of election data suggests that sectionalism and antislavery idealism have been exaggerated, in regard to both their importance among other influences in the 1850s and their long-run effects.[20]

Germans do not appear to have hated slavery more than other groups did. They disliked blacks perhaps as much as or more than did native Americans, but they did not display the Negrophobia found among Irish Catholics.[21] If the Republican party successfully appealed to certain Germans on moral grounds, it probably was because they were attracted by its moral stance which stressed ascetic Protestant middle-class values of disciplined, temperate conduct rather than because of German attitudes toward slavery.

This Protestant German rapport with Republicanism received no better expression than that given it in a public letter by Nicholas Greusel, Jr., Republican candidate for city marshal

20. Alan S. Brown, "Southwestern Michigan in the Campaign of 1860," *Michigan Heritage* 2 (Winter 1960): 71; Detroit *Advertiser*, October 22, 1858; Grand Rapids *Daily Eagle*, March 30, 1859. The Saginaw German is quoted in Floyd B. Streeter, "History of Prohibition Legislation in Michigan," *Michigan History* 2 (April 1918): 297.

21. Voting returns by township on an 1850 state referendum on extending equal suffrage to colored persons and other data relating to attitudes to blacks are analyzed in my unpublished paper, "The Edge of Caste: Colored Suffrage in Michigan, 1827–1861." In 1860 Republican speakers told Germans, as they told other voters, that Republicans knew the Germans had not immigrated so that "their children should labor side by side with the African slave" (Detroit *Tribune*, October 26, 1860).

of Detroit in 1856. His Democratic rival, a German saloonkeeper in the fourth ward, had apparently attacked him for being rather strait-laced. Greusel answered that his opponent believed that to be fit for marshal a man "must have the qualification of drunkenness; he must regularly attend a saloon, spend his money, lose his senses, and be called a good fellow." The city, he said, had had enough of such officers. "I do not wish you to think that I do not take a glass of lager beer when I feel like taking one; most of my German friends know this, and the better class of them will vote for him of whom they well know that he never disgraced them by being carried home on a dray," wrote Greusel, further describing his opponent as "a man who despises religion, and sets all laws at defiance."[22]

The Republican party also attracted the political radicals who fled Germany after the revolutions of 1848. In 1856 at the "Black Republican" display at the Michigan State Fair the editor of the Detroit *Catholic Vindicator* noticed "some 200 German Red Republicans of the very worst stamp, comprising the association of young German turners . . . and the other secret German radical associations of this city." One Republican candidate for state legislator was in fact "a member of this priest-hating fraternity of dangerous infidels." The *Vindicator* advised German Catholics to vote against such men and after the election claimed that the "entire Infidel Red Republican German vote" was cast for Republicanism.[23] Unfortunately, there is very little other information available regarding the German "radical associations." They probably supported the Republicans not only because of their antagonism to Catholic authoritarianism, but also because of their unusual political consciousness which made them more vulnerable than average Germans to appeals to sectional pride and the interests of the North. Moreover, of all the German groups, these young, idealistic radicals probably despised the institution of slavery the most. Ironically, this kind of revulsion to slavery has often been attributed to the radicals'

22. Detroit *Advertiser*, February 25, 1856; also ibid., September 8, 1856; Thomas, *Nativism in the Old Northwest*, pp. 211–12.
23. Detroit *Catholic Vindicator*, October 11, November 8, 1856.

very strange bedfellows in Republican ranks, pietistic German Protestants.

Republican inroads on German Democratic voting strength were also related to continued Irish support of the Democracy. Although the Irish found themselves uncomfortable in the factionalized party of 1853–55, Fusion and Republican actions drove them back into the Democratic fold. They really had nowhere else to go. If the Irish saw themselves as special targets of anti-Popery, they had considerable reason for it. Actually, by serving as a negative reference group for many voters who would choose the Republican party in reaction against them, the Irish may have contributed much to the Republican cause. In any case, Republicans tended to write off Irish Catholic votes.

Although a new Irish military company might march in Detroit's 1853 Fourth of July celebration, symbolically suggesting Irish participation in the community, still the flourishing of Know-Nothingism made Irish Catholics well aware that "the native American hate is more fiercely directed against the naturalized citizens of Irish descent than of any other foreign extraction."[24] The Irish became more firmly entrenched in their Democratic loyalty (or anti-Republicanism) even while their position in the Democratic party remained uncomfortable. Tension existed between them and not only native Protestant Democrats but also French Canadian and German Democrats. The ethnic rivalries among different Catholic groups also pervaded the churches, where, indeed, they originated to some extent. The Irish complained, for example, all during the ante-bellum years of having non-English-speaking priests of French, German, or Dutch origin.[25]

Thus, in the 1850s Irish Catholics felt increasingly isolated. A habitual Irish-baiting publication, the Detroit *Advertiser,* per-

24. Detroit *Catholic Vindicator,* July 9, 1853, January 27, 1855.
25. Detroit *Advertiser,* March 3, 1855; Richard R. Elliott, MS Index to *Vindicator,* University of Detroit Library, microfilm; M. Dolorita Mast, *Always the Priest: The Life of Gabriel Richard* (Baltimore and Dublin, 1965), pp. 318–19; Detroit *Advertiser,* August 3, 1858; Frank A. O'Brien, "Le Père Juste," *Michigan Historical Collections* 30 (1906): 263.

mitted itself unmitigated wrath when in 1858 it saw "miserable Irish rowdies, who had not the right to vote in their own country, and who where bought up like swine, at so much a head, bluffing and insulting all who dared to vote. . . . They are *owned* by the Locofoco demagogues of this city as much as Southern slaves are owned by their masters."[26] But more revealing, and more offensive perhaps to the Irish as a group, was a casual satirical account of politicking in "Corktown" in which a Democratic politician described how "a barrel of whiskey on the night previous to the election properly administered" would take care of Irish voting. In 1859 a Grand Rapids editor expressed a prevailing Republican attitude when he observed the unqualified support given to the "Dimmicratic" ticket by the Irish and judged the Democrats welcome to it: "We want no slaves or cravens in our ranks." The great mass of Irish were unlike other foreign groups, he wrote; "The Germans, Hollanders, Scotchmen, and people of all other nations, except the Irish, are divided in their political action, like the natives of our own country. . . . this difference is respected by all." Though Germans and Hollanders had at first been strongly "prejudiced" for the Democrats, they were now beginning to grow more "independent." Thus the Irish had no one's respect.[27]

Election returns and other data support the impression of massive Irish Catholic voting for the Democrats in the period 1854–60. It was easily 95 per cent, possibly more. In 1860, when Irish Catholics accounted for some 50 per cent of the voters of Detroit's eighth ward, "Corktown" remained strongly Democratic, going for Douglas by 60 per cent. Southeast of Detroit, the village of Adrian in Lenawee County had a concentration of Irish and other Catholics in its first ward, which bordered the railroad yard where many of the immigrants worked. That was Adrian's

26. Detroit *Advertiser,* November 3, 1858; see also *Cass County Republican,* December 2, 1858.

27. Detroit *Advertiser,* February 7, October 30, 1856, November 11, 1858; Detroit *Catholic Vindicator,* April 4, 1857; Grand Rapids *Daily Eagle,* March 30, also April 6, 1859.

only Democratic ward (57 per cent) in 1860.[28] Far to the west, the first ward in Grand Rapids also contained a heavy Irish vote. In 1854 a local politician promised Irish votes for the Fusion ticket, then applied to the new state administration for a reward. A local Republican, however, told Governor Bingham that while the applicant may have done what he could, "as the Irish Catholics generally gave their votes against us, I have supposed that he did not effect much." The first ward continued to vote Democratic—by 62 per cent in 1858 and 60 per cent in 1860.[29]

Irish Catholic farmers also maintained a strong Democratic loyalty. Erin, Macomb County, received some German Lutherans in the 1850s but was still voting over 80 per cent Democratic in 1860 as it had in 1852. Nearby Emmet Township in St. Clair County, purely Irish and 98 per cent Democratic in 1852, slipped to 81 per cent Democratic in 1859 after its population became more heterogeneous. Washtenaw County's Northfield also continued to be a strong Democratic township of German and Irish Catholic voters, and Irish Catholics probably helped give the Democrats majorities in 1860 in Bunker Hill and White Oak townships, Ingham County.[30] Thus, urban or rural, east or west, Irish Catholics voted as their friends and enemies said they did.

The Dutch voters of western Michigan were much like the Germans. Their allegiance shifted during the 1850s, primarily away from the Democracy. But the popular notion that anti-slavery sentiment caused a sudden huge Dutch switch is grossly inaccurate. In 1854 the Dutch voted strongly Democratic. *De Hollander* supported not only the Democracy but the Kansas-Nebraska bill as well. The Dutch disliked abolitionists and

28. W. A. Whitney and R. I. Bonner, *History and Memoirs of Lenawee County, Michigan* (Adrian, 1879), 1: 503; Frank Krause, *City Map of Adrian* (Ann Arbor, 187?), Burton Historical Collection, Detroit Public Library (BHC).

29. Lovell Moore to Gov. Kinsley Bingham, January 10, 1855, Executive Records, Elections, MHCom; Grand Rapids *Daily Eagle,* March 30, 1859.

30. Samuel W. Durant, *History of Ingham and Eaton Counties, Michigan* (Philadelphia, 1880), p. 228. There is also evidence that the Irish in Kent and Berrien counties voted Democratic: Detroit *Catholic Vindicator,* November 20, 25, 1854; Index to *Vindicator;* Niles *Republican,* November 8, 1856.

blacks, and both these prejudices influenced their first reactions to Fusion-Republicanism.[31]

Fusion continued to represent the old threat and arrogance of Whig evangelicalism with its potential threat to Dutch separatism. Although prohibition appealed to many Dutch, enforcement of the liquor law in Ottawa County led to incidents offensive to them. The tendency of Republicans to stereotype "Hollanders" probably confirmed the impression of the Dutch that the *Nietweters*—Know-Nothings—were allied with the new party.[32] Yet even in 1854 some erosion from the nearly monolithic Dutch support of the Democrats could be discerned. In 1856 it became a beachhead. Ministers and other influential persons seem to have numbered disproportionately among the early Republican boosters. Frémont clubs were formed in Grand Rapids and in Holland, and Dutch defections to the Republican party were threatening enough for *De Hollander* and the Kalamazoo *Gazette* to denounce the recusants as dupes of the Know-Nothings.[33]

Republican activity among the Dutch continued in the later 1850s but remained mostly superficial, leaving the mass of voters still Democratic. By 1857 Republicans at least had a newspaper, Henry Chubb's *Clarion,* in the Ottawa County area. *De Hollander* stayed Democratic, however, and two new Democratic newspapers appeared, the *Grand Haven News* in 1858 and the *Ottawa County Register* in 1859. In June, 1860, a Republican

31. Henry S. Lucas, ed., *Dutch Immigrant Memoirs and Related Writings* (Assen, Netherlands, 1955), 1: 545, 536; in February, 1855, *De Hollander,* published in Holland, Michigan, said that natural laws guided by God would eventually destroy slavery; meanwhile "political abolitionists" were having the opposite effect (quoted in ibid. 1: 547); Centreville *Western Chronicle,* November 2, 1854; one descendant of the Holland pioneers remembered a book in his father's library defending slavery as "not contrary" to the Bible (Martin Ten Hoor, "Dutch Colonists and American Democracy," *Michigan History* 31 [December 1949]: 357).

32. Grand Haven *Grand River Times,* March 15, 1854; Marshall *Statesman,* May 16, 1855; Lucas, ed., *Dutch Memoirs,* 1: 547–48; Thomas, *Nativism in the Old Northwest,* 229–30.

33. Lucas, ed., *Dutch Memoirs,* 1: 545, 551–56; Detroit *Advertiser,* July 21, October 30, 1856; Grand Rapids *Grand River Times,* October 29, 1856; Kalamazoo *Gazette,* April 11, 1856.

paper, *De Grondwet*, emerged in Holland itself, published by John Roost. Meanwhile, in the 1859 legislature Henry Barns, one of the architects of Republicanism, delivered a eulogistic report on the Holland Colony and asked the state to grant swamplands to the colony to aid its plans for internal improvements.[34] Yet that same year supreme court justice election returns from Holland and Zeeland clearly showed that "the colony still sustain[ed] the Sham Democracy." The Republican cause was "steadily gaining ground," but the Democrats nevertheless won a majority.

Holland elected John Roost, who was running for supervisor, and the rest of the Republican township ticket in April, 1860, but then gave a solid majority for Douglas in the fall.[35] Unfortunately, returns for only Holland Township are available for 1860. Yet Democratic strength there, plus Democratic emphasis on Republican contempt for the Dutch, and the energetic campaigning of the Douglasite "Holland Invincibles," suggest that in 1860 Dutch voting in general closely resembled that of the

TABLE IV

PARTY VOTING, 1852–60, IN STRONGLY DUTCH TOWNSHIPS

	HOLLAND (OTTAWA COUNTY)				ZEELAND (OTTAWA COUNTY)				FILLMORE (ALLEGAN COUNTY)			
	Dem.		Rep.		Dem.		Rep.		Dem.		Rep.	
	No.	%	No.	%	No.	%	No.	%	No.	%	No.	%
1852	123	96	5	4	128	91	11	9	47	78	13	22
1854	105	63	61	37	24	28	62	72	16	50	16	50
1856	129	63	74	37	55	60	36	40				
1857	154	72	59	28	139	94	9	6	24	47	27	53
1859	182	53	159	47	112	64	64	36				
1860	208	66	105	34								

34. Grand Rapids *Daily Eagle*, April 6, 1859; letter to Detroit *Advertiser*, April 7, 1859; *Michigan Senate Journal, 1859*, pp. 245–58.

35. A. S. Kenzie, "Newspapers in Ottawa County," *Michigan Historical Collections* 9 (1886): 295–300; Detroit *Advertiser*, April 5, 7, 1860; Aleida Pieters, *A Dutch Settlement in Michigan* (Grand Rapids, 1923), p. 158.

still loyal township of Holland.[36] A leading historian of the Dutch pioneers, Professor Henry Lucas, has observed that although some Dutch areas in the Midwest voted Republican in 1860, "the Hollanders were generally unwilling to forsake the Democratic party."[37]

Dutch loyalty to the Democracy sometimes is explained in terms of Dutch revulsion to Republican prohibitionism. In this view the Democracy was "the party of license . . . more liberal with other people's rights and with strong drink."[38] But this interpretation overlooks the religious asceticism of the great majority of western Michigan rural Dutch in 1860. The "license-strong drink" appeal may have counted favorably with some Dutch men in the villages of Grand Rapids and Kalamazoo, or among the Detroit Dutch, uprooted from any community; but for the great majority of pietistic Dutch immigrants, the Democratic philosophy of laissez faire was appealing because it meant freedom to control their own communities, even to the extent of establishing near theocracies in the early settlements. The Dutch rejected the Whigs and then Republicans at first not because of any small concern over drinking, but because of the Protestant Party's broad evangelical Christianizing bent, which,

36. Centreville *Western Chronicle,* September 27, 1860; Kalamazoo *Gazette,* October 5, 19, 1860. Olive Township, Ottawa County, an extension of the Dutch colonies, voted 100 per cent Democratic in 1857.

37. Lucas claimed, however, that a majority of the Dutch in Grand Rapids and Kalamazoo voted Republican in 1860 (Lucas, ed., *Dutch Memoirs,* 1: 560–61, 562). Unfortunately, the data to test that claim are not available. For example, Lucas said that the Grand Rapids third ward was "heavily Dutch" and voted Republican by 285 to 190, with 80 votes going to minor candidates. But scrutiny of the United States census population schedules (on microfilm) for Grand Rapids in 1860 shows that no more than 15 per cent of the adult males in the third ward were actually born in Holland, though the third did contain a proportionately large number of the Holland-born compared to other wards. On the other hand, the Republican majority in the third was probably related to the fact that almost 60 per cent of its adult males were from New York or New England and were probably Yankee Protestants; there were four clergymen living in the ward: one Presbyterian, one Baptist, and two Methodists, all from New York or New England.

38. Adrian Van Koevering, "The Dutch Colonial Pioneers of Western Michigan," MS, Michigan Historical Collections, Ann Arbor, pp. 490–91.

however vaguely, raised the threat of church and state problems they had left behind in Europe. Whigs and then Republicans had too active an attitude toward government, combined with too serious a concern for morality and religion, for the comfort of the early Dutch.

Among the rural pietists, party divisions probably did not reflect cleavages between pietists and secularists—consensus existed on piety—but rather divisions along status, class, occupational, geographic, or other cultural lines. The question of assimilation, for example, was such a line of disagreement, coinciding apparently, with party divisions. Thus, religious Dutch leaders who were willing to assimilate into American society understood that they had to adopt the dominant values as well. These assimilationist leaders also tended to embrace Republicanism. Other equally pious Dutch, including probably the mass of the rank and file as well as older leaders, desired rather to preserve their ethnic heritage, resisted assimilation, and were far more reluctant to move away from the Democracy.[39]

One influence working on both assimilationists and conservatives to erode their allegiance to the Democracy was anti-Popery. Signs of Dutch attitudes to Catholicism in the 1850s were few but unmistakably hostile. Years later a local politician, explaining why Zeeland was then heavily Republican, said that the "great change" in Dutch politics began "in the trying period of the war." Promoting Republicanism were "first, the Democratic party's record on secession and rebellion, finance and tariff; second, the intense jealousy with which the Zeelanders regard their civil and religious rights and our public schools system, all of which they regard in constant danger from the Catholic hierarchy which, together with the liquor interest of the country, is a standing menace to free institutions." The importance of "free schools"

39. On different attitudes toward assimilation, see Martin Ten Hoor, *Michigan History* 31 (December 1949): 363–64; Paul Honigsheim, "Religion and Assimilation of Dutch," *Michigan History* 26 (Winter 1942): 54–55, 59–61; Lucas, ed., *Dutch Memoirs,* 1: 224, has a Zeeland settler remembering the assimilation issue arising as early as 1850.

in this Republican's mind, in fact, overshadowed any other issue.[40] The postwar Republican ideology expressed in this explicit and articulate statement did not necessarily exist in the 1850s, but its foundations were laid then.

Recent British immigrants generally displayed formidable anti-Democratic tendencies throughout the 1850s. The New British had earlier favored the Whigs, and as the Republican party emerged, most Protestants among them sought its ranks. This attachment was intensified by Catholic Democrats who identified Know-Nothingism and "Irish Orangeism" with the Republicans. In the 1850s E. B. Ward led a group of Republican capitalists in locating the Eureka Iron Company and the Wyandotte Rolling Mills in Ecorse Township, Wayne County, where Wyandotte village grew as English, German, and Irish workers poured in. Nearby Monguagon Township's percentage of New British rose from 12 in 1850 to 44 in 1860. The simultaneous influx of Irish and German Catholics probably balanced the political impact of the increase of British Methodists and no great declines of Democratic strength took place in these towns. The Republicans, however, underlined their New British connection in 1856 by nominating Duncan Stewart, a "sound gallant Scotchman," to run for state senator in the district including Wyandotte and Monguagon. Moreover, the leaders of the new Republican association of Ecorse in 1856 were predominantly English. Even the New British of Sanilac County, who had voted strongly Democratic through 1854, switched to Republicanism late in the decade. So rapid was the change that whereas 70 per cent of 358 voters in 1852 were Democrats, 80 per cent of the county's 1,005 voters in 1856 were Republicans, as were 70 per cent of 1,304 voters in 1860. In nearby Lapeer County a mixed group of English, Scots, and New Yorkers settled Burlington

40. Lucas, ed., *Dutch Memoirs*, 1: 251, 248, 250, also 548 and 512; Pieters, *Dutch Settlement*, p. 109.

Township in the 1850s. Methodist in religion, this town of newer New British gave the Republicans 80 per cent in 1860.[41]

The New British were one of the largest groups among the 149,000 foreign-born persons in Michigan in 1860. Less noticeable than the Germans or Irish because of their English language and Protestant religion, the 26,000 English and 6,000 Scots together exceeded the Irish total of about 30,000 persons but were less than the German group of nearly 39,000. However, part of the Irish group were Northern Irelanders, allied with the New British Protestants in religion and sentiment, as were many of the 36,000 Canadian-born immigrants in 1860, a group which contained many English, Welsh, and Scottish Protestants.[42] Thus, while the dramatic activities of some German and Dutch voters received a great deal of attention, the most numerous immigrant group in the Republican coalition was the New British.

The ethnic variable in the 1860 election clearly operated as one of the most important influences on party choice. Ethnocultural consciousness was an element which party politicians ignored only at their peril. Along with religious heritage, the ethnic factor was perhaps one of the two most important shapers of party loyalty. But any generalization such as this must be qualified by the recognition that human beings, no matter what social classification one chooses to give them for purposes of behavioral analysis, are extraordinarily complex. Ethnicity and

41. Silas Farmer, *The History of Detroit and Michigan* (Detroit, 1884), 1: 100; Detroit *Advertiser*, November 3, July 11, 1856; Mrs. Joseph DeWindt, *Proudly We Record: The Story of Wyandotte, Michigan* (1955), pp. 21, 27, 29, 49, 229–30; "Lake Superior Iron," *Michigan Pamphlets* 5 (1860); E. P. Christian, "Historical Associations Connected with Wyandotte and Vicinity," *Michigan Historical Collections* 12 (1887): 323–24; *The Village of Wyandotte: Its Present and Prospective Advantages* (1856), 1–3; Farmer, *Detroit*, 1: 1328–29; Thomas H. Christian, "History of St. Stephen's Parish, Wyandotte," MS, BHC; *Portrait and Biographical Album of Sanilac County, Michigan* (Chicago, 1884), pp. 560, 478 (the core of New British settlers in Sanilac had been Lexington Township, which voted 72 per cent Democratic in 1852 and 70 per cent Republican in 1860); *History of Lapeer County, Michigan* (Chicago, 1884), pp. 196–202.

42. For a convenient summary of United States census data for 1860, see United States Civil War Centennial Commission, *The United States on the Eve of the Civil War* (Washington, D.C., 1963), p. 63.

religion, moreover, did not operate independently, but acted more or less in concert with a great many variables: status, class, wealth, occupation, education, length of residence in country or locality, and degree of assimilation, to name only a few. Any one of these variables opens a Pandora's box of measurement problems on its own.

Each ethnic group could experience a mass of conflicting pressures. Many of their nominal members lived apart from the group, physically and psychically, and generalizations about group norms and behavior do not apply to them. Estimates of the voting behavior of the group as a whole refer to central tendencies, and while historians usually know *something* about the majority bloc in each group—say, the 95 per cent Irish Catholics who were Democrats—they often know almost nothing about the minority blocs—for example, the 5 per cent of Irish Catholics who did not vote Democratic. Describing the relative significance of ethnicity and religion in the election of 1860 (or any other in the nineteenth century) is not arrival at a promised land; it is discovering one of many frontiers whose internal mysteries need to be explored and charted, then placed in perspective on the historical and social horizon.

Adapted from a chapter in *The Forming of American Mass Parties: Michigan, 1829–1861* (Princeton, N.J.: Princeton University Press, forthcoming).

James M. Bergquist (b. 1934) is a specialist in the political history of the Germans in the United States. He received his Ph.D. from North-western University in 1966 and is now an associate professor of history at Villanova University in Pennsylvania. His article provides the first full-scale analysis of the political behavior in the 1850s of the Germans of Illinois, the home state of both Lincoln and Douglas. He finds that even though the religious diversity of the Germans precluded the possi-bility of their acting as a political unit, a majority preferred the Re-publican party, which in Illinois had escaped the stigma of nativism.

People and Politics in Transition: The Illinois Germans, 1850-60

JAMES M. BERGQUIST

If we seek to understand the political outlook of the German immigrants and the mark that they left upon their times, it is not enough merely to measure the weight and division of their vote in 1860. Rather must we look upon that election as the result of a complicated process of readjustment, both political and social, for the German-Americans as a group—a process which had been going on over most of the preceding decade. For one thing, the German community itself was a vastly different entity in 1860 than it had been in 1850; for another, the Germans faced the same problem that all Americans faced of defining their political loyalties in a period when the political party structure was changing rapidly. The confusion and uncertainty which re-sulted, and the almost inevitable diversity of response, can be seen by examining the process in one crucial western state, Illi-nois.

Sheer growth in numbers, of course, accounted for much of what was happening to America's German immigrants during the fifties. That decade (and particularly its first half) was marked by America's highest rate of immigrant arrivals, considered in proportion to the existing population of the country. The wave of Irish newcomers reached its peak about 1851, and in the next few years the Germans replaced them as the largest incoming element. The German-born population of the United States grew from 584,720 in 1850 to 1,301,136 in 1860, and the effect was especially notable in the burgeoning northwestern states. About one-eighth of this increase occurred in Illinois alone; the German-born population there rose from 38,451 to 130,804, an increase greater than in any other state in the Northwest and exceeded only by New York in the entire Union.[1] Illinois had had some centers of German population since the 1830s, and to an extent these served as focal points for the settlement of newcomers: the rural counties of Illinois across the Mississippi from Saint Louis, elsewhere along the Mississippi, and regions of the Illinois River valley. But perhaps as many of the newcomers came to the northern part of the state, since that was the area being opened up by the rails to settlers of all sorts in those years. By 1860, about half the Illinois German population lived in the northern four tiers of counties: about one-sixth of the state's total within the city of Chicago, another sixth in rural areas within twenty miles of Lake Michigan, and another sixth scattered westward along the new railroads leading to the Mississippi.[2] The statistics alone hint at their importance in some politi-

1. J. D. B. De Bow, comp., *Statistical View of the United States . . . Being a Compendium of the Seventh Census* (Washington, 1854), p. 117; Joseph C. G. Kennedy, comp., *Population of the United States in 1860, Compiled from the Original Returns of the Eighth Census* (Washington, 1864), pp. xxix, xxxii. Figures for increase of German population are not the same as numbers of arriving German immigrants; the former statistics are influenced by deaths of foreign-born, emigration, and internal migration. The "increase" figure demonstrates more adequately the politically significant aspect of German-born distribution among states. Ohio had more German-born than did Illinois in 1860, having received more of the pre-1850 influx. The German-born formed a larger proportion of the population in Wisconsin than in Illinois in 1860.

2. Published census data for 1860 list only the number of foreign-born, not the number of individual nationalities, in each county. These rough estimates rest on study of manuscript census records and local history materials as well as the published census data. For elaboration, see James M. Bergquist, "The Political Attitudes of the German Immigrant in Illinois, 1848–1860" (Ph.D. diss., Northwestern University, 1966), pp. 22–46.

cally critical areas, but it may well be added that they were also a highly "visible" group. Indeed, the politicians of the day may have been unduly impressed by the appearance of the close-knit German rural communities and the fast-growing neighborhoods on Chicago's *Nordseite* (as even native Americans often referred to it), where one could walk for blocks and hear only German.

It is natural enough that astute politicians would consider cultivating such a group. And when political parties dissolved into uncertain flux in the mid-fifties, it is natural as well that politicians would hope to garner the German vote in toto for one side or the other—especially given the overwhelmingly Democratic political allegiance of the Germans in the period before 1854. That hope, however, was in vain; the one conclusion most easily drawn from all the scholarly discussion of the Germans' voting habits is that they were not at all as united behind any single party in 1860 as they had been behind the Democracy in 1850. The variations among Germans were apparent not only between states, but within them. Some of those variations arose from differences among the Germans themselves; some arose from differing relationships that developed in states and localities between the German community and the particular political party structure.

The growth and maturing of the German group to a position of considerable strength in the western states, and the economic stability its members slowly but steadily were gaining, served at the same time to foster a diversity that had not been possible when Germans were fewer in number and more often gathered in small homogeneous communities. The impressive and growing lists of German congregations, singing societies, lodges, workers' organizations, and cultural groups may from one point of view be seen as the beginning of a social separatism that was to become the German-America of later years. But from another point of view, these proliferating institutions may also be seen as the breaking up of the group into ever more numerous parts as the interests of its members became more diverse. The remarkable expansion of the German population in the West brought together, it must be remembered, people of very different backgrounds from widely separated areas of a Germany that was itself still divided. The possible variations among Germans (who often thought of themselves first as Saxons or Rhinelanders or Bavarians) were greater than the variations between a New Englander and a Mississippian; even the common link of language was marked by variations in dialect more striking than any in American speech. When these Germans of many different political, cultural, and religious backgrounds were brought together, then, they faced the problem of adjusting to an amalgamated German community as well as to American society as a whole. That problem militated against the easy maintenance of solidarity in the new milieu of American politics.[3]

The weakening of the close-knit fabric of the German community is most easily observed in its growing religious dissension. In the Germans' earlier years in the West, Protestants in their widely scattered settlements had felt lucky to obtain the services of any itinerant preacher who was willing to hold services in the German tongue. Thus congregations very often practiced latitudinarianism out of necessity; if the minister now was a Calvinist, the next one along might be a Lutheran, and the potential church members in the locality might have been brought up in religious traditions anywhere in the theological spectrum. The doctrinal indefiniteness that resulted was not unlike that of the "united" state churches that had been formed in Prussia, Saxony, and other German states, and thus many Germans did not object. But as their numbers grew, those who did care could be more discriminating about the kind of religious congregations they formed, and doctrinal squabbles multiplied. Congregations split over whether they would be Evangelical or Lutheran. The newly organized Missouri Synod, representing conservative adherence to the "unaltered Augsburg confession" of Luther, inveighed against more liberal theologies of all sorts. German

3. Many of the writings of the Forty-eighters reflect their frustration over lack of German-American unity. For general discussion of the subject, see Heinz Kloss, *Um die Einigung des Deutsch-amerikanertums* (Berlin, 1937); Heinrich H. Maurer, "The Earlier German Nationalism in America," *American Journal of Sociology* 22 (1917): 519–43. Compare also Bayrd Still, *Milwaukee: The History of a City* (Madison, 1965, pp. 111–32.

Methodists, relatively few in number, nevertheless raised antagonism by preaching temperance and Sabbath reform like their native-American counterparts. German Catholics especially felt themselves under attack all at once by American nativists, German Protestants, and the growing element of vocal German freethinkers. Unlike many immigrant groups in America, the Germans never were identified with one dominant religious tradition. The differences among them were emerging more clearly in the fifties as German-America became more firmly established.[4]

Unusual developments among their leadership also played a role in the growing divisions of the Germans. Among the many newcomers was the relatively small group of Forty-eighters, political activists who had come as refugees from the most recent revolutions in Germany. While they added resources of talent such as few American immigrant groups have enjoyed, that hardly meant that all German-Americans immediately rallied to the banners they raised (at times somewhat ostentatiously). In many places Germans had already produced their own political leaders, some of them political refugees of the 1830s, most of them seasoned in the ways of American politics. The "Grays," as they came to be called in the feuding of the early fifties, were not disposed to yield quietly to the newer "Greens." The "Greens," frequently of strong ideological bent and much given to doctrinal squabbling among themselves, would often join to turn their criticism upon the supposed irrationality and lack of principle of the entire American party system. Older German leaders, they argued, were servile and unidealistic in agreeing to work within such a system. In the case of Illinois, the noise of the recriminations should not obscure the fact that the outcome was

4. General works on German-American religious development include Carl E. Schneider, *The German Church on the American Frontier* (St. Louis, 1939); Philip Schaff, *America: A Sketch of its Political, Social and Religious Character*, ed. Perry Miller (Cambridge, Mass., 1961), the most recent edition of an 1854 work; Walter O. Forster, *Zion on the Mississippi* (St. Louis, 1953); Colman J. Barry, *The Catholic Church and German Americans* (Milwaukee, 1953); Heinrich H. Maurer, "Studies in the Sociology of Religion: III, The Problems of a National Church before 1860," *American Journal of Sociology* 30 (1925): 534–50.

never very much in doubt. The "Grays" were already in firm political control—the older German leader Gustave Koerner was elected lieutenant governor as a Democrat in 1852—and the "Greens" generally came to terms with the established political leadership and with traditional concepts of party structure.[5] Yet the newer element made its influence felt, especially in the field of German-language journalism, which improved significantly in quality and in number of publications during the decade. But this adjustment was not made without releasing tensions within the group, and the "Greens" remained as an abrasive social and religious element in the eyes of some Germans.[6]

What has been said about religious dissension and about factionalism among leaders might be said as well about many of the German institutions proliferating in the West: far from uniting Germans in the cohesive sort of political force that American politicians and German leaders might hope for, they usually served to divide. Time and again, would-be German leaders who envisioned one forceful organization that would rally all German-Americans to exercise the influence they deserved met with disillusionment. Although Germans might sometimes rally together on an issue, especially if they felt themselves under attack as German immigrants, they could nevertheless find other issues that transcended the immigrant community, and still others that might divide the immigrant community against itself.

These forces of fragmentation were already at work when the Kansas-Nebraska Act of 1854 brought to an end a long tradition of established ties between the Germans and the Democratic

5. See also the succinct discussion in Carl Wittke, *Refugees of Revolution: The German Forty-Eighters in America* (Philadelphia, 1952), pp. 72–75 and passim. The best reflection of the struggle of the two elements in Illinois may be seen in the files for 1850 and 1851 of the *Belleviller Zeitung* (Belleville, Ill.), in which Koerner frequently wrote for the "Grays"; his most frequent adversary for the "Greens" was Heinrich Boernstein, who edited the Saint Louis *Anzeiger des Westens* during the same period.

6. Since many readers tend to think of Carl Schurz when Forty-eighters are mentioned, it should be specifically pointed out (as many scholars have done) that he hardly fits the generalizations made here, but rather criticized the doctrinaire views of many of his contemporaries. See especially Chester V. Easum, *The Americanization of Carl Schurz* (Chicago, 1929), pp. 137–40 and passim.

party; and so, in the situation that resulted, it was by no means clear what the future course of the immigrants would be, nor even whether the old solidarity might be restored in some new political system. In general, the Germans of Illinois regarded the Kansas-Nebraska bill as a betrayal on the part of Stephen A. Douglas, whom they had unstintingly supported through his previous political career. Now he seemed to have moved to court the southerners and to be joining them in a twofold effort: to create new opportunities in the West for slavery, and at the same time to deny such opportunities to the foreign-born. The latter suspicions grew among Germans because of the southern attempts to restrict immigrant voting and officeholding in the new territories. The tone of protest in the German press and in German public meeings rose noticeably after such nativist amendments were added to the Kansas-Nebraska bill. Although these provisions were ultimately defeated and Douglas did not advocate them, immigrants felt that the Little Giant did not speak their part by denouncing the southerners who wanted them.[7] At any rate, Illinois Germans reacted overwhelmingly against pro-Douglas candidates in the congressional elections of late 1854. Study of sample precincts with heavily German-born electorates throughout the state suggests that over 75 per cent of the German vote was directed against Douglas and his cohorts. The picture of voting behavior is not a perfectly even one; there were many types of anti-Douglas candidates, including former Whigs, nativists, and men who still considered themselves Democrats. But it is a fairly safe generalization that, as long as Germans' fears of nativism were not aroused by the anti-Nebraska congressional candidates, their decision to reject the forces of Douglas was clear and definite.[8]

7. Files of the *Belleviller Zeitung,* the Freeport *Deutscher Anzeiger* and the Saint Louis *Anzeiger des Westens* for 1854; Frank I. Herriott, "The Germans of Chicago and Stephen A. Douglas in 1854," *Deutsch-Amerikanische Geschichtsblätter: Jahrbuch der Deutsch-Amerikanischen Historischen Geselleschaft von Illinois* 12 (1912): 381–404. This journal is hereafter cited as *DAG.*

8. Some examples of specific precincts will be discussed hereafter for this and later elections; for fuller statistical elaboration, see Bergquist, "Political Attitudes of the German Immigrant," pp. 158–62.

But that heavy vote against Douglas did not mean a definite transfer of allegiance to a new political organization, for the anti-Nebraska movement in Illinois was not to coalesce into a new Republican organization for fully two years thereafter. In the meantime, the question of what path the German immigrant should follow was complicated by the emergence of nativist and temperance agitation in 1855. That March, a slate of candidates proposed by Know-Nothings won the Chicago city elections and immediately began vigorous enforcement of the Sabbath laws and saloon regulation laws, to the great disgust of all immigrants. The tension between the city administration and the immigrants erupted into violence at the "beer riots" of April 21, 1855; one man was killed, many were injured, a state of siege was invoked for four days, and the city's emotions were raised to a high state.[9] In Springfield about the same time a new anti-Nebraska legislature showed great interest in drafting a new liquor prohibition law, which was submitted to a public referendum in June. It was defeated decisively after a bitter campaign. In the process, many immigrants were transformed from political apathy into political action, and Germans particularly were taking a closer look at the anti-Nebraska candidates they had aided a year before.[10]

As the presidential election year of 1856 began, all supporters of the anti-Nebraska cause had finally to confront the problem, too long deferred, of achieving a more permanent organization in Illinois. It was now quite clear that if the German immigrant was to be enrolled in such an organization, his dislike of the nativist-temperance forces had to be taken into account. The immigrants helped to drive the point home in March at the annual municipal elections in Chicago. The ticket which tried to

9. The heated state of Chicago municipal politics may be followed in the Chicago English-language newspapers for early 1855. Although no files remain of the *Illinois Staats-Zeitung* (Chicago) for this period, its accounts of the "beer riots" may be read in the Saint Louis *Anzeiger des Westens* (daily ed.), April 24 and 25, 1855, and in *Belleviller Zeitung*, May 1, 1855.

10. Arthur C. Cole, *The Era of the Civil War*, vol. 3 of *Centennial History of Illinois* (Springfield, 1919), pp. 207–9. Study of German precincts shows much greater voter participation in the prohibition referendum of 1855 than in the congressional election of 1854.

"fuse" anti-Nebraska and temperance candidates was overwhelmingly rejected in favor of the Douglas organization. Chicago's
North Side, with the heaviest concentration of immigrants, voted
72.6 per cent for the mayoral candidate of Douglas. The lesson
was not lost on those seeking to organize Illinois Republicanism;
any new party would have to be purged of nativist characteristics
if it hoped to win at least part of the German vote, which it clearly needed in the larger towns and cities.[11] Indeed, accommodating
the immigrants seemed much more urgent than accommodating
the nativist element. If the Germans were lost by the Republicans, they would doubtless return to the camp of Douglas—a
course not likely to be taken by the advocates of nativism and
temperance.

Such considerations made Republican organizers particularly
amenable to the influence of the Germans as they laid the foundations of the new party. The first step was a meeting of Republican newspaper editors at Decatur in February, 1856, which issued
a call for a state convention and attempted to define in a platform the character of the new party. At the behest of Charles
Ray, editor of the *Chicago Tribune,* and of George Schneider,
editor of the state's most influential German newspaper, the
Illinois Staats-Zeitung of Chicago, the Decatur platform included
a declaration against Know-Nothingism. As Schneider later re-
counted it, the decisive influence for adopting the statement
came from Abraham Lincoln, who had joined the journalists'
meeting as an interested observer.[12]

The statewide convention that the editors had called for
met at Bloomington in May. Much of the German press maintained a "wait and see" attitude; so, too, did the influential
lieutenant governor, Gustave Koerner, who had clearly been out

11. The fullest discussion of these issues in Chicago politics is in the
Chicago Tribune and the *Chicago Democrat* for the period. See especially
the *Daily Tribune,* March 6, 1856. Canvass for 1856 municipal election, Chi-
cago City Council documents, 1855–56, No. 2144, City Clerk's office, Chicago
City Hall.
12. "Address by Honorable George Schneider," McLean County Historical
Society *Transactions* 3 (1900): 87–91; Paul Selby, "The Editorial Convention,
February 22, 1856," ibid., pp. 30–43; Jay Monaghan, *The Man Who Elected
Lincoln* (Indianapolis, 1956), pp. 60–64; *Illinois Staats-Zeitung,* April 21, 1898.

of sympathy with Douglas over the Kansas-Nebraska issue even while still a member of the state's Democratic administration.[13] Republican organizers continued to pursue the urgent task of having the Bloomington convention repudiate nativism. Much of the work toward that end was done behind the scenes by Orville Hickman Browning, a Quincy attorney and former Whig who served as platform committee chairman, working closely with the convention's president, John M. Palmer. The plank adopted gave assurances "that we will proscribe no one, by legislation or otherwise, on account of religious opinions, or in consequence of place of birth."[14] An even stronger assurance was given by the act of nominating a naturalized German, Francis A. Hoffmann of Chicago, for the post of lieutenant governor. The fact that the former Whig element of the new party was induced to yield both the governor's and lieutenant governor's positions on the state ticket to former Democrats reflects the especially conciliatory mood of the convention toward the immigrant.[15]

The direction of the national Republican party, however, was yet to be determined, and there was reason to fear that the party would feel the influence of nativist-minded former Whigs in many eastern states. Concern there was more prevalent about keeping Know-Nothing support behind the anti-Nebraska party, and in particular about getting cooperation from the nativists' North American splinter element, which was meeting in New

13. Koerner stated his views in letters published in the *Belleville Advocate,* March 5, 1856, and in the Peoria *Illinois Banner* (translation in *Weekly Chicago Democrat,* May 17, 1856). See also *Memoirs of Gustave Koerner, 1809–1896,* ed. by Thomas J. McCormack, 2 vols. (Cedar Rapids, 1909), 2: 3–5.

14. Record of Bloomington convention in McLean County Historical Society *Transactions* 3 (1900): 160–61. The same volume presents various accounts of the convention. See also *The Diary of Orville Hickman Browning,* ed. Theodore C. Pease and James G. Randall, 2 vols. (Springfield, Ill., 1927), 1: 237–38.

15. Hoffmann had to drop out of the election race subsequently when it was discovered that he had not been a citizen long enough to satisfy the Illinois requirement for officeholding. He admitted his own inadvertence and there is no evidence that the turn of events alienated many Germans. See clippings in F. A. Hoffmann scrapbook, Concordia Historical Institute, Saint Louis; Karl Kretzmann, "Francis Arnold Hoffmann," *Concordia Historical Institute Quarterly* 18 (1945): 47–49.

York at the same time that the Republicans convened in Philadelphia. The western Republicans concerned about immigrant support achieved their most critical step in securing as convention president a man who would agree on a course favorable to their views. Such a man was found in Henry Lane of Indiana; he appears to have used his influence to get the resolutions committee to produce a platform statement that would reassure the Germans. It was a vague and innocuous plank about "liberty of conscience and equality of rights among citizens," but eastern delegates nevertheless began to protest when it came to the floor. Lane, however, gaveled down the opposition and declared the resolution accepted. Even its supporters confessed in later years that there may have been more votes against it than for it.[16]

The question of the North Americans had to be dealt with in a more gingerly fashion. A committee of them was waiting in Philadelphia to confer, in direct response to invitations previously sent by the Republican National Committee; yet the friends of the immigrant feared any sort of formal recognition of an organization identified in any way as nativist. As Illinois's Owen Lovejoy told the convention, "if the North Americans were received as an organized body of Know-Nothings, that demagogue, Stephen A. Douglas, would tickle the senses of the foreign-born citizens of Illinois, and Illinois would be lost."[17] The Republicans finally sent their platform committee, which had already demonstrated its sensitivity toward the immigrants, to meet the North Americans; but there was no agreement on a joint ticket involving a North American vice-presidential nominee or on any formal amalgamation. Eventually, as the hopes of the North

16. *Proceedings of the First Three Republican National Conventions* (Minneapolis, 1893, especially pp. 44–45. On the more specific involvement of the Illinois Republicans, see A. T. Andreas, *History of Chicago from the Earliest Period to the Present Time*, 3 vols. (Chicago, 1884–86), 1: 390, and the jubilee edition of the *Illinois Staats-Zeitung*, April 21, 1898; both apparently base their accounts on recollections of George Schneider; also *Belleviller Zeitung* (weekly ed.), July 15, 1856.

17. *Proceedings of the First Three Republican National Conventions*, p. 57.

Americans waned, they had to join the Republican ranks either as individuals or not at all.[18]

Thus the new party emerged from the Philadelphia convention of 1856 committed, on paper at least, to the course desired by the West in its efforts to win over the Germans. The organizational steps of that year had afforded immigrant spokesmen and their native-born sympathizers an opportunity to mold the party to their desires, and they used the opportunity well. The fact that the party gradually took shape in the West, and eventually in the nation, as one that avoided nativist and temperance positions, was in large part due to the pressure of the Germans. This positive contribution to the character of the new party constitutes the most important influence of the German immigrant upon the politics of the fifties.

The campaign strategies of the two major parties in Illinois in 1856 demonstrated the awareness of both that the Germans were a critical element. The Douglas forces, despairing of regaining most of the German-language newspapers that had defected to the Republicans, made strenuous efforts to build a new German Democratic press. The theme repeated to the Germans by both Democratic papers and stump speakers was that nativism and its dangers still lay hidden behind the conciliatory facade of the Republican party. Had not the Germans already been deluded once by the anti-Nebraska men they had aided in 1854?[19] Recognizing the threat of the argument, the Republicans made every effort to show that the Germans were a functioning part of the party's structure, not just an outside group being appealed to. Fortunately, they could demonstrate this with an impressive group of Illinois German leaders, and it was the Democrats who more often had to rely on German-language speakers brought in from other

18. Arthur W. Crandall, *The Early History of the Republican Party, 1854–1856* (Boston, 1930), pp. 179–87; Roy F. Nichols, "Some Problems of the First Republican Presidential Campaign," *American Historical Review* 28 (1923): 492–96; Murat Halstead, *Trimmers, Trucklers and Temporizers: Notes of Murat Halstead from the Political Conventions of 1856,* ed. by William B. Hesseltine and Rex G. Fisher (Madison, 1961), pp. 72–79, 102–3.

19. The Democratic appeals to the immigrant are best followed in the files of the *Chicago Daily Times* for the period; see also Freeport *Deutscher Anzeiger,* August 6, 13, 20, 27, 1856.

states. In addition to Francis Hoffmann, the Republicans could make use of one of the most popular and romantic figures of the revolutions of 1848, Friedrich Hecker, who had settled on a farm in Saint Clair County. His torrents of German oratory usually enlivened Republican rallies with the enthusiasm of 1848, as he identified the Republican cause with Kossuth and Mazzini and the southern slaveholders with the Bourbons and Hapsburgs.[20]

Perhaps more significant was the campaign work of Gustave Koerner, who had now completed his break with the Democrats. Having done so after a period of soul searching and indecision, he realized that the appeals of 1848 were not enough to win over many moderate Germans from their long-standing allegiances into the new political alignment. Much of his campaign argument thus dwelt on tradition rather than radical liberalism. He stressed repeatedly that the ideals of democracy that had once tied Germans to the party of that name were no longer there; "true democracy," true allegiance to Jacksonian principles, was now to be found in Republicanism. Germans, he argued, need not look upon a Republican alignment as a radical break, nor on the new party as a strange, hostile camp. If they would only look around them, they would see familiar principles and familiar political leaders. Koerner made special efforts to attract the vote of Catholic Germans, even though they had never been his most ardent supporters; he realized that they were the group most sensitive about nativism and least receptive to the appeals of men like Hecker.[21]

20. See the files of the *Belleviller Zeitung* on Republican campaign efforts. On Hecker, see *Belleviller Zeitung* (weekly ed.), August 12, 26, September 16, 1856; *Chicago Daily Tribune*, August 16, 1856; *Weekly Chicago Democrat*, October 25, 1856; Geo. S. Hecker and James E. Gleichert, "Lincoln Writes to Friedrich Hecker: A New Letter," *Lincoln Herald* 69 (1967): 159–61; Lincoln to Hecker in *Collected Works of Abraham Lincoln*, ed. Roy P. Basler et al., 9 vols. (New Brunswick, 1953–55), 2: 376; speech at Belleville, ibid., pp. 379–80.

21. Koerner, *Memoirs*, 2: 18–36; Koerner to Richard Yates, October 25, 1856, Yates MSS, Illinois State Historical Library. Koerner's appeals to German moderates were set forth most fully in a series of essays signed "X" in *Belleviller Zeitung* (weekly), July 22, September 2, 1856; his authorship is acknowledged in ibid., January 6, 1857, but was probably widely recognized when the series appeared.

The November election of 1856 showed that a majority of German voters in Illinois had been reconciled to Republicanism. It was not an overwhelming majority, but something like 55 or 60 per cent (only rough estimates are possible), and with wide variations among German communities. In rural townships in northern Illinois which had been more recently settled by Germans, the Republicans polled over 85% of the vote; in longer established German communities in the same area, the returns were more often 65 to 70 per cent Republican. Republican support was generally not quite so strong among the southern Illinois Germans. In the larger German communities of Saint Clair County, the Republican vote ran from 48 to 60 per cent. But most precincts there showed some native-born voters turning to Millard Fillmore, who polled one-fifth of the county's total; thus the Republican vote among Germans often ran higher than the precinct percentages alone would indicate. German Lutheran areas were more often divided between parties in both north and south; Catholic German communities remained 70 to 80 per cent Democratic. Koerner had correctly perceived that it was the moderate German group, mostly of longer residence and with Catholic or Lutheran religious ties, that most needed to be courted. It was apparent that the Republicans had not had overwhelming success in doing so.[22]

Nevertheless, if the 1855 reaction of the Germans against nativism is taken into consideration, the Republicans rightly considered it a success to have won back nearly as much German support against Douglas as had been shown in 1854. But the election also posed another problem, the wavering of a critical but troublesome portion of the conservative Whig-nativist element. Their inconstancy showed obvious results in the statewide returns. The party had won the state administration but the Democrats had taken the presidential electoral vote. It did not take much electoral analysis to see the reason: about 6 per cent of the state's voters had showed themselves willing to support the Republican state ticket while at the same time denying the

22. For statistical elaboration, see Bergquist, "Political Attitudes of the German Immigrant," pp. 234–40.

Republican presidential candidate, John C. Frémont, their presidential ballots and giving them instead to the American party candidate, Millard Fillmore. Republicans therefore were to show concern in subsequent elections about winning these Fillmore voters of 1856, at the same time balancing off that consideration with the one of retaining Germans in the ranks. But this attempt was not seen as completely hopeless; many of the Fillmore men were not rabid nativists but simply old conservative Whigs, and their concern was not so much with the party's platform or with the participation of Germans, but rather with the choice of Frémont as a candidate deemed too radical on the slavery question.[23]

The year 1856 thus appears as the crucial one in Illinois in which the Germans aligned themselves with the Republican party; their electoral support, having been set at about 60 per cent of the German vote, remained somewhere near that level through 1860. The Republicans' strategies were now directed more at maintaining this support, and that became increasingly easier as the party found many practical ways to allay the Germans' fears about nativism. The state administration was in Republican hands after 1856, and so was the Chicago city hall from 1857 on. Both patronage and party policy were used to demonstrate good faith toward the immigrant. Friction between nativist and immigrant remained an ever present threat as the party continually sought to accommodate both; the contention between the two in the Madison County organization, for instance, seriously weakened Republican efforts there, and the party lost the county narrowly in the critical legislative election of 1858.[24] But on the state level the party could demonstrate consistently its acceptance of the Germans.

23. The problem is perhaps best illustrated by Abraham Lincoln's concern over it in his private calculations on campaign strategy in 1858, and his persistent letters to Koerner and to Joseph Gillespie. See *Collected Works*, 2: 476–81, 502–3, 523–24; 8: 416. Also Gillespie to Lincoln, July 18, 1858, Robert Todd Lincoln Collection, Library of Congress.

24. *Alton Weekly Courier*, September 25, November 11, 1858; Saint Louis *Anzeiger des Westens* (daily ed.), October 6, 1858; Edwardsville *Madison Press*, February 16, 1859.

The Republican party faced another perplexing question when Stephen A. Douglas broke with President Buchanan in December, 1857, over the issue of a constitution for Kansas. Douglas's position rejected outright the southern-oriented Lecompton constitution, and the course he advocated would in all likelihood eventually result in a Kansas free from slavery; how, then, would this influence moderate free-soil opinion, and what should be the Republican response? Illinois's Republican leaders flatly refused any idea of collaboration with the Little Giant, even though some eastern Republicans advocated it, and the party adhered to its opposition to all future extension of slavery (an absolute position not taken by Douglas).[25] Douglas himself, however, sensed that moderate free soilers were a prime political target, and that that critical element might include many Germans, who could now resolve the nativist–free soil dilemma in their minds by turning once again to Douglas. Thus his 1858 campaign resurrected the specter of nativism among the Republicans, and added appeals to the immigrants' racial fears that the "white basis" of American government might be undermined by Republican ideas of Negro equality. Abraham Lincoln in reply sought to use some of Douglas's own words against him, and to show that the Little Giant's arbitrary definitions of human rights and constitutional protection might someday be turned against the foreign-born.[26]

The Democratic vote in 1858 across Illinois was two to three percentage points above that of 1856. That small gain was of course important in the narrow winning of the legislature which enabled Douglas to retain his Senate seat. The German voters as a group, however, seem only to have reflected the general trend of the electorate; about 2 or 3 per cent of them seem to have switched to Douglas. In some cases German areas about the state reflected gains of seven to fourteen percentage points for the Democrats, with a few ranging higher; these were very often

25. See the cogent discussion in Don E. Fehrenbacher, *Prelude to Greatness: Lincoln in the 1850's* (Stanford, 1962), pp. 48–69.
26. See, for example, Douglas's remarks to a group of German Democrats of Chicago in *Weekly Chicago Times*, July 22, 1858; Lincoln's speeches of July 10 and July 17, *Collected Works*, 2: 499–501, 519–20.

older German communities, especially of Lutherans and Catholics. There were Republican gains in other Lutheran areas and in some of the more recently settled German townships. The general picture still showed the moderate free-soil Germans to be hanging in the balance. While Douglas made gains among them, he was disappointed in his hopes for a wholesale reconversion of the Germans.[27] By this time, it seems clear, it was no longer merely a matter of the Democrats' reviving old loyalties broken by some temporary aberration among the Germans. Rather they faced the problem of trying to attack some firmly established new political loyalties—a much more difficult problem of political strategy.

The Republicans' stance by 1860 was, conversely, a defensive one of holding these established German loyalties. The principal threat of disruption was, as before, from the vestiges of nativism still among some party adherents. But that threat came not from within Illinois, where active nativism among Republicans had virtually vanished, but rather from those eastern states where nativists remained more strongly situated in party councils. The Republican legislature of Massachusetts created a particular problem in 1859 by passing the so-called two-year amendment to the state's constitution, requiring two years' residence after naturalization before the foreign-born could vote. Immigrants correctly pointed to the unusual discrimination inherent in the amendment; it created in effect two classes of citizenship, one of which was denied the franchise for a longer period of time. Republican organizations in most of the western states, including Illinois, showed themselves willing to undertake a protest within the party in the immigrants' behalf. When Massachusetts Republicans could not be dissuaded in 1859, efforts turned to securing a disavowal of such restrictions from the Republican national convention in 1860.[28] The other principal concern of German Republicans was with the possibilities for presidential candidates.

27. For statistical elaboration, see Bergquist, "Political Attitudes of the German Immigrant," pp. 268–72.
28. Frank I. Herriott, "The Premises and Significance of Abraham Lincoln's Letter to Theodore Canisius," *DAG* 15 (1915): 181–254.

Many German leaders favored William Henry Seward, although it is more difficult to divine the wishes of the rank and file. An even stronger current, however, was the Germans' general resistance to any contender with previous nativist connections. The most likely prospect of this sort was Edward Bates of Missouri, who was being advanced in some quarters as the man most able to attract a following among moderate and conservative former Whigs.[29]

As Germans and their western sympathizers saw it, then, the 1860 convention presented a challenge similar to that which they had faced in the Republican convention of 1856. By persistent and skillful demonstration of the need to retain German votes in the West, they were able to impress their views on national leaders, on the platform committee, and on several critical state delegations. With remarkably little difficulty, a platform statement was obtained against any federal or state legislation diminishing the rights of naturalized citizens.[30] As to the choice of a presidential candidate, the Germans probably made their influence felt most strongly in spoiling the chances of Edward Bates. Other elements found Seward unacceptable, and the result was to clear the way for Abraham Lincoln. If Lincoln's chief merit in 1860 was seen by party leaders as his acceptability, the Germans were certainly among those who could accept him without protest. His own political record in Illinois was free from nativist positions and he had been among those working steadily in state politics to make the Germans part of the party.[31]

29. Koerner, *Memoirs*, 2: 79, 85; *Illinois Staats-Zeitung*, quoted in *Belleviller Zeitung*, December 29, 1859; *Belleviller Zeitung*, March 8, 1860; Koerner to Lyman Trumbull, December 23, 1859, Trumbull MSS, Library of Congress; Marvin R. Cain, "Edward Bates and the Decision of 1860," *Mid-America* 44 (1962): 109–24.

30. Saint Louis *Anzeiger des Westens* (weekly), May 24, 1860; Koerner, *Memoirs*, 2: 86–90; Edward Younger, *John A. Kasson: Politics and Diplomacy from Lincoln to McKinley* (Iowa City, 1955), p. 104; Reinhard H. Luthin, *The First Lincoln Campaign* (Cambridge, Mass., 1944), pp. 148–53.

31. My estimation of the work of German Republican leaders rests mainly on reports in the German-language press for May, 1860, and especially the reports of the *Belleviller Zeitung*, Saint Louis *Anzeiger des Westens*, and transcripts of the Davenport *Demokrat* in F. I. Herriott MSS, Iowa Department of History and Archives, Des Moines. All of these republish reports of

Thus in 1860 the national Republican party continued along the course set in 1856 in its relationship with the immigrant. The national party showed itself willing to appeal to the immigrant with specific declarations, even to the point of implying disapproval of nativist actions in some state organizations; it was not willing to make its official policies conform to nativist viewpoints, only agreeing to passive acceptance of support from nativists. Of importance also was the broadening of Republican appeals in the late fifties beyond issues of slavery and free soil to such matters as the homestead law and tariff protection. The homestead appeal was of special value in winning over additional support from moderate free-soil Germans; like other free-labor elements, they could see the relevance of aiding the expansion of the free farmer in the West while curbing the expansion of plantation slavery. In Illinois, the increased stress upon the Germans' self-interest can be clearly seen in the Republicans' efforts among the more doubtful, moderate-to-conservative German communities. Carl Schurz, for example, added such appeals to his free-soil idealism when he toured German areas in central Illinois, and the *Belleviller Zeitung* repeated the theme in the southern part of the state.[32]

The Illinois Republicans had accumulated by 1860 many valuable cards which they played wisely in the campaign of that year: the proven reliability of the state party in its treatment of the immigrant; an array of German speakers, many of them Illinois residents, more distinguished than those the Democrats

many other German newspapers. The most used account of the German role at the convention is F. I. Herriott, "The Conference in the Deutsches Haus, Chicago, May 14–15, 1860," Illinois State Historical Society *Transactions,* 1928, pp. 101–91. I disagree with Herriott's emphasis on the conference of Germans and would attribute more influence to German Republican leaders who operated independently of the "Deutsches Haus" meetings—and who, in fact, disapproved of the meetings. For discussion, see Bergquist, "Political Attitudes of the German Immigrant," pp. 280–83, 293–307.

32. Saint Louis *Anzeiger des Westens* (weekly), August 2, 1860; *Quincy Whig,* July 18, 1860; *Belleviller Zeitung,* July 26, September 27, November 1, 1860. The relationship of the homestead issue to the immigrant is discussed well in Luthin, *The First Lincoln Campaign,* passim; and in George M. Stephenson, *The Political History of the Public Lands from 1840 to 1862* (Boston, 1917), especially pp. 221–39.

could produce; an important German-born candidate, Francis Hoffmann, once again on the slate for lieutenant governor; a presidential candidate with whom the state's Germans were acquainted and who aroused no fears of nativism; effective specific appeals such as the homestead, which western Democrats might advocate but could never deliver. In comparison to this, the materials used by the Douglas Democrats to construct a campaign among the Germans seemed rather shopworn. The scare talk about nativism was simply not confirmed by the established record of Illinois Republicanism, and the "Negro equality" threat seems to have moved few Germans to desert the ranks of the Republicans. Such appeals might serve to reinforce those German Democratic loyalties that still remained, but not to win back Republicans.

The most remarkable feature (though not a spectacular one) of the 1860 election returns from German areas of Illinois is their consistency in comparison with the 1858 election. The fact that there was no striking change in the German orientation in general and in the political leanings of most individual precincts shows that the political transformation of the German community begun in 1854 was now complete. The Republicans held nearly all the votes that they had won in 1858 and added some of the moderate Germans they had been hoping for. In some older German communities, from 4 to 15 per cent of the voters switched their allegiance to the Republicans; there were fewer instances of Democratic advances. The Republicans showed more success among Lutherans in the northern part of the state, but only slight gains, if any, among rural Catholics. A very rough estimate of the overall German vote would show the Republican predominance to have grown slightly since 1858, taking into consideration especially the Republican increases in the more populous areas. A fair estimate might place the Republican portion of the German vote at from 60 to 65 per cent.[33]

Both the German-born electorate's general course through the 1850s and some of its variations can be illustrated more con-

---

33. For statistical elaboration, see Bergquist, "Political Attitudes of the German Immigrant," pp. 317–21.

cretely by an examination of the election returns from some specific Illinois precincts. One would use the word "typical" with great caution about any of the precincts, nor can they be taken all together to represent any well-balanced cross section of Illinois Germans. Since the choice of examples is dictated primarily by the availability of election returns, census data, and background information on these communities, it is best to consider them as illustrating some possible varying political reactions, and not to see them as proving anything in themselves.

DEMOCRATIC PARTY PERCENTAGES OF TOTAL VOTES CAST,
SELECTED GERMAN-POPULATED PRECINCTS OF ILLINOIS,
BIENNIAL ELECTIONS, 1850–60

Precinct and county	1850	1852	1854	1856	1858	1860
Addison, Du Page	91.7	47.8	5.6	32.7	35.8	30.8
New Trier, Cook	82.6	97.5	21.1	63.7	70.8	64.7
Bremen, Cook	83.9	83.7	0.0	1.1	14.4	15.4
Belleville, St. Clair		77.8	45.8	34.4	42.4	38.6
Mascoutah		68.0	13.9	18.2	33.1	28.0
Benner poll, St. Clair		94.0	19.8	71.3	53.7	65.3
Centreville, St. Slair		93.0	64.5	75.7	38.7	35.8

SOURCES: Cook County returns are from MS election returns in Illinois State Archives and from *Chicago Daily Tribune,* November 6, 1860 (for 1856) and November 10, 1860 (for 1860). Addison Township returns are from *Weekly Chicago Democrat,* November 16, 1850, November 20, 1852; *Chicago Daily Democratic Press,* November 9, 1854; *Naperville Sentinel,* November 11, 1858, November 8, 1860 (for 1856 and 1860). Saint Clair County returns are from State Archives, 1852 and 1854, and from *Belleville Advocate,* November 12, 1856, November 10, 1858, November 16, 1860. Returns are for the presidential vote for 1852, 1856, and 1860; for congressional candidates in 1850, 1854, and 1858. No returns appear for Saint Clair County in 1850 because the Democratic congressional candidate in that year was unopposed. Because of variations in county government structures in Illinois, the units in Saint Clair County were officially precincts, those in Cook and Du Page counties were townships.

The table shows German communities from the area near Chicago (the ones in Cook and Du Page counties) and from southern Illinois areas near Saint Louis (Saint Clair County). Most were rural communities; Mascoutah was a slightly larger town of about two thousand population in 1860, Belleville a county seat with population totaling about seventy-five hundred.

The proportion of German-born in the potential electorate (adult white males) was in every instance more than 70 per cent in 1860,[34] although their populations had been developing in a variety of ways before that point. The figures used are the percentage of the total vote given to the Democratic party (specifically, to Stephen Douglas's organization, excluding any Democratic splinted groups), since other parties came and went and the Democratic organization in Illinois, while under strain, at least held together as some sort of constant. A very brief examination will illustrate two main points already discussed about the Germans' political tendency: their strong support of the Democrats vanished generally in 1854; German precincts were sorting themselves out in various ways by 1856 and pursued a variety of political courses through 1860.

The first two townships listed were both among the oldest of the German rural townships near Chicago, dating from the late 1830s and early 1840s. Addison Township, eighteen miles northwest of Chicago, had by the fifties developed as a center of German Lutheranism, becoming a stronghold of the Missouri Synod after that body was organized in 1847. It should also be noted that it was a community where the important German Republican Francis Hoffmann had once served as minister; that may have helped to influence many there in the direction of the Republicans. New Trier was a community with a large Catholic population, on Lake Michigan fifteen miles north of Chicago.[35] While the election figures show that both communities turned against Douglas in 1854, the Catholic community

34. Tabulated from MS census returns for 1860 in the National Archives. The figures for Saint Clair County are approximate since the census takers did not use precinct boundaries.

35. The background information on all the communities studied is drawn from MS census reports (1850 and 1860), and from local history and published church history materials and contemporary newspaper descriptions. These may be pursued in Bergquist, "Political Attitudes of the German Immigrant," pp. 325–401, which also examines numerous other German communities. The number of votes cast in Addison Township for the elections examined was, in chronological order, 60, 94, 72, 156, 95, 182. For New Trier the total vote for the same elections was 86, 79, 52, 102, 107, 181. Addison polled 45 votes (47.8 per cent) for the Free Soil party in 1852; this was uncommon in German communities.

returned to the Democratic ranks in 1856, while the Lutheran one did not. This general pattern continued through 1860; in both places Douglas managed to gain some adherents in 1858 and the Republicans won back about as many in 1860. The point most needing comment is perhaps the greater reluctance of the Catholic group to join the Republicans. Although that party was carefully purging itself of appearances of hostility toward the foreign-born, some of its elements (including at times the *Chicago Tribune*) retained the theme of hostility to Catholicism. The issue could be used against the Democratic Irish, and even had some value as a common ground on which to unite nativists, German Protestants, and German freethinkers. While some Republicans did not give up bidding for German Catholic support, it is understandable that many of the Catholics had misgivings about the alliance they saw within the new party.[36]

Bremen Township, on the northern reaches of the Illinois prairie twenty-three miles southwest of Chicago, was a more recently settled area opened up by the building of the Illinois Central Railroad in the early fifties. It lay some miles from the railroad itself, however, and most of its land was purchased by individuals from the federal government. Its population of adult males grew fivefold during the fifties; study of the census manuscripts of 1860, and especially of the birthplaces of the immigrant children, indicates that most of the Germans came between 1850 and 1856 and were newcomers to the United States when they arrived.[37] The township may be characterized as recently established, without many traditional loyalties in American politics, somewhat more North German than South German in origins

36. On anti-Catholicism and Republicanism, see Don E. Fehrenbacher, "Illinois Political Attitudes, 1854–61" (Ph.D. diss., University of Chicago, 1951), pp. 130–35. Fehrenbacher discusses the subject more briefly in his *Prelude to Greatness*, pp. 13–14.

37. The growth in number of voters reflects this development. For the elections discussed, the number of votes cast, in chronological order, was 37, 43, 24, 91, 104, 175. Since after 1848 citizenship was required for the franchise in Illinois, many who immigrated in the wave of the early fifties were entering the electorate in the last years of the decade. As the discussion will bring out, this expansion of the German-born voting population just before 1860 generally favored the Republicans.

of its population, but for the most part religiously heterogeneous. Such areas seem to have been among the most strongly Republican of German precincts.

The remaining precincts, chosen from among the heavily German areas in southern Illinois, reflect the same general picture. The area as a whole had been regarded since the 1830s as a German cultural and intellectual center as well as a center of German population, since many refugees of the political upheavals of the thirties had chosen to settle there. Nevertheless, it had its prairie areas still being opened up to new settlement in the 1850s. Belleville, the county seat, was clearly the center of this Germanized countryside; but its population, while still growing, was more stable during the decade and, one may assume, more accustomed to older American traditions of politics. Mascoutah, while founded in the 1830s, was located on the prairie farther east in the county and so received a greater proportion of its population from the influx of the fifties. The Mascoutah population tended to be drawn from the areas of Germany that were Protestant, but the town was otherwise religiously diversified. Belleville as a larger town was quite cosmopolitan in its Germanism. Both became Republican in 1854 and remained so through 1860, but Mascoutah did so more strongly.[38] Two likely explanations suggest themselves: first, that the longer established population of Belleville found it harder to give up Democratic loyalties; second, that the Catholic and Lutheran influences may have been felt a little more strongly there. It is not possible to sort out the two possibilities very successfully in these examples.

The Benner poll (actually part of a precinct) and Centreville precinct give two examples from among rural German areas. Benner encompassed the heavily Catholic German community

38. The number of votes cast in Belleville for the elections discussed, 1852–60, in chronological order, was 1,166, 858, 1,345, 1,397, 1,946. West Belleville, developing rapidly, was a separate precinct in 1858 and 1860 but is included here in the Belleville total for consistency. Like other more recently settled German areas, West Belleville was more Republican. The number of votes cast in Mascoutah in the elections discussed, 1852–60, in chronological order, was 342, 280, 450, 339, 635. In Belleville in 1856, 16.6 per cent of the vote was cast for Fillmore; in Mascoutah, 22.0 per cent. Presumably these were native-born voters.

around the church of Saint Libory at Mud Creek, in the southeast corner of Saint Clair County; the settlement had existed since the 1830s. Centreville, in the southwest portion of the county, was an area with many Lutherans and Catholics, but with the Lutherans in greater predominance; the precinct's population seems more related socially to adjacent Catholic and Lutheran areas of Monroe County than to Saint Clair County. We can clearly classify the Benner poll as a German Catholic community, and, with more reservations, the Centreville precinct as under Lutheran influence. The voting behavior of the Benner poll seems not greatly different from that of the Catholic township of New Trier in northern Illinois. The main exception is that in the Benner poll Douglas lost some strength in 1858 and regained it in 1860; this was one of only a few precincts found where that happened. The general orientation of the precinct, however, remained Democratic, except for the 1854 reaction against the Kansas-Nebraska Act. In Centreville, however, the 1854 reaction was not so strong; the precinct was three-quarters Democratic in 1856 (so were some nearby Lutheran precincts in Monroe County); between 1856 and 1860, the Republicans made inroads on the electorate.[39] Taken with other examples from the north and some incomplete voting records from other southern Illinois areas, the general picture seems to be that both Lutheran and Catholic areas were more reluctant to forsake Democratic allegiances for the Republican coalition than were other groups, but that the Republicans had more success between 1856 and 1860 in persuading Lutherans than in persuading Catholics.

The numerous German electorate in the city of Chicago can hardly be ignored, yet it can hardly be the subject of statistical analysis as precise as in small country precincts. The most heavily foreign-born ward (there were no smaller voting divisions), the

39. The number of votes cast in the elections discussed, 1852–60, in chronological order, was Benner, 117, 81, 153, 106, 216; Centreville, 354, 206, 202, 398, 551. The proportion of the vote cast for Fillmore in 1856 (presumably from native-born) was Centreville, 12.4 per cent; Benner, 15.7 per cent. The precinct of Centreville lay about the present-day town of Millstadt; the town called Centerville today is several miles to the north, and was not within the precinct discussed here.

seventh on the city's North Side, serves to illustrate the complexities. The ward was large in area, and its population, like that of the city as a whole, mushroomed, rising from 3,560 in 1850 to 17,937 in 1860.[40] It changed in ethnic make-up, too, with the city's shifts in population; while the electorate probably remained more than 80 per cent foreign-born throughout the decade, the Irish outnumbered the Germans in the early fifties, while the Germans were clearly in predominance by 1860. While that general picture of transformation is clear, we have no precise statistics on separate nationalities in the ward at any one time.[41] The balance of the two groups seems to have been very close about 1857 and 1858. In the former year, there was a tense and hectic municipal election in the ward, with violence between the two groups resulting in the death of a German. In contention particularly was the office of alderman; the choice was between an Irish Democrat and a German Republican. The Democrat won, amid outraged cries of fraud from the Republicans; the next year, with John Wentworth's Republican city administration carefully watching the polling, a German Republican alderman, Henry Wendt, was elected by the ward for the first time.[42] The choice of an alderman, resolved by a bare majority within the ward, could stir emotions more easily than state and national contests. Indeed, there is considerable evidence in the newspapers of the time that the ethnic rivalries were becoming identified with parties. The effect seems to have been particularly to make Republicans out of Germans more rapidly than was usual across the state. After the 1857 disturbances, some German Democratic spokesmen complained openly and bitterly that Irish rowdies

40. J. D. B. De Bow, comp., *Seventh Census of the United States: 1850* (Washington, 1853), p. 705; Kennedy, *Population of the United States in 1860,* p. 90.

41. For population shifts in the city in general and the seventh ward in particular, see Bergquist, "Political Attitudes of the German Immigrant," pp. 327–35.

42. *Chicago Daily Tribune,* March 4, 5, 7, 1857; January 22, 23, March 2, 3, 6, 1858; *Belleviller Zeitung,* March 10, 17, 1857; *Chicago Daily Journal,* March 4, 5, 1857; *Weekly Chicago Times,* March 12, 1857; Peter H. Olden, "Anton C. Hesing: The Rise of a Chicago Boss," Illinois State Historical Society *Journal* 35 (1942): 271.

were roughing up German voters as though all of them were Republicans; the Chicago party, they said, seemed simply to have written off the Germans.[43]

Some general impressions of the German vote may be gotten from the election returns of the seventh ward if one makes the assumption, suggested by virtually all contemporary accounts, that the Irish remained solidly Democratic (with some possible exceptions in 1854). Most changes in the ward's party division, then, are probably due to changes among the German voters (including the addition of more of them to the populace); we thus have some indication of what direction they were going politically but lack enough ethnic data to estimate the number of German votes for one side or the other. The general trend seems to have followed that of Germans elsewhere in the state: a sharp reaction against Douglas in 1854, a more cautious return to Republicanism in 1856 after the nativist interlude of the previous year, and apparently some slow growth of Republican strength in ensuing years until 1860. As to the election of 1860 itself, a few more definite statements may be made. In that election, the party proportions of the seventh ward (44.8 per cent Democratic) approximated those of the whole city (42.6 per cent Democratic).[44] In order to produce that outcome, if the Irish remaining in the seventh ward turned in their usual strongly Democratic vote, it must have been offset by a heavily Republican vote from the Germans, the other principal element in the ward. Again, lacking precise ethnic breakdowns of the adult males, only rough estimates are possible, but a fair one would seem to be that the Germans were voting at least 75 per cent Republican. That would suggest that even a greater proportion of German Catholics were voting Republican here than elsewhere; and contemporary accounts suggest that they were experiencing friction with the Irish Catholics, too. There is no particular reason to think that the German vote differs elsewhere

43. Peoria *Illinois Banner,* quoted in *Belleviller Zeitung,* March 31, 1857.
44. Sources of election returns: see sources for Cook County data in Table I.

in the city; the same ethnic and political factors prevailed throughout Chicago, even if they were dramatized more clearly in the seventh ward.

Purely on the basis of the examples cited here, one might begin to think of the estimate already stated of the German vote (60 to 65 per cent Republican) as too low. One has to temper the assessment of these precincts with the observation that the most complete returns we have from the period seem more often to be from Republican areas; sketchy returns and newspaper references from some more remote areas very often indicate more instances of Democratic majorities. In other words, we have to curb somewhat the temptation to generalize freely upon those examples where the evidence is most abundant. In the hinterland of the southwest Illinois German area, for example, in places like Washington, Monroe, and Clinton counties, precincts which resemble Benner and Centreville in their electoral behavior seem to outnumber those which resemble, say, Mascoutah, although all three types are found. In Madison County, as we have noted earlier, the Republicans were more often torn by feuding between Germans and nativists; and while the German voting there seems to have followed the trend of Saint Clair County, it seems to have been consistently less Republican by several percentage points. Along the Illinois River valley, the evidence is very sparse, but disposes one to see a much more even balance of party strength. On the other hand, in the area of most rapid growth of new German population, the northeastern prairies, the fervent Republican German areas like Bremen Township were more common. There were similar townships to be found across northern Illinois between Chicago and the Mississippi, but also perhaps as many whose voting records looked more like that of Addison. Any estimate, then, will have to be very tentative, and must take into account the numbers of Germans in these areas of concentration as well as the variations described. One can make with confidence the statement that the Republicans gained a majority of the Germans; that majority, again, seems not to have been an overwhelming one, and 60 to 65 per cent seems a reasonable estimate.

The diversity of reactions of Germans in the politics of one state can give us some clues to the reasons for their varying political courses in other states of the West. Among possible variables are the social and religious make-up of the immigrant group itself; the nature of its leadership; relationships with other elements of the population, both immigrant and native-born; length of residence of immigrants and their degree of older political loyalties; and the strength, character, and timing of the nativist-temperance movement. The success of the Republican party depended on how it dealt with all of these factors, but most especially on how, in the view of the Germans, the party handled the questions of nativism and temperance.

A few examples from other states may serve to show especially the importance of how Republicanism evolved at the state level. In Wisconsin, the Republican party developed more quickly on the organizational base of a previous People's party. That party, consisting of Whigs, free soilers, and temperance advocates, had helped to bring about a "Maine law" in 1853. The Republicans from the outset seemed to be identified with prohibition; and although German Forty-eighters joined the anti-Nebraska coalition, it was much more of an uphill fight in the late fifties to win over the rank-and-file Germans than in Illinois. The newer leaders clashed more frequently with the older, established German leaders, who more often had grown out of the conservative Lutheran and Catholic communities which seem to have been more prevalent in Wisconsin.[45] In Iowa, too, temperance became more firmly identified with Republicanism—a "Maine law" was enacted during the first Republican state administration, and Republican legislators kept it in force, although modifying it slightly in reaction to German protests. While the Iowa Republicans did grapple with the problem of satisfying both nativists and

---

45. Ernest Bruncken, "The Political Activity of Wisconsin Germans, 1854–1860," Wisconsin State Historical Society *Preceedings* 69 (1901): 190–211; Aaron Boom, "The Development of Sectional Attitudes in Wisconsin, 1848–1861" (Ph.D. diss., University of Chicago, 1948), pp. 77–88, 117–22; Sr. M. Hedwigis Overmoehle, "The Anti-clerical Activities of the Forty-Eighters in Wisconsin, 1848–1860: A Study in German-American Liberalism" (Ph.D. diss., Saint Louis University, 1941), pp. 119–21; Still, *Milwaukee*, pp. 151–55.

Germans, the party's orientation more often was seasoned to the tastes of the prohibitionists and "Americans" than in Illinois. Slight differences of that sort seldom escaped notice by the Germans—especially when they were constantly reminded of them by the Democrats.[46] In Indiana, the anti-Nebraska fusion was under the control of a People's party, which gave nearly equal stress to temperance and free soil during much of the period 1854–58. It was not until 1858 that the Republican title was adopted. By that year the party was making conscious attempts to court the immigrant, but a swift change of heart by the Germans at that point was probably too much to expect. Slow gains, however, were apparently being made by the Republicans by 1860.[47] These briefly stated comparisons help to show the special importance in Illinois of the time at which the anti-Nebraska groups achieved organization in a formal Republican party. Since that step lagged until 1856, the new party could more easily abjure nativist and temperance sentiment, which had already caused trouble while the anti-Douglas forces remained a loose and unorganized coalition.

The classic question of how "decisive" the German vote was in Illinois may be approached briefly if we translate the estimates previously made of the 1860 vote into round figures. Lincoln won Illinois in 1860 by a vote of about 172,000 to Douglas's 160,000. The number of German-born adult males in the state was about 57,000; on the basis of sample areas studied, perhaps two-thirds of them, or 38,000, voted. An approximate division of the German vote would be 23,000 for Lincoln, 15,000 for Douglas.

46. David S. Sparks, "The Birth of the Republican Party in Iowa, 1854–1856," *Iowa Journal of History* 54 (1956): 1–34; Frank I. Herriott, "The Germans in the Gubernatorial Campaign of Iowa in 1859," *DAG* 14 (1914): 451–622; Charles W. Emery, "The Iowa Germans in the Election of 1860," see above, pp. 16–45.

47. Emma L. Thornbrough, *Indiana in the Civil War Era, 1850–1880* (Indianapolis, 1965), pp. 57–96, and other secondary works cited therein; Elmer D. Elbert, "Southern Indiana Politics on the Eve of the Civil War, 1858–1861" (Ph.D. diss., Indiana University, 1967), pp. 214–19, 231, and passim. Incipient state Republican movements are also surveyed in Clifford S. Griffin, *Their Brothers' Keepers: Moral Stewardship in the United States, 1800–1865* (New Brunswick, 1960), pp. 219–41.

How this affected the outcome boils down to hypothetical considerations of possible alternatives. But such conjectures in themselves really tell us very little; the same kind of argument for decisiveness might be made by singling out many other voting elements.[48]

The calculations, however, do show, as many political observers knew in 1860, that the decision was close and that the thing to do was to go after every doubtful, wavering vote. The Germans fell in that category in Illinois; even though the party allegiance of a majority of them had been set in 1856, the knowledge that the loyalties of some were still in doubt was enough to make them worth seeking out. Filiopietistic Germans, and some historians as well, who later spoke of the unswerving Republicanism of the Germans as being decisive missed the point. What made them really "decisive" was the tentative nature of their support, usually because of the varying pressures of nativism and free-soil sentiment. German Republican leaders, in fact, perhaps exaggerated the picture of the uncertainty of German support in order to obtain acceptable party policies and candidates. As in other years after 1856, the Republicans in 1860 oriented their appeals toward the Germans, mounted a special campaign to reach them, and adjusted the party platform in the immigrants' favor because they never considered them "safe." Thus the Germans were able to influence the party, the candidates, the election, and the future course of events far beyond what their numbers alone warranted. The election of 1860 may serve as a reminder for political analysts that, although the ballot box may be the final arbiter, policies and candidates are influenced not merely by how men *did* vote, but also by the fear of how men *might* vote.

48. I have revised upward here the estimates of German adult males made in 1966 in Bergquist, "Political Attitudes of the German Immigrant," pp. 405–7. Because of a misstep in statistical logic I then set the number of votes of German-born at about 22,000. My estimate of the party division remains the same. The calculations include Austrians and Swiss. The newer estimate of course enhances the importance of the German vote, but my basic argument about the limited relevance of these figures remains.

DATE DUE

MT. UNION		
FEB 2 0 1973		
MT. UNION		
MAR 1 4 1973		
GAYLORD		PRINTED IN U.S.A.